W9-BUY-605

A Tentative Autobibliography
YAKOV MALKIEL

With an Introduction by Henry Kahane

Romance Philology
Special Issue, 1988–1989

Special Editors
Joseph J. Duggan
Charles B. Faulhaber

University of California Press
BERKELEY AND LOS ANGELES

University of California Press
Berkeley and Los Angeles, California

ISBN: 0-520-06592-1
Printed in the United States of America

Contents

Tabula Gratulatoria

SPONSORS

Manuel Alvar
Samuel G. Armistead
Arthur L-F. Askins

Ana María Barrenechea
Jonathan Beck
Berkeley's Northside Travel
Curtis and Barbara Blaylock
William Brinner
Kevin and Marina Brownlee
Bulletin of Hispanic Studies

The University of California Press
Catherine A. Callaghan
Dwayne E. Carpenter
Diego Catalán
Frank M. Chambers
Matthew Chen
Dorothy Clotelle Clarke
William G. and Louise George Clubb
Alice M. Colby-Hall
The College of Letters and Science, University of California, Berkeley
Kathleen Connors
Noel L. Corbett
Gustavo Costa and Natalia Costa-Zalessow
Mary Cozad

Manuel DaCosta Fontes
Ralph and Lisa De Gorog
Peter F. and Yolande Dembowski

A. Richard Diebold Jr.
Joseph J. Duggan and Annalee C. Rejhon

Murray B. Emeneau
Arthur R. Evans, Jr.

Jamy and Charles Faulhaber
Charles J. Fillmore
Suzanne Fleischman
Anne Flexer
Freie Universität Berlin
August Frugé

Leanna Gaskins
Walter E. Geiger
Philip O. Gericke
Joaquín and Rosalie Gimeno
Prof. and Mrs. Arthur E. Gordon
The Graduate Division, University of California, Berkeley
Carol Grigsby
†John L. Grigsby

Robert A. Hall, Jr.
Doris and Tulio Halperin
M. Roy Harris
James A. Haug
Albert Henry
Leanne Hinton
Gary B. Holland

Angela M. Iovino

Margret Jackson
William H. Jacobsen, Jr.
Fred M. Jenkins

Henry and Renée Kahane
Lloyd Kasten
M. Emilie Keas
Dean Geoffrey Keppel
Sheldon Klein
Christopher Kleinhenz
Antoinette Knapton
Karen H. Kvavik

Nicholas J. Lahey
Margaret Langdon
Rafael Lapesa
Isaías and Lía Schwartz Lerner
Dr. Emilio and Mrs. Rebeca Lida
Ilse Hempel Lipschutz
Lewis D. Lipschutz
Paul and Joan Lloyd
Juan M. Lope Blanch

Donald S. and Judith B. Marshall
María Rosa Menocal
Alicia and Luis Monguió

Isabel Lida and Ricardo Nirenberg

Mrs. Leonardo Olschki

William D. Paden

Marie-Claude Paris
Dr. and Mrs. David A. Pharies
Beverley and John Polt
Rebecca Posner
Flora Praszker

Alain Renoir

Norman P. Sacks
Barbara N. Sargent-Baur
Martha E. Schaffer
Dayle Seidenspinner-Núñez
Ian Short
Michael Silverstein
Mary B. Speer
Ruggero Stefanini
Charlotte Stern

Edward F. Tuttle

Karl D. Uitti and Michelle A. Freeman
Barbara Ullrich

Albert Valdman
Alberto Vàrvaro and Rosanna Sornicola

†Ronald N. Walpole
John K. Walsh
Thomas J. Walsh
Raymond S. Willis
Lenora D. Wolfgang
Benjamin M., Jr., and Mary S. Woodbridge
Hensley C. Woodbridge

DONORS

Franca Brambilla Ageno
Andrew S. Allen
Roberto Antonelli
Grace M. Armstrong

Françoise Bader
Kurt Baldinger
Clarence L. Barnhart
Jeannie K. Bartha
John Benjamins North America, Inc.
†Thomas G. Bergin
Emilie Bergmann

R. Howard Bloch
Morton W. Bloomfield
Woodrow W. Borah
Benito Brancaforte
Robert Brentano
Boris and Johabed Bresler
R.W. Burchfield
Frances Butler
Joan L. Bybee

Frederic G. Cassidy
Patricia M. Clancy
Concepción Company

Jane E. Connolly
Michael A. Covington

Agnes Liakos Dimitriou
Anne and Larry Donaker
Steven N. Dworkin
Nancy Joe Dyer

Ernst A. Ebbinghaus
Sanford S. Elberg

Joan M. Ferrante
Anna Ferrari

†Alfred Foulet
Victoria A. Fromkin

Roger S. Gammons
Boris Gasparov
John S. Geary
Anne Iker-Gittleman
Edith Gladstone
Valerie M. Gomez
Raïssa N. Gorline-Bloch (*in memoriam*)
Prof. and Mrs. Jonas C. Greenfield
Gregory and Joan Grossman
J. Gulsoy
Basil J. Guy

Vladimir S. and Noemi Halpérin
Eric P. Hamp
Mary-Louise Hansen
Martin Harris
Emmanuel Hatzantonis
Einar Haugen
Walter W. Horn
Fred W. Householder

Italica

Soledad H-D. Jasin
Carol F. Justus

Braj B. and Yamuna Kachru
Simon Karlinsky
Keith E. Karlsson
Paul Kay
Hans-Erich Keller and Barbara G. Keller
Kathleen Kish
Flora P. Klein-Andreu
Renate Blumenfeld-Kosinski and Antoni Kosinski

Sydney M. Lamb
D. Terence Langendoen
Joan S. Leopold
John F. Levy
Charles N. Li
María Rosa Lida de Malkiel (*in memoriam*)
Humberto López Morales

Sally McLendon
Arlene Malinowski
Léon and Claire (née Saitzew) Malkiel (*in memoriam*)
James A. Matisoff
Roy Andrew Miller
Thomas Montgomery
Mrs. Edwin S. Morby
Anna Morpurgo Davies
Jenni K. Moulton
William G. Moulton
Louis A. Murillo
Charles Muscatine
Oliver T. Myers

John J. Ohala
Robert L. Oswalt

W. Keith Percival
Miriam Petruck
Elizabeth Wilson Poe
Claude Poirier
Ernst Pulgram

Irmengard Rauch and Gerald F. Carr
Erica Reiner
Robert J. Rodini
Aurelio Roncaglia
David S. Rood
Thomas G. Rosenmeyer
Cecilia Ross

Aldo Scaglione
John and Simone Scott
Joseph H. Silverman
Joseph Snow
Eve E. Sweetser

Karl V. Teeter
Paola and Nicholas Timiras
Lenora A. Timm
Máximo Torreblanca
Elizabeth Closs Traugott

Calvert Watkins

Ladislav Zgusta
Viktor M. Žirmunskij (*in memoriam*)

CONTRIBUTORS

Arthur S. Abramson
Karen T. Akiyama
Harold B. Allen

Philip Baldi
Menahem Banitt
Moshe Barasch
Paul Barrette
Jeanette Beer
Natasha A. Beery
Paola Benincà
Henrik Birnbaum
Thomas N. Bisson
Ariel A. Bloch
Allan R. Bomhard
Veronica Bonebrake
Georg Bossong
Sue Bremner
Bela Brogyanyi
Francesco Bruni
Victoria A. Burrus

Brigitte Cazelles
Giovanni Cecchetti
Bernard and Jacqueline Cerquiglini
Diane Chaffee-Sorace

Fredi Chiappelli
Carol J. Clover
Gerald L. Cohen
Harold C. Conklin
Lincoln Constance
Lidia Contreras
José Luis Coy
Susanna Peters Coy
Mechthild and Philip Cranston

Barbara De Marco
Marta De Pierris
Alan Deyermond
Constance L. Dickey
John W. Du Bois
Wolfgang Dressler
Peter Dronke
Meghan C. Ducey
Catherine Bloc Duraffour

Søren C. Egerod

Michael S. Flier
María Beatriz Fontanella de Weinberg
W. Nelson Francis
Hans H. Frankel

David Gaatone
Beatriz Garza Cuarón
E. Michael Gerli
Eliza Miruna Ghil
Harriet Goldberg
Olga Grlić
Maria Grossmann
Otto Gsell
John J. Gumperz

Mary R. Haas
Claude Hagège
Jean Halpérin
Friederike Hassauer
Richard Herr
Gabriele L. Hoenigswald
Henry M. Hoenigswald
Mrs. Harry Hoijer
Günter Holtus
Moira A. Hughes
Robert and Olga Hughes

John L. and Harriet Isaack

Richard D. Janda
Frede Jensen
David B. Justice

Alan S. Kaye
Mary Ritchie Key
Anne Draffkorn Kilmer
Robert W. Kingdon
Jurgen Klausenburger
Kathryn Klingebiel
Konrad Koerner
Johannes Kramer

Ronald W. Langacker
Randy J. Lapolla
Anita Benaim Lasry
Yolanda Lastra de Suárez
Ilse Lehiste
Ruth P. M. Lehmann
Winfred P. Lehmann
Giulio and Anna Laura Lepschy
Joan H. Levin
Anita K. Levy
Hans Lewy
Ricarda Liver
Bengt T.M. and Leena Lõfstedt
Alf Lombard
Luce López-Baralt
Alexandre Lorian
Julián Errasti Lubizarreta

James H. McGregor
Hugh McLean
John Manea
Maria Manea-Manoliu
Vera Mark
Francisco Márquez-Villanueva
Artemio Martínez-Moya
Francine Masiello
Carlo Alberto Mastrelli
Philippe Ménard
Gordon M. Messing
Luis Michelena Elissalt
John S. Miletich
Shelomo Morag
Žarko Muljačić
Albert M. Muth

Donna Jo Napoli
Virgil Nemoianu
Frank Nuessel

Eileen C. Odegaard
Boris Oguibénine

Mina Rainès-Lambé Parsont
José A. Pascual
Massimiliano Pavan
Giovan Battista Pellegrini
Herbert Penzl
Rosa Perelmuter Perez
Harvey Pitkin
Edgar C. Polomé
Glanville Price
Dawn Ellen Prince
Jaan Puhvel
Paul Pupier

Ambrosio Rabanales
John A. Rea
David W. Reed
Graciela Reyes
Barbara Reynolds
Nicholas V. Riasanovsky
Geoffrey Ribbans
Francisco Rico
Carol G. Rosen
Merritt Ruhlen
Ciriaco Ruiz
Hans Runte

Tilde Sankovitch
Rüdiger Schmitt
Christoph Schwarze
Christine Schwarze-Hanisch
Armin Schwegler
Hansjakob Seiler
Arié Serper
Salvatore Claudio Sgroi
Thomas F. Shannon
Alice Shepherd
Hava Bat-Zeev Shyldkrot
Carmen Silva-Corvalán
Michael Solomon
Blake Lee Spahr
Sarah Spence
Frits Staal
Patricia Harris Stablein
Edward Stankiewicz
Donca Steriade
Mrs. Gleb Struve

Pierre Swiggers

Ana Tătaru
Sarah G. Thomason
Jürgen Trabant
Bernard Tranel
Jeffrey S. Turley
Katherine Turner

E.M. Uhlenbeck

Veikko Väänänen
Paolo Valesio
Amelia E. Van Vleck

Dieter Wanner
Linda R. Waugh
Paul Wexler
Max W. Wheeler
Francis J. Whitfield
Prof. and Mrs. Harry F. Williams
Margaret E. Winters
Brian Woledge

Marion A. Zeitlin
Karl E. Zimmer
Michel Zink
Paul Zumthor

Acknowledgments

It gives me keen pleasure to tender my sincere thanks to several parties that, in an unusual display of generosity, have made possible this project of a critical autobibliography. My colleagues and junior friends Joseph Duggan and Charles B. Faulhaber, *qua* consecutive editors-in-chief of the *Romance Philology* quarterly, have assumed a heavy administrative responsibility for the entire venture; additionally, Dr. Faulhaber read the finished typescript in his role of sophisticated critic, advantageously known for his punctilio.

My senior friend Henry Kahane, who preceded me by a narrow margin as a student enrolled at the old Friedrich-Wilhelms Universität (Berlin) and, consequently, often understands better than myself what I have been aiming at all along, has sketched, by way of introduction, a pen portrait far in excess of my actual merits.

Placing her cerebral talent and impressive digital skill at our disposal, Karen Akiyama has prepared, as a fruit of several painstaking revisions, the definitive text which, in the end, was processed by the printer. Barbara De Marco excelled herself and, by an even wider margin, surpassed me in the rigor of her proofreading and in the intensity of her longing for consistency.

The officers of our University Press, including Ellie J. Young as the journal manager, had their significant share in the administrative underpinning of the project.

Two among the highest officers of the Berkeley Campus of my university, namely Provost and Dean of the College of Arts and Science Dr. Leonard V. Kuhi and Dean of the Graduate Division Dr. Joseph Cerny, have each sponsored a major intramural grant.

Last but certainly not least, an unexpected three-digit number of relatives, colleagues, academic and social friends, former students, and just plain well-wishers have generously contributed to a specially established fund, which alone has made it possible to expand this initially modest project on an unusually liberal scale, which no one could have foreseen at the outset.

In certain respects this autobibliography may give the impression of being experimental. This qualifier applies in particular to the system of cross-references adopted—an innovation meant to help fellow researchers to locate as speedily as possible items devoted to comparable topics or similar in approach. Less original but, one hopes, equally useful is the mention of critical reactions to the given piece. No special justification seems to be needed for the summaries provided. Should this apparatus appear too heavy for the taste of some readers, they are cordially invited to blame for this "extravagance" the many benefactors, as a result of whose munificence the space made available for this purpose had to be used in some imaginative fashion heretofore rarely tried out.

Berkeley, July 22, 1987

List of Sigla and Abbreviations

(A) SIGLA

AA	*American Anthropologist*
AC	*L'Antiquité classique*
AEM	*Anuario de estudios medievales*
AF	*Anuario de filología* (Barcelona)
AGI	*Archivio glottologico italiano*
AJPh	*American Journal of Philology*
AL	*Anuario de letras*
ALH	*Acta Linguistica Hafniensia*
AM	*Annales du Midi*
Arch	*Archivum* (Oviedo)
ArL	*Archivum Linguisticum*
ASNS	*Archiv für das Studium der neueren Sprachen und Literaturen*
BA	*Books Abroad*
BBMP	*Boletín de la Biblioteca de Menéndez y Pelayo*
BÉP	*Bulletin des études portugaises*
BF	*Boletim de Filologia* (Lisboa)
BFUCh	*Boletín de filología de la Universidad de Chile*
BH	*Bulletin hispanique*
BHS	*Bulletin of Hispanic Studies*
BICC	*Boletín del Instituto Caro y Cuervo (= Thesaurus)*
BNF	*Beiträge zur Namenforschung*
BRAE	*Boletín de la Real Academia Española*
BSLP	*Bulletin de la Société de Linguistique de Paris*
CA	*Current Anthropology*
CanJL	*Canadian Journal of Linguistics*
Čas	*Časopis pro moderní filologii*
CCM	*Cahiers de civilisation médiévale*
Cel	*Celestinesca*
Cer	*Cercetări de lingvistică* (Cluj)
CFS	*Cahiers Ferdinand de Saussure*
CJRL	*Canadian Journal of Romance Linguistics*
CL	*Comparative Literature*
CM	*Classica et Mediaevalia*
CN	*Cultura neolatina*
Cor	*La Corónica*
CS	*Cuadernos del Sur* (Bahía Blanca)
DL	*Deutsche Literaturzeitung*
EB	*Encyclopaedia Britannica* (edd. 1964, 1970)
ELT	Y.M., *Essays on Linguistic Themes* (Oxford: Blackwell, 1968).
Em	*Emerita*
Er	*Erasmus: Spiegel der gelehrten Welt*
ER	*Estudis romànics*
FeL	*Filologia e letteratura*
Fil	*Filología*
FLa	*Foundations of Language*
FLi	*Forum Linguisticum*

FM *Le Français moderne*
FS *French Studies*

GL *General Linguistics*

HL *Historiographia Linguistica*
HR *Hispanic Review*
HUS *Hebrew University Studies in Literature*

IARB *Intern. American Review of Bibliography*
IF *Indogermanische Forschungen*
IJAL *International Journal of American Linguistics*
IJb *Indogermanisches Jahrbuch*
IJSL *International Journal of the Sociology of Languages*
IL *Incontri linguistici* (Trieste)
Íns *Ínsula* (Madrid)
IR *Iberoromania*
It *Italica*

JAOS *Journal of the American Oriental Society*
JEGPh *Journal of English and Germanic Philology*
JF *Jornal de filologia*
JL *Journal of Linguistics*

KN *Kwartalnik Neofilologiczny*
Kr *Kratylos*
(K)RQ *(Kentucky) Romance Quarterly*

Lat *Latomus*
LBB *Leuvensche Bijdragen—Bijblad*
LEA *Lingüística española actual*
Lg *Language*
LG Y.M., *Linguistica generale, filologia romanza, etimologia*, tr. Ruggero Stefanini (Firenze: Sansoni, 1970)
LGRPh *Literaturblatt für germanische und romanische Philologie*
Lgs *Linguistics*
LiS *Language in Society*
LN *Lingua Nostra*
LS *Lingua e stile*
LSc *Language Sciences* (Indiana University)

MA *Le Moyen Age*
MeLR *Mediterranean Language Review* (Tel Aviv)
MLF *Modern Language Forum*
MLJ *Modern Language Journal*
MLN *Modern Language Notes*
MLQ *Modern Language Quarterly*
MLR *Modern Language Review*
MPh *Modern Philology*
MR *Medioevo romanzo*
Mus *Museum*

Neoph *Neophilologus*
NM *Neuphilologische Mitteilungen*
NR *Die Neue Rundschau*
NRFH *Nueva Revista de Filología Hispánica*
NSpr *Neuere Sprachen (Neue Folge)*

Paid *Paideia*
PBLS *Proceedings of the Annual Meetings of the Berkeley Linguistics Society*
PCPh *Pacific Coast Philology*
PGL Y.M., *From Particular to General Linguistics* (Amsterdam: Benjamins, 1983)
Phil *Philologica*
PhP *Philologica Pragensia*
PhQ *Philological Quarterly*
PMLA *Publications of the Modern Language Association of America*

QBR *U.S. Quarterly Book Review*
QIA *Quaderni ibero-americani*

RB *Revue belge de philologie et d'histoire*
RCCM *Rivista di cultura classica e medievale*
RDTP *Revista de dialectología y tradiciones populares*
REL *Revista española de lingüística*
RÉL *Revue des études latines*
RevPh *Revue de philologie, de littérature et d'histoire anciennes*
RevR *Revue romane* (Copenhagen)
RF *Romanische Forschungen*
RFE *Revista de filología española*
RFH *Revista de filología hispánica*
RIO *Revue internationale d'onomastique*
RJb *Romanistisches Jahrbuch*
RL *Ricerche linguistiche*

RLaR *Revue des langues romanes*
RLiR *Revue de linguistique romane*
RN *Romance Notes*
Ro *Romania* (Paris)
RPF *Revista Portuguesa de Filologia*
RPh *Romance Philology*
RR *The Romanic Review*
RRL *Revue roumaine de linguistique*

SCI *Spanish Cultural Index*
SCL *Studii şi cercetări lingvistice*
Scr *Scriptorium*
SEE *Southeastern Europe*
SF *Studi francesi*
SiL *Studies in Linguistics*
SIL *Studi italiani di linguistica teorica ed applicata* (Padova)
SN *Studia Neophilologica*
Spec *Speculum*
Spr *Die Sprache*
StL *Studies in Language*
StPh *Studies in Philology*
Symp *Symposium*

TLL *Travaux de linguistique et de littérature* (Strasbourg)
TLS *Times Literary Supplement*
TrAut *Traduction automatique*

UCPL *University of California Publications in Linguistics*

VD *Via Domitia*
VR *Vox Romanica*

YRS *Yearbook of Romanian Studies*
YW *The Year's Work in Modern Language Studies*
YWES *The Year's Work in English Studies*

Zb *Zbornik za filologiju i lingvistiku* (Novi Sad)
ZPh *Zeitschrift für Phonetik, Sprachwissenschaft und Kommunikationsforschung*
ZRPh *Zeitschrift für romanische Philologie*

(B) NOTEWORTHY ABBREVIATIONS

Ac(c). Academy (Accademia, etc.)
Anon. Anonymous
Bibl. Bibliography (-phic, etc.)
cf. compare (refers to related studies, by others)
Chap. Chapter
Coll. Colloquium
Contr. Contribution
Cr. Criticism; reviewed by
dir. directed by
disc. discussed by
due due to appear in
ed(d). edited by
edn. edition
et al. and others
Exc. Excursus
exp. expanded in
FS *Festschrift*
Hom(m). *Hommage (Homenaje*, etc.)
In: Included in (a volume)
Intern. International (-cional, etc.)
LSA Linguistic Society of America
Mél. *Mélanges*
Mem. *Memorial*
Misc. *Miscellany* (etc.)
N, num. number (número, numéro, etc.)
N.S. New Series
rev. revised
rpr. reprinted
See also signals a cross-reference to author's own studies
Ser. Series
Suppl. Supplement
Symp. *Symposium*
Test. *Testimonial*
Trans. *Transactions*
tr. translated by
UP University Press
With In collaboration with

Introductory Essay

HENRY KAHANE

I. Yakov Malkiel's extraordinary œuvre has been attracting in recent years ever-increasing attention, assuming international proportions and evidently related to the sheer quantity of his scattered publications. They truly call for the comprehensive view which a systematic bibliography provides. Large as the number of items is, varied as the topics are, as one man's life work they nevertheless take on, in their totality, a unified character and style, and an eminent scholar's thoughts on language yield the contours of their author's portrait.

Malkiel's *Bildung* is marked by his exposure to various cultures: he was born in Russia, studied in Germany, was married to an Argentinian, and spent most of his professional life in California. In Germany, he was a refugee from Russia, and in the United States, a refugee from Germany. But insight and knowledge resulting from a change of cultures are balanced by the inexorable pressures toward adaptation. In one of his necrologies, commemorating a fellow expatriate (*RPh* 35 [1982]:522), Malkiel defines the strategy for a refugee's survival: "the business of self-extrication." I read his "self-extrication" as the blending of the former and latter stages, which have given to his scholarly attitudes and performance their characteristic stamp. Being a European transplanted to America meant to him, above all, two metamorphoses: as a Romanist he turned into a general linguist; as a historian of grammar he felt attracted by functional interpretations.

The predicament of the American Romanist is a story that weighs heavily upon the Editor of *Romance Philology*. He sees that the discipline is "crumbling" (*RPh* 35:515), and attributes the decline, in part, to the mutations of its image (*RPh* 35:iv). The field, still flourishing at the beginning of the century, succumbed to the winds of change, which signaled the search for an American identity: Romance linguistics was too closely tied to German humanism and elitist European scholarship; it was too esoteric, a medieval tradition resting on dead languages. For the mid-century scholar coherent integration, wide applicability, and language structure became the new rallying points. The spirit prevalent at Berkeley, where Malkiel settled, as a Hispanist, in 1942, eased for him the difficult crossing from Romance to general linguistics (*RPh* 35:520).

The magnificent journal which Malkiel created at Berkeley and which he guided for thirty-six years, *Romance Philology,* manifests its Editor's change of viewpoint. By the middle forties the two key terms were, still, *Romance* and *Philology*. Looking back in 1983, Malkiel conjures up (*RPh* 37:17–18) his early collaborators: Corominas, Orr, Dauzat, Gougenheim, Paul Barbier, and María Rosa Lida, indeed a phalanx of Romanists, and he contrasts the rationale of their selection, their stardom in Romance, with the policy of his latest years, in which theory was increasingly stressed. The journal, in short, reflects the changes of *Romance* from a discipline in its own right to a corpus of data subject to the general rules of analysis.

His diachronic approach to language, which was still the foundation of a linguist's training when Malkiel left Berlin, in the dark days of the late thirties, also had to conform, once he was in America, to the new currents. The blend of tradition and innovation, which he developed in this particular ambience and which he subsumes under the key term 'glottodynamics', became a hallmark of Malkiel's scholarship. Baldinger (in an address delivered on the occasion of Malkiel's *Ehrendoktorat,* Berlin, 1983, p. 5) shrewdly observes that Malkiel's gift for sensing the forces activating linguistic change was *in nuce* already present in his dissertation of 1938, on *Das substantivierte Adjektiv im Französischen*. (Perhaps, I am tempted to add, Malkiel's inclination was stimulated by his teacher, Ernst Gamillscheg, who liked to dwell on the "psychological" causes of linguistic change.) Among the various features of this first work which anticipate the later Malkiel, Baldinger singles out the insistence on function and the focus on the *energeia* inherent in language as a trigger of change. A binomial structure of titles, which for Baldinger embodies Malkiel's typical correlation between the "specific" and the "general," often encapsulates also the tie between the event of the "change" and the "function" which motivated it. The changes, in themselves, are the usual ones, phonological or morphological. We list, from among Malkiel's titles, just the terms for the causes, to substantiate his concept of 'glottodynamics': "paradigmatic resistance," "morphological analogy," "derivational transparency," "differentiation of near-homophones," "hierarchizing the components," "Interferenzerscheinungen," "phonological irregularity." An ever more intensive recourse to functional explanations of linguistic change provides the diachronic linguist with an Archimedean Point (*Essays on Linguistic Themes* [Berkeley and Los Angeles, 1968], 71): "the pendulum of taste and preference in linguistics may soon start swinging back toward dynamics; . . . a vigorous revival of diachronic grammar is a strong and pleasant possibility."

We described the impact which the move from the Old World to the New had on Malkiel the linguist as an intricate and seminal intertwining of the two strata of his scholarly education; and this cognitive duality is mirrored in his hero-worship for two masters of his craft, the one a European, the other a European-born American. The European is Hugo Schuchardt, a Romanist and diachronist. Malkiel singles him out as "dynamically curious" on both levels of his primary concern, the Romance domain and linguistic theory (*Essays,* 68). He calls Schuchardt "incomparable" (ibid.) and uses in reference to him the metaphor (rarely applied to linguists) of a "meteoric rise to stardom" (*Historiographia Linguistica* 9 [1982]: 473). In Sapir, to whom Malkiel has devoted a study of conceptual redefinitions (*Language* 57 [1981]: 535–570), he praises the virtues of which Romance scholarship, at least for Malkiel, is largely devoid: "glorious elasticity and ability for forceful synthesis" (*Essays,* loc. cit.); and Sapir's *Language* he calls "hauntingly suggestive" (*RPh* 35:3 [1982], 479). Both Schuchardt and Sapir were pioneers and they shared the bent for theory, central to Malkiel's work, as well as the flair for new directions.

II. Several Romance scholars, above all Europeans and his American disciples, have written perceptive appreciations of Malkiel's achievement and its impact. As to the basic features they are in accord. Uitti's succinct phrasing provides the leit-motif (*Hispanic Review* 34 [1966]:255): "M[alkiel]'s work has done much to reveal the several "American" and "European" schools to one another; to a large extent it constitutes a successful blending of approaches, tastes, and traditions."

Each one of the writers highlights this or that particular feature in a way I found interesting enough to draw attention to: taken together they establish the image.

Rebecca Posner added, in 1970, to Iordan's and Orr's *Introduction to Romance Linguistics* a survey of the previous thirty years, in which she singled Y. M. out as the dominant figure in contemporary Romance scholarship. She describes his achievements in a set of antonyms headed by the oxymoron Neo-Traditional: for her, Malkiel bridges the gap between yesterday and today, positivism and formalism, traditional meticulousness and innovative thought. As to the processes of linguistic change which he investigates, Malkiel aims at *explanation* rather than mere *description,* and he tends to stress *interaction* rather than *separation* of levels. As an etymologist he sees words not *static* as isolated units of research but *dynamic* as interpenetrating members of word families. In his perception of lexis, he is torn between two poles of analysis: between *lexicalization,* the anti-abstract European approach, which applies such techniques as linguistic geography, the Words-and-Objects view, and the areal rules of "idealist" linguistics, and *grammaticalization,* which subsumes the methods fashionable in post-bellum America, aiming at the building of an abstract structural model. Posner regards Malkiel's typologies as sophisticated bibliographies, classified in a way which contrasts and compares their items. They reveal an inimitable grasp of bibliographical detail combined with an extraordinary breadth of vision. The material is organized on the basis of "distinctive features."

Baldinger (in his address), expressing Malkiel's achievement in terms of his style, approaches him from two angles. Malkiel, as he sees him, lives in the field of tension between "rule" and "reality" (7), and he skillfully concentrates on key terms to substantiate this thesis. Malkiel's etymological, i.e., morpholexical, reconstitution of word families, which forms a large part of his efforts, vindicates the assumption of their inherent and rule-defying complexity and concatenation, and Baldinger's roster of the respective key terms (8–9) underpins the fact. There are, above all, the *inter*-compounds such as *interlocking, interaction, interplay, interference, interpenetration, intertwining*. Several other morphemes, some of them prefixes, fill the same slot: *cross-connection/amalgamation/continuum/infiltration/transition/fluidity/gradualism*. The second feature of style which to Baldinger reveals basic phases of Malkiel's scholarship consists in the changing structure of his titles (16–18). Baldinger recognizes an earlier stage in Malkiel's productivity, in which the first part of the title provides the specific, and the second part, the general: e.g., "Hispanic *algu(i)en* and Related Formations: A Study of the Stratification of the Romance Lexicon in the Iberian Peninsula" (1948) and "The Latin Background of the Spanish Suffix *-uno:* Studies in the Genesis of a Romance Formative" (1950). Then, from 1959–1960 on, the "base" titles isolate the particular themes (hidden behind the subtitles) which stimulate the study, e.g., "Form Versus Meaning in Etymological Analysis: Old Spanish *auze* 'luck'" (1966) and "The Fluctuating Intensity of a 'Sound Law': Some Vicissitudes of Latin *ĕ* and *ŏ* in Spanish" (1980).

Otto Gsell organizes his beautiful *Forschungsbericht* on Malkiel's linguistic œuvre (*Iberoromania:* 13 n.s. [1980], 1–29) around the key concepts of "coherence" and "integrationism" (23). The customary parts of grammar lose their autonomy, and linguistic change is explained through multiple etiology. Phonological change, for example, results from morphological and analogic interference. In word formation, morphology intersects with lexicology, and the genesis of suffixes is stimulated through "lead words," which shift the process into the domain of etymology. Etymology itself, the "most integrated" branch of them all, evolves, in Malkiel's hands, into a metadiscipline: the single word history becomes a microcosm. With language development consistently perceived as interaction, traditional Romance linguistics merges into general linguistics.

Peter Dembowski (*RLiR* 36 [1972]:167), on the other hand, tries to vindicate the paramount role of Romance within M.'s unified theoretical framework. He even senses a "self-portrait" in Malkiel's description of the Romanist as a scholar who approaches the Romance languages with the particular methods imposed by the "Romanicity" of that family of languages. The Romanist re-creates the data enclosed in them, on both the literary and the dialectal levels, as a dynamic process, with a harmonious integration of the grammatical and lexical features.

The various assessments of Malkiel's work usually dwell on his stance between tradition and innovation but they hardly ever go into the "influence" specific predecessors have had on him. In regard to Malkiel's two "heroes" whom we identified and whose views on language were, in many respects, akin to his own, we noticed that Karl Uitti (op. cit., passim) mentions the same two names to establish some link between Malkiel and his sources of inspiration. Uitti is reminded of Schuchardt by Malkiel's "converging" method, by his "imaginative" style in a lexical exposition, and by his inclination to perceive each linguistic relation (such as that of one phoneme to another) as unique, i.e., to be interpreted according to the specific "context." Uitti is reminded of Sapir by Malkiel's labeling a certain process "paradigmatic resistance to sound change."

III. One of Malkiel's characteristic approaches to linguistics (well outlined by Gsell: 17–20) is his substantial, and constantly developing, work in what is now called historiography. We consider it characteristic for two reasons: On the one hand, it is for him the essential medium for criticism; on the other, Malkiel's historiographic vision of linguistics tends to transcend the traditional borderline of *sachbezogen,* fact-conditioned scholarship, and becomes a personal form of expression in which the dominant experiences of his life are tangibly present.

A programmatic essay, "History and Histories of Linguistics" (rpt. [from *RPh* 22 (1969)] in *From Particular to General Linguistics* [Amsterdam, 1983]:51), is quite explicit: Malkiel examines the qualities which make the historiographer, and, in addition to the professional talents which one would expect, posits four conditions as "most desirable." They describe his own life and circumscribe his preparation for the task: having personally witnessed the rise and decline of "fashions"; having lived in several countries and their intellectual "climates"; having cultivated more than one genre of linguistic investigation; and having focused attention on a period definitely closed. And he adds, quite convincingly, a fifth (somewhat toned-down) qualification (53): "Scholars gravitating toward the descriptive approach will, on the average, make for less satisfactory historians of linguistics."

A few examples will illustrate Malkiel's personal engagement in his historiographic work, in particular his inclination to identify with, or dissociate himself from, the doctrines or movements he analyzes. Frequently his position mirrors the pressures on the European linguist in the New World, on the historian in a synchronic environment, with its fast-changing theories and techniques. The pressures are, for example, terminologically echoed, in Malkiel's writings, by the recurring epithets *tone-setting, trend-setting, mainstream, modernist, avant-garde,* applied to currents, scholars, issues, and journals. From the same angle, a study on "Romance and Indo-European Linguistics in Italy" (*Historiographia Linguistica* 9 [1982]:471–93) is interesting. It calibrates the up-to-dateness, in linguistic matters, of an entire culture. Yesteryear's pride in the Italian contribution, the linking of *filologia* and *glottologia,* which led to impressive achievements in fields such as substratum, glotto-diachrony, Words-and-Objects, is depicted as leaving behind a climate of conservatism, isolation, and *passatismo,* which sharply contrasts with Ascoli's century-old insistence (supported by Malkiel) on the integration of Indo-European and Romance linguistics, praised as living heritage.

Again in the context of yesterday vs. today, yet concentrating on the assessment of one man, the Swedish linguist Ernst G. Wahlgren (1879–1938), Malkiel ties the work of the portrayee to his own (*Studia Neophilologica* 49 [1977]:69–85). The two, of course, never met, and the bond between them is one of purely scholarly affinity. M. isolates four "grands problèmes" treated by the Scandinavian master which today, forty years after his death, still call for renewed attention. All four problems are central to Malkiel's own forays into new territory and are increasingly heeded by American linguists. They are: (a) the semi-learned transmission of the lexicon, i.e., the disregard of phonological rules caused by the impact of learnèd doublets; (b) etymological research strongly tied to the history of grammar; (c) linguistic change resulting from multiple causation; and (d) the acceptance of morphological causes, i.e., analogy, as the explanation of phonological irregularity. The last feature is the most relevant to Malkiel's linguistic creed, and he entitles the essay accordingly: "Ernst G. Wahlgren—et les perspectives d'une réhabilitation de la morphologie."

The historiographical view, natural to Malkiel, emerges in a wide range of his approaches to linguistics. We shall briefly comment on the ones most affected.

1. The *historique* of any problem that Malkiel attacks is an integral feature of his argument: It throws into relief the specific facets of the problem; it presents an opportunity for evaluating the previous solutions; and it leads up to the chronicler's own position.

Malkiel's way of perceiving the chain of interpretations as "the fascinating story of a protracted scholarly debate" is well evidenced in his essay on "Gender, Sex, and Size, as Reflected in the Romance Languages" (rpt. in *From Particular to General Linguistics,* 155–75). The debate rests on more than fifty items, stretching from the middle of the 19th to the late 20th century: "The discussion started in low gear . . . , reached a much higher plateau . . . New voices, including young ones, have been heard over the last few years . . . We still have no truly satisfactory answers to [various] basic facets of the problem." The many viewpoints are, at the end of the study, recapitulated in the condensed form of a chronologically arranged bibliography (173–75).

In the hands of Malkiel, with his extraordinary knowledge of personalities and currents linked to a flair for the historical process, an annotated bibliography changes effortlessly into a dramatic narrative. A set of discontinuous quotations taken from his derivation of *desire* in Romance ("Between Monogenesis and Polygenesis," *Amsterdam Studies in the Theory and History of Linguistic Science,* IV:13 [1982], passim) illustrates the genre:

> First let us quickly recapitulate how scholars, after 1850, went about cutting a path through the jungle./ The derivation seemed too obvious to deserve mention./ The situation changed abruptly in the mid-19th century, with the flourishing of a historically oriented comparatism. Diez recognized that. . . ./ Diez's idea was accepted *in nuce* by some immediate followers./ Interestingly, it ran very soon into stiff resistance in certain quarters. Thus, W. Foerster (1879) disliked the older scholar's semantic analysis . . . in an effort to do justice to an OProv. variant, heretofore neglected./ Meyer-Lübke, on the other hand, starting with his doctoral dissertation (1883) and until the bitter end, defended a different conjecture./ As if these three explanations were insufficient, two more "theories" were launched in quick succession. Almost simultaneously with the appearance of Meyer-Lübke's thesis, an, all told, less than prestigious etymologist, namely, F. Settegast, ventilated a possibility (1883), which, though initially brushed off—e.g., by an almost sarcastic Gaston Paris (1883)—or merely listed without approval, . . . almost won out./ True, this supposition required some semantic legerdemain; but Settegast, for once, turned out to be an astonishingly adroit juggler, and his partisans, half a century later, accomplished even more in keeping this explanation afloat./ Finally, a scholar of the first magnitude, and a spokesman, from the start, for provincial Latinity, namely, H. Schuchardt, came up with a fifth explanation, whose chief characteristic is that its advocate had abandoned all hope of offering a single base for all Romance offshoots (1889)./ Compared to the liveliness of discussions in the period between 1853 and 1889, which produced five independent hypotheses in thirty-six years, the following decades may be described as uneventful, even dull./ . . . Even reputable specialists were willing to settle on various sorts of unexciting compromises./ It is difficult to avoid the impression of a spell of doldrums, if not a certain stagnancy./ Though there has occurred . . . no genuine breakthrough over the last few decades, Settegast's once weakly-argued thesis has been generally reinforced by better-prepared and more qualified sympathizers./ In the mid-forties, J. Corominas produced such examples./ Corominas's mentor and senior friend, Leo Spitzer, [focused] attention on a characteristic Arthurian passage./ Soon after, . . . Corominas threw in for good measure a few more illustrations . . . and reaffirmed his earlier thinking./ With so much and such strong support flowing of late in the direction of the Settegast hypothesis, I incline to join the trend.

2. *Etymology* ranks high in Malkiel's life work. He felt attracted to the field not only as a "word biographer" but also, with the profound change in its status and its foundation, as a historiographer. In a lucid lecture of 1975, "Etymology and Modern Linguistics" (now in *From Particular,* 497–511), he correlates downfall and rebirth of the (once glamorous) subfield with the change of the epistemological climate. The ever more ahistoric, ever more theory-directed linguist looks skeptically at the culturally-embedded word history of Western tradition. Malkiel traces the metamorphoses of attitudes through the last century, from Whitney and Hermann Paul through Saussure and Vendryes to Sapir and Bloomfield. The new meaning of etymology has,

of course, been frequently and variously discussed; as Malkiel reads it, "advanced diachronic linguistics" pushes lexicology toward the borderline of grammar: etymology has to provide the explanations of morphological opaqueness, frequently caused by irregular phonological change. "Etymology fulfills an important function within a morphological framework." The etymologist-historian of the past has become an etymologist-grammarian.

3. *Typology* refers to the comparative description, according to the various techniques employed, of the literature available in a specific scholarly genre. Malkiel has developed the method with his analysis of Spanish dictionaries (1958–1960), Romance historical grammars (1960), and etymological dictionaries (1976). Although the basic outline of the material goes by "distinctive features" (such as time, depth, range, and scope), thus giving to typology a synchronic character, the change of techniques is reported along the time axis, in terms of development and progress, not only moving the method into the realm of historiography but providing the historian of linguistics with a powerful tool. To be specific, Malkiel's essay on *Etymological Dictionaries: A Tentative Typology* (Chicago, 1976) is larded with temporal key terms, stressing the tenet of historiography that each school, each technique analyzed functions as a link between what was practiced before and what came after.

Examples: *successive* schools of thought (1), *shifts* in tastes and in criteria (2), the thinking . . . has undergone considerable *change* (20), the *evolutionary* line (24), over against the *older* compilations . . . stand the *younger* dictionaries (24), the *history* of philological scholarship (25), . . . the *next step* (43), one recognizes, then, the *emergence* of . . . (44), our survey of *progressive* formalization (44), the prerogatives of the *history of a discipline* must be carefully safeguarded (83).

4. *Pen portraits,* i.e., person-centered historiography, are a form of linguistic history frequently cultivated by Malkiel. They sometimes deal, as in the case of Diez or August Friedrich Pott, with scholars of times past and then they usually center on some new phase of Romance linguistics. Mostly, however, they deal with contemporaries who have recently died, and in these necrologies (frequently published in *Romance Philology*) Malkiel developed a particular style, with the interlocking accounts of the portrayee's milieu, personality, and achievement. The necrologies also represent essentially linguistic criticism. On a human scale, the spectrum may extend from warmth to chilliness, but the main theme is always Malkiel's assessment of the impact of the scholar's work. Some names are quite familiar, some, I am sure, largely forgotten; but even the forgotten ones are shown to have had their role in the development of linguistics. A few examples:

The memoir about Georg Cohn (1866–1945?) (*Historiographia Linguistica* 5 [1978]:237–52) tells the story of a maverick, whom Malkiel, just before leaving Germany, met in the late thirties. The background is the state of linguistics in Berlin at the turn of the century. Cohn, a disciple of Adolf Tobler, the Romance philologist, and Heymann Steinthal, the general linguist, published in 1891 a provocative and still stimulating study, in the field of diachronic morphology, on *Suffix Changes in Vulgar Latin,* but was unable to live up to his promise and, an "incurable *cunctator,*" spent the rest of his life under pressure from unfulfilled expectations.

In this context belongs also one of Malkiel's particular accomplishments, in which his pen portrait introduces the posthumous selection of the portrayee's essays: his edition of Elise Richter's *Kleinere Schriften zur allgemeinen und romanischen Sprachwissenschaft* (Innsbruck, 1977). Here the struggles of a pioneer in the field of unified diachrony are told from two angles: through Malkiel's description of the academic milieu together with his interpretative remarks on some of the essays, and on the other hand, through various autobiographic pieces by Richter herself, which are included in the volume.

The third example concerns the pen portrait as a medium to express human relationship. Malkiel lost his wife in 1962, more than twenty-five years ago. María Rosa Lida de Malkiel was a superb scholar and author, the acclaimed expert on the classical tradition of medieval Spain. She had a magnificent record of publications and left unpublished studies behind, and in numerous articles Malkiel kept her memory and her work alive. These contributions, written from many angles, stretch over all these years since her death. They begin with a necrology in *RPh* 17 (1963–64), 9–32; two of the most recent are: "María Rosa Lida como investigadora de las letras coloniales" (1980) and "A Brief History of M. R. Lida de Malkiel's *Celestina* Studies" (1982). In this kind of work, the borderlines between portrait, assessment, and *Geistesgeschichte* are even more tenuous than normally.

■ ■

I wrote this "portrait" of Yakov Malkiel as a personal expression of admiration and friendship. We share much: we both came from Romance to general linguistics; we studied at the same University, Berlin, and wrote our dissertations under the same advisor; we both emigrated in the thirties to the United States, and ever since have tried to blend our European past with the American present. We met in 1940, and our relationship has been a close one ever since.

The present autobibliography certainly demonstrates *ad oculos* the truly staggering dimensions of Malkiel's vigor and devotion. The fitting epithet that comes to mind is the ancient characterization of Didymos, the learned and prolific grammarian, as *chalkénteros,* the man with the iron persistence.

Organization of the Booklet

In the Golden Age of humanistic (including Romance) scholarship it was customary for a university professor of some distinction who was fortunate enough to have reached a ripe age to receive, as an integral part of a testimonial volume in his honor, a scrupulously compiled bibliography of his writings. The person in charge of such a venture was, typically, a former favorite student who had meanwhile become a junior friend and perhaps even the equal of the honoree in farsightedness and sophistication. One thinks of Elise Richter's efforts to prepare an exemplary bibliography of Adolfo Mussafia's publications as the opening piece of the rightly famous miscellany, *Bausteine zur romanischen Philologie* (1905), or of the roughly simultaneous, if posthumous, guide, by Mario Roques, to the writings of his erstwhile preceptor Gaston Paris.

With the passage of time, a certain unevenness of performance began to set in. If Angelina Pietrangeli's two consecutive bibliographies of the explorations of her friends and colleagues Henry and Renée Kahane remain models of finely-chiseled bibliographic performance (1962, 1973), the same, alas, cannot be said of María Luisa Vázquez de Parga's record (1964[–66]) of the publications by a figure as impressive as Ramón Menéndez Pidal–a record marred by gaps and inconsistencies, chargeable to the annalist, and a host of plain misprints. Worse, if one Romance scholar had so recklessly scattered his writings as to make a well-organized bibliographic clue to them nothing short of mandatory, it was Leo Spitzer (1887–1960); yet to this day there exists, to my knowledge, no handy, readily accessible listing of his *varia scripta minora,* i.e., of the bulk of his production.

Given this depressing course of events, there seems to be no alternative to an honoree's overcoming his or her scruples, however well-founded, and preparing a straight autobibliography–if properly encouraged by relatives, personal friends, former or present students, and colleagues. The present booklet, with all its predictable limitations, is one tentative step in this direction.

Since the project of this semi-centennial autobibliography has been launched for the sole purpose of providing a time-saving tool for fellow-scholars (and, on a small scale, even for the compiler himself), a few introductory comments on its organization may be in order. All the items captured have been numbered, chiefly to facilitate cross references. In several respects, but not in all, the pattern of the older "Breve autobibliografía analítica", prepared at Francisco Rico's behest for Vol. 6 (1969[–72]) of the *Anuario de Estudios Medievales* (Barcelona), has served as a model. Mark G. Littlefield's *Bibliographic Index to "Romance Philology", Vols. I–XXV,* of the year 1974, has also proved to be useful.

Had unlimited space been available, it might have been attractive to provide abstract-style summaries, not only for the major items. This luxury had to be dispensed with (but note the inclusion, in recent years, of numerous items in the well-known series Sociological Abstracts). By way of partial compensation, references have been furnished to such critical reactions as had come to my attention, and to plain epitomes in certain reviewing media as well. (Mere mention of an item, however, even if accompanied by a few noncommittal descriptive remarks, as a rule has not been taken into account.) No distinction has been drawn between favorable and unflattering critical assessments, and no attempt has been made at any sort of rebuttal or apologia. I have also curbed the temptation to correct certain non-trivial misprints.

Only on rare occasions have I deemed it useful to specify any such oral presentation of a given topic as may have preceded the publication of the relevant paper, usually by a margin of less than one year. Several exceptions from this norm seemed to me justified in situations where the original context of delivery (e.g., presidential address) may actually have colored content and style of the article in question. Also excluded from further consideration have been, consistently, research papers never meant to be published, but not necessarily those whose anticipated publication was thwarted (e.g., through the collapse of a publishing house or for some other extraneous reason)– provided the underlying research has been completed.

Since accuracy and reasonable completeness of bibliographic information have been the principal goals, I have included allusions to second editions, sometimes vastly improved on the typographic side (e.g., through absorption of a journal article, or of a contribution to a testimonial or memorial volume, into a collegiate reader, or into some other unhurriedly-assembled book-length collection of scattered papers). Translations of certain articles (e.g., into Spanish or Italian) have also been recorded, not least because a few translators have, obligingly, in the process, enriched the documentation adduced. This holds especially for my esteemed colleague Ruggero Stefanini.

The critical reactions hinted at above comprise not only formal book reviews (including review articles, standard-sized appraisals, book notices, and the like), but also digests of periodicals, decennial surveys of periods and genres of research, "état présent des études" types of balance sheets, counterproposals (e.g., in etymology) published as independent articles or notes, etc., with occasional attention to such attempts at alternative solutions of a given problem as have failed to take into account my own earlier gropings. A modicum of attention has further been paid to pertinent entries in etymological dictionaries bibliographically underpinned. What I have succeeded in gathering by way of collateral information undoubtedly represents only a small selection of the material actually extant; omissions have been random and unintentional; let me thank in advance those willing to alert me to any possible lacunae. Cross-references to topically or methodologically related studies of my own have been listed separately, even where they involve elaborations and self-corrections. In general, cross-references may imply different things: a return to the same subject (sometimes from a different angle), mutual topical affinity or mere resemblance, use of the same approach or technique, etc. Their number could easily have been doubled.

The break-up of a mass of ca. 850 items into certain categories, with the chronological sequence prevailing only inside each class thus established, will not be to everyone's liking; let me parry in advance certain possible objections and show how I have tried to remedy a few foreseeable shortcomings of this arrangement. It has, e.g., been argued that most historians of scholarship, any future necrologists, and the like would instead have favored a straight chronological ordering (such was, e.g., the philosophy of my late friend Antonio Rodríguez-Moñino, an acknowledged master bibliographer). To humor those who hold such a belief, I should perhaps have offered the entire array of data, properly foreshortened, in an annalistic counterview (Appendix A). At the crucial moment, however, I felt that an essayistically phrased "Candid Retrospect" would provide a more welcome balance to the array of barren data. Another category of potential users, the theorists, grammarians, and etymologists, could not care less about chronological sequences of analyses; what they need for speedy consultation is a handy list of key terms, and a parallel one of key words, both alphabetically arranged. I have tried to cater to the legitimate needs of these categories of colleagues by compiling Appendices B and C. Finally, I readily visualize a third group of users—let me identify them as those bio-bibliographically curious or inspired—who are eager to find out, in a matter of seconds, the names of those authors of books (and, occasionally, of monographs and lengthy articles) which it has been my privilege, over the years, to examine in a critical vein; or the names of those colleagues whom it has been my sad duty to memorialize—in obituary notices and other "minor genres" of research: dedications and the like. To satisfy this gamut of tastes, I have organized separate, complexly-structured Appendices D and E. These five appendices, obviously, are skeletal, containing as they do only bare numbers.

With two or three exceptions (marked by such tags as "unassigned" or "acceptance pending"), I have included in this survey, toward the end of each rubric, items actually researched, edited, accepted for publication, and awaiting appearance in a given journal or miscellany. In regard to forthcoming pieces any strict chronological order is obviously unattainable; should an asterisk have set off those items that have already been proofread? It seemed unrealistic to me to inflate a forbiddingly long list even further through allusions to books, articles, necrologies, comments, etc., which, true enough, I have committed myself to preparing, but which are not yet available in definitive shape at this cut-off point; to be specific, toward the beginning of August 1987. A bibliography, after all, aims at being a record, and as such must not be confused with a titillating "sneak preview" of projects and bare possibilities, however well-meant.

The categories themselves are not, it is hoped, controversial, but a few, nevertheless, invite some preliminary explanations. On a handful of occasions I have run into classificatory difficulties. Certain special (typically, expanded) issues of periodicals have also appeared as separate volumes, under titles devised *ad hoc;* a famous example in point is *Linguistics Today* (1953), which corresponds word by word—but, of course, not page by page—to Vol. X:2–3 of the journal *Word.* To avoid duplication, I have opted for listing such pieces as journal articles alone, sometimes indicating in parentheses any alternative way of recording them. I have deemed it wise to subdivide the necrologies, of widely varying scope, into (a) full-scale necrological essays, of up to forty printed pages, hence comparable in potential weight to articles and review articles, and (b) briefer obituary notices, whose writing presupposed a modest quota of research on my part. In the category subsuming my efforts, starting with 1962, to make posthumously available and to interpret certain writings by my late wife, María Rosa Lida de Malkiel, an even subtler network of subcategories had to be devised, according to the specific service I was, in each instance, aiming to perform. It has further seemed defensible to me to precede the whole with a list of general critical surveys or appreciations of my endeavors frequently cited. After some wavering, I decided against including in additional Appendices an assortment of books or articles generously dedicated to me, as well as the titles of doctoral dissertations, which it has been my pleasure and privilege to direct or co-direct on the Berkeley Campus. I am aware of certain testimonial volumes (e.g., the one in honor of the noted historian Herbert Boulton) in which the entire corpus of each former student's scholarly production has been itemized and thus "morally" credited to the teacher, at least in part. With this adjudication of merit I happen to be in disagreement: No former student is obliged to remain beholden to one of his or her former teachers beyond the contractual relationship represented by the supervision of a thesis—although it certainly is a marvelous dividend if a few students choose to remain loyal to their mentors beyond that point.

By way of honest retrospective self-criticism let me confess that the single major difficulty I have encountered was with the collection of experts' responses. Formal reviews of book-length publications were relatively easy to catch. A higher degree of selectivity has, perforce, prevailed in tracking down assessments of entire volumes into which the given piece from my pen happened to enter: Much depended, under this set of circumstances, on sheer luck (and, one hopes, on the relative weight of the pertinent segment of the book review). Completely impossible to verify in their entirety were the scattered reactions to my writings in reference works, introductory manuals, grammatical treatises, histories of scholarship, counterviews of the same problems in all sorts of publications. I was lucky enough to run across miscellaneous specimens of such responses, often merely descriptive, but may easily have missed a few crucially important items or, conversely, have recorded far too numerous fleeting or flimsy references. To achieve significantly better results might have cost me several years of concentrated and, to be frank, slightly tedious (or else improperly narcissistic) research. Aware as I am of these shortcomings, I apologize in advance for any imbalances and omissions of this sort, in addition to disappointments which possible inaccuracies, in page references and the like, may cause.

And these flaws and infelicities are not even the worst. Like many other people in my position, I suppose, I cannot help realizing, on the occasion of this retrospective survey, that certain articles, polemic notes, and hasty page fillers should never have been written, let alone published, in the first place; and that the tone of not a few review articles, book appraisals, and necrologies might well have been more restrained, or that some different, and, all told, more pleasing modulations might have been better-advised. *Si c'était à recommencer*. . . .

Berkeley, April 22, 1984–August 14, 1987–February 5, 1988

I. General Appreciations by Critics; Joint Assessments of Numerous Writings

Alvar/Pottier: Manuel Alvar & Bernard Pottier, *Morfología histórica del español*. Biblioteca Románica Hispánica, 3:57. Madrid: Gredos, 1983. Passim.

Baldinger (a): Kurt Baldinger, *La formación de los dominios lingüísticos en la Península Ibérica*$_2$ (rev.). Tr. Emilio Lledó & Monserrat Macau. Biblioteca Románica Hispánica, 1:10. Madrid: Gredos, 1972. Passim.

Baldinger (b): Kurt Baldinger, "Yakov Malkiel", *Ehrenpromotion Y.M. am Fachbereich Neuere Fremdsprachliche Philologien der Freien Universität Berlin am 6. Oktober 1983*, 18–50. Berlin: Duncker & Humblot, 1984.

Catalán: Diego Catalán [Menéndez-Pidal], *Lingüística ibero-románica: crítica retrospectiva*. Biblioteca románica hispánica, 3:34. Madrid: Gredos, 1974.

Corbett: Noel Corbett, "Romance Studies in North America", *Trends in Romance Linguistics and Philology,* ed. Rebecca Posner & John N. Green, vol. 4: *National and Regional Trends* . . . The Hague, etc.: Mouton, 1982. Pp. 81–126, esp. 111–3, 124.

Corominas: Juan Corominas, *Diccionario crítico etimológico de la lengua castellana*. 4 vols. Bern: Francke, Madrid: Gredos [1954–57]. Passim.

Corominas/Pascual: Juan Corominas & José A. Pascual, *Diccionario crítico etimológico castellano e hispánico*. 6 vols. Madrid: Gredos, 1980–. Passim.

Craddock, Dworkin, & Poghirc: Jerry R. Craddock, Steven N. Dworkin & Cicerone Poghirc, "Romance Etymology", *Trends in Romance Linguistics and Philology,* ed. Rebecca Posner & John N. Green, vol. 1: *Romance Comparative and Historical Linguistics,* 191–240. The Hague/Paris/N.Y.: Mouton, 1980.

González-Llubera: Ignacio González-Llubera, Contributions to Vols. 11 (1940–49)–22 (1960) of *The Year's Work in Modern Language Studies,* especially under the rubric "Spanish Language".

Green: John N. Green, Contributions to Vols. 31 (1969)–48 (1986) of *The Year's Work in Modern Language Studies,* especially under the rubric "Romance Linguistics".

Gsell: Otto Gsell, "Das wissenschaftliche Œuvre Yakov Malkiels: ein Forschungsbericht (1958–1978)", *Iberoromania,* N° 13 (1981), 1–29.

Huberman: Gisela Bialik Huberman, *Mil obras de lingüística española e hispanoamericana; un ensayo de síntesis crítica.* Madrid: S.A. Playor, 1973. Summaries of 41 papers; for a list see p. 806.

Hymes/Fought: Dell Hymes & John Fought, "American Structuralism", *Current Trends in Linguistics,* ed. Thomas A. Sebeok, vol. 13:2. The Hague/Paris: Mouton, 1975. Pp. 903-1176. Passim.

Justice: David Justice, "Biographical Essay: Yakov Malkiel", *Proceedings of the Eighth Annual Meeting of the Berkeley Linguistics Society,* ed. Monica Macaulay & Orin Gensler, 1–9. Berkeley, 1982.

Kahane: Henry Kahane, "Introductory Essay", in the present *Autobibliography,* pp. xvii–xxv.

Kuhn: Alwin Kuhn, *Die romanischen Sprachen* (= Romanische Philologie, 1), Wissenschaftliche Forschungsberichte, 8. Bern: A. Francke, 1952. Passim.

Laca: Brenda Laca, *Die Wortbildung als Grammatik des Wortschatzes: Untersuchungen zur spanischen Subjektnominalisierung.* Tübinger Beiträge zur Linguistik, 286 (Tübingen, 1986). *Kr,* 32 (1987), 122:5.

Meier: Harri Meier, *Notas críticas al DECH de Corominas/Pascual. Verba,* Supl. 24 (1984).

Otero: Carlos-Peregrín Otero, *Evolución y revolución en romance: mínima introducción a la fonología.* Barcelona: Seix, 1971. Pp. 142–3, 146–9, 151–60, 197–9.

Pensado Ruiz: Carmen Pensado Ruiz, *Cronología relativa del castellano.* Acta Salmanticensia, Filosofía y Letras, 158. Salamanca, 1984. Passim.

Posner (a): Rebecca Posner, Contributions to Vols. 24 (1962)–31 (1969) of *The Year's Work in Modern Language Studies,* under the rubric "Romance Linguistics", sometimes in collaboration with John N. Green and Joseph A. Cremona.

Posner (b): Rebecca Posner, "Thirty Years On", Supplement (393–579) to I. Iordan & J. Orr, *An Introduction to Romance Linguistics: Its Schools and Scholars*$_2$ (rev.). Language and Style Series, dir. S. Ullmann, 8. Oxford: Blackwell, 1970. Esp. pp. 434–47.

Trabant: Jürgen Trabant, "Yakov Malkiel und die Berliner Romanistik", *Ehrenpromotion Y.M. am Fachbereich Neuere Fremdsprachliche Philologien der Freien Universität Berlin am 6. Oktober 1983.* Berlin: Duncker & Humblot, 1984. Pp. 5–17.

Uitti: Karl D. Uitti, Introduction, *Trends in Romance Linguistics and Philology,* ed. Rebecca Posner & John N. Green, vol. 3: *Language and*

Philology in Romance, 3–42. The Hague, etc.: Mouton, 1982. Esp. pp. 6–7, 11, 18, 20, 31–2.

Wilkinson: Hugh E. Wilkinson, Long series of contributions, in English, on miscellaneous problems of Romance linguistics, to the Japanese periodical *Aoyama Gakuin "Ronsha"* (from sixties to eighties).

Wright/Wheeler: Roger Wright & Max W. Wheeler, Contributions to *The Year's Work in Modern Language Studies,* Vols. 41 (1979)–48(1986), under the rubric "Spanish Studies: Language".

II. Books and Book-Length Monographs

1 *Das substantivierte Adjektiv im Französischen.* [Inauguraldissertation, Friedrich-Wilhelms-Universität Berlin]. Berlin: Jüdischer Buchverlag Joseph Jastrow, 1938; printer: Speer & Schmidt. Pp. viii, 142. Title page varies.

[Mere torso, due to a political emergency, of the monograph as originally planned, with a Prefatory Note replacing the Introduction, the Conclusion entirely absent, any comparison with Spanish, as initially foreseen, omitted, and only four chapters salvaged and loosely strung together: (1) Substantivization in chromonyms; (2) The signaling of a part; (3) The neuter abstract, and (4) Designations of persons.]

Cr.: L.J. Corbeau, *Mus,* 47 (1939), 144–6; C. Fahlin, *SN*, 12 (1939–40), 241–5; G. Gougenheim, *BSLP,* 40:3 (1939), 88–90; U.T. Holmes (Jr.), *Lg,* 15 (1939), 205–7; E. Lerch, *ZRPh,* 60 (1940), 286–90; H. Rheinfelder, *LGRPh,* 62 (1941), 44–5; M. Roques, *Ro,* 67 (1942–3), 281; K. Sneyders de Vogel, *Neoph,* 26 (1940–1), 63; L. Spitzer, *MLN,* 54 (1939), 148–50.

See also 73, 127, 136.

2 *The Development of the Latin Suffixes* -ANTIA *and* -ENTIA *in the Romance Languages, with Special Regard to Ibero-Romance. UCPL,* 1:4 (1945), 41–186.

[Careful survey of the announced situation in older Spanish, Portuguese, and Catalan, on the basis of newly-collected source material, with only superficial attention to the remaining cognate languages, for the sake of the contrast they often afford.]

Cr.: J.H.D. Allen, Jr., *Lg,* 27 (1951), 394–9; M. Alvar, *ZRPh,* 71 (1955), 299–303; V. Buben, *Čas,* 31 (1948), 321; C.G. Echegaray, *BBMP,* 22 (1946), 282–5; L. Deroy, *AC,* 18 (1949), 474; A. Ernout, *RevPh,* 22 (1948), 111–2; C. Fahlin, *SN,* 19 (1946–7), 190–1; G. Gougenheim, *BSLP,* 43:2 (1946), 71; H. Guiter, *RLaR,* 69 (1947), 335–8; U.T. Holmes (Jr.), *Spec,* 20 (1945), 495–7; J. Horrent, *Er,* 2 (1948), 89–93; F. Lecoy, *Ro,* 70 (1948), 133–4; E. Lerch, *RJb,* 3 (1950), 179–90; B. Migliorini, *LN,* 8 (1947), 120; L. Mourin,

RB, 26 (1948), 838–40; K.S. Roberts, *HR,* 14 (1946), 86–8; A.H. Schutz, *Word,* 1 (1945), 292–4; K. Sneyders de Vogel, *Neoph,* 31 (1947), 216; L. Spitzer, *AJPh,* 67 (1946), 380–2; J.A. van Praag, *Mus,* 53 (1948), 158; H.F. Williams, *MLJ,* 33 (1949), 156–7; M.A. Zeitlin, *MLF,* 30 (1945), 129–30.

See also 131.

3 *The Hispanic Suffix -(I)EGO: A Morphological and Lexical Study Based on Historical and Dialectal Sources. UCPL,* 4:3 (1951), 111–214.

[Study of the vicissitudes of a pre-Latin formative, with equal attention to historical and to modern dialectal Peninsular sources of information. Contacts with -ICU, -IACU, -AECU, and other Latin and Graeco-Latin derivational suffixes; miscellaneous etymological problems.]

Cr.: E. Alarcos Llorach, *Arch,* 1 (1951), 184–5; M. Alvar, *ZRPh,* 71 (1955), 312–4; W.C. Atkinson, *ArL,* 4 (1952), 92–3; K. Baldinger, *ZPh,* 8 (1954), 267–9; W. Belardi, *RL,* 2 (1951), 233; O. Deutschmann, *RJb,* 4 (1951), 408–15; W.D. Elcock, *MLR,* 48 (1953), 113; A. Ernout, *RevPh,* 26 (1952), 145; I. González-Llubera, *YW,* 13 (1951–2), 118; G. Gougenheim, *BSLP,* 47:2 (1951), 164; O. Gsell, 12; H., *Íns,* 8:85 (15. I. 1953); U.T. Holmes (Jr.), *Spec,* 27 (1952), 234–5; J.E. Iannucci, *HR,* 21 (1953), 258–60; H.V. King, *SiL,* 10:1 (1952), 12–3; F. Krüger, *NRFH,* 11 (1957), 207–8; M.M. Lasley, *Word,* 8 (1952), 186–7; H. Lausberg, *DL,* 74 (1953), cols. 90–1; P.M. Lloyd, *RPh,* 17:4 (1964), 759; B. Pottier, *Ro,* 73 (1951), 286; G.R. Solta, *Spr,* 9 (1963), 217; H. Stimm, *BNF,* 3 (1951–2), 355; J.A. van Praag, *Mus,* 57 (1952), cols. 187–8, and *Lingua,* 4:4 (1955), 435–6. Cf. U. Schmoll, *Die Sprachen der vorkeltischen Indogermanen...* (Wiesbaden, 1959), 54, 122 and, additionally, K. Baldinger (a), 81, 198.

See also 20, 22, 30, 154–5, 160, 165–6.

4 *Studies in the Reconstruction of Hispano-Latin Word Families* (1. The Romance progeny of Vulgar Latin *(re)pedāre* and cognates; 2. Hispano-Latin **pedia* and **mania;* 3. The coalescence of *expedīre* and *petere* in Ibero-Romance), *UCPL,* 11 (1954); pp. viii, 224.

[Although each of these three studies can be assessed on an individual basis, they have as a common denominator the author's concern with the Latin *ped-* stem suggestive of 'foot'. The first article marks an attempt to reconstruct, in the speech of Roman soldiery, an entire subfamily of which only REPEDĀRE is recorded in a few texts. The second article involves an instance of lexical polarization; in addition, it bespeaks an attempt at justifying the reconstruction of *INTERPEDIĀRE, the starting point for Sp. *tro(m)peçar,* orig. *entre-, entro-peçar* 'to stumble'. The third piece aims at demonstrating that Sp. Ptg. *despedir* 'to dismiss', refl. 'to take leave', not only echoes EXPEDĪRE, but also involves an encroachment of PETERE. Conversely, Ptg.-Gal. *(d)espir* represents a pure reflex of *expedīre.*]

Cr.: M. Alvar, *NRFH,* 10 (1956), 205–13; W.C. Atkinson, *ArL,* 7 (1955), 68–9; D. Catalán Menéndez-Pidal, *RFE,* 39 (1955), 412–42; C. Crews, *VR,* 14 (1955), 375–80; W.D. Elcock, *MLR,* 51 (1956), 444–6; I. González-Llubera, *YW,* 16 (1954–5), 169–70, and 18 (1956–7), 172; E. González López,

Lat, 14 (1955), 482–3; J. González Muela, *BHS,* 33 (1956), 51–2; G. Gougenheim, *BSLP,* 51:2 (1955), 75–6; H. Guiter, *RLaR,* 72 (1955–8), 250–1; M.M. Lasley, *Symp,* 10 (1956), 141–3; H. Meier, *RJb,* 6 (1953–4), 382–4, and *RF,* 69 (1957), 72–92; G.M. Messing, *Spec,* 32 (1957), 382–3; L.J. Prieto, *Word,* 14 (1958), 97–100; H. Rheinfelder, *Er,* 11 (1958), 78–82; N.P. Sacks, *HR,* 24 (1956), 251–5; H. Stimm, *BNF,* 7 (1956), 211–2; H.L.A. van Wijk, *Mus,* 61 (1956), 228–30. In addition see Horst Bursch, *Die lateinisch-romanische Wortfamilie von "*interpedāre" und seinen Parallelbildungen.* Romanistische Versuche und Vorarbeiten, 52. Bonn, 1978, and the reviews produced by that dissertation.

See also 14, 37, 167, 169–71, 183; and, on the impact of the language of soldiery, 198 and 251.

5 *Essays on Linguistic Themes.* Language and Style Series, dir. S. Ullmann, Vol. 6. Oxford: Basil Blackwell, 1968 (American edn.: Berkeley & Los Angeles: California UP); pp. viii, 415.

[This is the first collection of scattered articles, chosen in consultation with the editor of the series. The items underwent only slight revision (updating and the like). Additional features include a rather full Preface, dated October 1966; a list of abbreviations; plus a careful Topical Index, in two columns, pp. 399–415.]

This collection includes the following items, in part slightly revised and with an occasional change in title: 808, 212, 207, 28, 203, 624, 206, 194, 191, 208, 331, 200, 213 (in this order).

Cr.: M. Balaban, *Lgs,* 99 (1973), 91–7; K. Baldinger, *ZRPh,* 84 (1968), 636–7; T. Berchem, *RJb,* 22 (1971 [–72]), 200–1; J. Blau, *Lešonēnu,* (1969), 312–6; P.F. Dembowski, *RLiR,* 36 (1972), 163–72; S.C. Dik, *Er,* 23 (1970), 345–7; W. D(ressler), *Spr,* 16 (1970), 89a; R.A. Hall, Jr., *GL,* 9 (1969), 185–95; H.M. Hoenigswald, *AA,* 71 (1969), 140–1; M.P.A.M. Kerkhof, *Neoph,* 55 (1971), 452–4; W.P. Lehmann, *FLa,* 8 (1972), 280–7; L. Lupaş, *RRL,* 14 (1969), 415–6; H. Meier, *ASNS,* 204 (1968), 385–90; Š. Ondruš, *Čas,* 52 (1970), 165–7; R. Posner, *Lg,* 45 (1969), 364–9; S. Potter, *MLR,* 65 (1970), 854–6; G. Price, *FS,* 24 (1970), 323–4; W. Roth, *RF,* 83 (1971), 97–103; K. Togeby, *SN,* 41 (1969), 166–8; M. Wilmet, *RB,* 47 (1969), 1327–9; M.G. Worthington, *RPh,* 23:1 (1969), 65–75 ("Theory and Practice in General Linguistics"); P. Wunderli, *VR,* 29 (1970), 171–2.

6 *Linguistica generale–Filologia romanza–Etimologia.* Manuali di Filologia e Storia. Tr. Olga Devoto (ed. Ruggero Stefanini); prefatory note ("Premessa") by Bruno Migliorini. Firenze: G.C. Sansoni Editore, 1970. Pp. xxiii, 308.

This collection includes the following 9 items, in part polished or enriched: 205, 194, 206, 187, 191, 184, 28, 195, 200 (in this order).

Cr.: A. Bohnet, *CanJL,* 18:1 (1973), 81–4; P.F. Dembowski, *RLiR,* 36 (1972), 163–72; J.N. Green, *YW,* 33 (1971–2), 19–20; R. A. Hall, Jr., *GL,* 14 (1974), 127–8; B. Migliorini, *LN,* 31 (1970), 130–1; V. Păltineanu, *CL,* 18 (1973), 189–92; E. Paratore, *RCCM,* 12 (1970), 99–105; R. Posner, *Lingua,* 27

(1971), 293–6; A. Scaglione, *D'Andrea's Yearbook of Italian Studies,* 1. 323–8; C. Schwarze, *IF,* 78 (1973 [–74]), 296–301; A. Vàrvaro, *ZRPh,* 86 (1970), 586–90; G.C. Vincenzi, *LS,* 6 (1971), 158–60.

See also 207, 243.

7 *Patterns of Derivational Affixation in the Cabraniego Dialect of East-Central Asturias. UCPL,* 64 (1970); pp. viii, 95.

Cr.: A. Alsdorf-Bollée, *RF,* 83 (1971), 339–41; H.H. Baumann, *ASNS,* 207 (1970–1), 385–9; P. Charaudeau, *BSLP,* 66:2 (1971–2), 137; J.R. Craddock, *Lingua,* 28 (1971–2), 383–92; D. S. Fagan, *Language Sciences,* April 1973, pp. 54–5; H. Goebl, *ZRPh,* 89 (1973), 385–8; O. Gsell, 13; W.H. Haverkate, *Er,* 23 (1971), 738–41; R.G. Keightley, *YW,* 33 (1971–2), 236–7; K.H. Kvavik, *RPh,* 29:1 (1975), 57–66 ("Patterns of Derivational Affixation in a Romance Dialect"); J.J. Montes Giraldo, *BICC,* 27 (1972), 142–3; V. Pisani, *Paideia,* 28 (1973), 126–8; M. Popescu-Marin, *SCL,* 22 (1971), 431–4; C.J. Pountain, *YW,* 37 (1975–6), 233; J. Purczinsky, *Lg,* 50 (1974), 185–6; R. St. Clair, *Lgs,* 114 (1973), 116–21.

See also 269.

8 *Linguistics and Philology in Spanish America: A Survey (1925–70).* Janua Linguarum, Ser. Minor, 97. The Hague & Paris: Mouton, 1972. Pp. 179.

[Basically a reprint of the chapter on "Hispanic Philology" prepared for Vol. 4 (*Ibero-American and Caribbean Linguistics,* 1968) of the *Current Trends in Linguistics* series. Additions include: the Prefatory Note; a tripartite list of abbreviations; a rather elaborate Supplement (126–60), bearing on (a) bibliographic surveys; (b) pioneers and trailblazers; (c) varying degrees of breadth of dialect surveys; (d) social aspects of language; plus (e) philological ingredients of literary scholarship; and two indices, compiled by Irene Hasenclever: one of names, the other of topics (161–79).]

Cr.: D.L. Canfield, *GL,* 15 (1975), 106–7 and *Hisp,* 57 (1974), 1022–3; M.B. Fontanella de Weinberg, *RPh,* 28:3 (1975), 372–9; D.J. Gifford, *YW,* 34 (1972–3), 309; G. de Granda, *RDTP,* 29 (1973), 280–2; J.N. Green, *IJAL,* 42 (1976), 277–8; O. Gsell, 18; R.A. Hall, Jr., *GL,* 14:2 (1974), 127–8; H. Kröll, *RF,* 87 (1975), 117–8; I. Lerner, *ZRPh,* 91 (1975), 599–605; C.J. Pountain, *BHS,* 52 (1975), 397–8; T. Şandru-Olteanu, *RRL,* 20 (1975), 85–6; A. V[àrvaro], *MR,* 1 (1974), 155–6.

See also 35, 76, 197, 601, 605, 607.

9 *Etymological Dictionaries: A Tentative Typology.* Chicago: Chicago UP, 1976. Pp. ix, 144.

[Aside from Preface (vii–ix), End Notes (85–95), the list of abbreviations and symbols (97–100), an elaborate but selective Bibliography (101–29), and a single-track, two-column Index (131–44), the booklet falls into ten chapters: Preliminaries and a panoramic view of the problem; time depth; direction of change; range; grand strategy; the total organization of the corpus; the structure of the individual entry: tactical preferences; breadth; scope; purpose and level of time; conclusion.]

Cr.: K. Baldinger, *ZRPh,* 96 (1980), 659–60; A. Bollée, *RF,* 90 (1978), 494–5; W.G. Boltz, *JAOS,* 97 (1977), 1407–8; H. Cottez, *BSLP,* 72:2 (1972), 52; H. Henne, *Germanistik,* 19:1 (1978), 30–1; G. Lepschy, *MLR,* 73 (1978), 130–1; G.J. MacDonald, *HR,* 46 (1978), 87–9; H. Meier, *RJb,* 27 (1976–77), 187–9; R. Schmitt, *Lg,* 54 (1978), 420–3; L. Thorpe, *RPh,* 32:2 (1978), 222–6; O.N. Trubačëv, *Ètimologija,* (1977–79), 172–4; L. Zgusta, *Kr,* 21 (1976–77), 184.

See also 203, 208–9, 751.

10 *From Particular to General Linguistics: Selected Essays 1965–1978.* Studies in Language; Companion Series, 3. Amsterdam / Philadelphia: John Benjamins, 1983. Pp. xxii, 659.

[Newly added are: Author's acknowledgments, Table of contents, Guide to abbreviations (v–xxii); Introduction (1–20); Supplement (559–91); Index of names (593–605); and Selective index of key terms (607–59). Included in the collection are 22 earlier articles, with numerous corrections, cross references, and elaborations: 34, 52, 55, 216, 218, 220, 222, 224, 229, 234, 236–8, 243–4, 246, 251, 253, 340, 345, 377, 386.]

Cr.: O. Gsell, *RJb,* 36 (1985–86), 140–2; G. Hilty, *Kr,* 31 (1986), 142–7; R. Martin, *RLiR,* 49:2 (1985), 427–8; M. Martinelli, *Linguisticae Investigationes,* 8:1 (1984), 213–4; X. Mignot, *BSLP,* 80:2 (1985), 28–30; J. Vizmuller-Zocco, *Lingua,* 67:1 (1985), 85–87.

11 *Prospettive della ricerca etimologica.* Strumenti linguistici. Napoli: Liguori Editore, 1988. Pp. 160. Contains translation, by Lucia Folena, of four items (45, 51, 238, 240), preceded by a prefatory note by Alberto Vàrvaro, a Supplement ("Appendice retrospettiva sul decennio 1975–85"), and various indexes ("Abbreviazioni", "Indice tematico", "Indice degli autori citati", "Scelta delle voci esaminate").

12 *A Tentative Autobibliography,* with an Introductory Essay by Henry Kahane. Preceded by a Table of Sponsors, Donors, and Contributors. Supplement to *RPh,* 41 (1988). Pp. xxxi, 186.

13 *Theory and Practice of Romance Etymology: Studies in Language, Culture, and History (1947–1987).* A selection of etymological essays, with an Editor's preface by Edward F. Tuttle. To include items 21, 25, 32, 143, 145, 147, 151, 155, 160, 178, 257, with a separate string of elaborations, plus a newly-written introductory piece titled: "Pure or Integrated Etymology?", plus a thoroughly revised and substantially expanded version of item 164. To be published by UCLA's Center for Medieval and Renaissance Studies, in collaboration with London's "Variorum": Revised Editions and Reprints. Edited by Carol D. Lanham. Scheduled for April 1989.

14 *Linguistica e cultura moderna: Ritratti di protagonisti.* Bologna: Società Editrice il Mulino. To include translations (*in toto* or in part) of pen portraits (originally necrologies) of some of the following figures: M. Bataillon, É. Benveniste, E. Gamillscheg, H. Hatzfeld, K. Jaberg, E. Kantorowicz, J. Kuryłowicz, R. Lida, R. Menéndez Pidal, C. Michaëlis de Vasconcelos, B. Migliorini, E. Richter, E. Sapir, L. Spitzer, A. Steiger, K. Togeby, M.L. Wagner, U. Weinreich.

14a *Etymology, or Verbal Archaeology.* [A book-length manuscript, under consideration by Cambridge UP]

III. Sections of Books

15 Some Contrasts between Spanish and Portuguese Pertaining to Verbal Derivation. *UWP,* 9 (1942), 53–67.

Cr.: A. Kuhn, 369, 373, 428.

See also items 45, 52, 91, 93, 100, 125, 139, 186, 188, 192, 235, 237, 260, 269, 274, 286, 290, 303, 352, 385, 580, 582, 586, 588, 651.

16 The Derivation of Hispanic *fealdad(e), fieldad(e), frialdad(e), UCPL,* 1:5 (1945), 187–211.

[The relation of Sp. *feo,* Ptg. *feio* 'ugly' to their respective abstracts *fealdad* and *fealdade* represents an anomaly, on account of the wedged-in *-al-* segment. There exist traces of older derivatives, in *-eza, -edad, -edumbre,* and *-adumbre;* these before long were dislodged by *fealdad,* taken over from the family of *fiel* 'true', where *fealdad* initially was a variant of *fieldad* < FIDĒLITĀTE. The modern language has opted for *fidelidad.* Similarly, *fri-or, -ez(a), -ura, -agem,* etc. gave way to *frialdad* (fig.) 'coolness, coldness', patterned on *fealdad.*]

Cr.: J.H.D. Allen, Jr., *Lg,* 27 (1951), 399; M. Alvar, *ZRPh,* 71 (1955), 297–8; V. Buben, *Čas,* 31 (1948), 321; G. Gougenheim, *BSLP,* 43:2 (1946), 71–2; A. Kuhn, 371; F. Lecoy, *Ro,* 69 (1946–7), 119–20; L. Mourin, *RB,* 26 (1948), 840–1; K.S. Roberts, *HR,* 14 (1946), 85–6; H.F. Williams, *MLJ,* 33 (1949), 157–8.

See also 24 and 250.

17 Three Hispanic Word Studies: Latin MACULA in Ibero-Romance; Old Portuguese *trigar;* Hispanic *lo(u)çano, UCPL,* 1:7 (1947), 227–96.

[Each of these three studies has been designed to stand on its own feet, except that *trigar,* often assigned to Germanic, is shown to be related to TRĪCAE and to be, consequently, of Latin stock, whereas OSp. *loçano,* Ptg. *louçano,* originally 'masterful, domineering, arrogant', is credited to Germanic, counter to prevalent opinions. MACULA is studied for the sake of its unusual ramification, due to nasal insert, vowel syncope, replacement of -ŬLA by -ĔLLA, etc.]

Cr.: J.H.D. Allen, Jr., *Lg,* 27 (1951), 400; M. Alvar, *ZRPh,* 71 (1955), 303–7; K. Baldinger (a), 25, 101, 219; V. Buben, *Čas,* 31 (1948), 383–4; M. Frenk Alatorre, *NRFH,* 4:2 (1950), 187–8; G. Gougenheim, *BSLP,* 44:2 (1947–8), 113–4; H. Guiter, *RLaR,* 70 (1948), 59–61; H., *Ins,* 3:25 (1948), 8; A. Henry, *Lat,* 9 (1950), 187–8; F. Lecoy, *Ro,* 72 (1951), 142–3; H. Meier, *RF,* 61 (1949), 413–4, and *RFE,* 34 (1950), 184–94; L. Mourin, *RB,* 26 (1948), 841; J.M. Piel, *RPF,* 2 (1949), 295–7; K.S. Roberts, *HR,* 16 (1948), 272–3; A.E. Sloman, *MLR,* 48 (1948), 438; J.A. van Praag, *Neoph,* 33 (1948), 60–1.

See also 143, 283.

18 Hispanic *algu(i)en* and Related Formations: A Study of the Stratification of the Romance Lexicon in the Iberian Peninsula, *UCPL,* 1:9 (1948), 357–442.

[A cluster of pronominal and adverbial formations traceable to such prototypes as QUĪ / QUEM; *ALTER-Ī, *-EM; ALIQU-EM, etc., with special attention to OPtg. *alguém, outrém, nen- / nin-guém* and to the change of OSp. *alguién* into mod. *álguien,* beside *alguno.*]

Cr.: J.H.D. Allen, Jr., *Lg,* 27 (1950), 401; M. Alvar, *ZRPh,* 71 (1952), 308–12; K. Baldinger (a), 184; C.G. Echegaray, *BBMP,* 28 (1952), 176–7; S. Fernández Ramírez, *Gramática española* (Madrid, 1951), 385–447; M. Frenk Alatorre, *NRFH,* 4 (1950), 187; I. González Llubera, *YW,* 11 (1940–49), 111; J. Horrent, *MA,* 55 (1949), 405–6; H.V. King, *SiL,* 10:1 (1952), 13–4; A. Kuhn, 374; H. Meier, *RF,* 61 (1949), 410–3; L. Mourin, *RB,* 27 (1949), 1094; V. Pisani, *Paid,* 4 (1949), 46; B. Pottier, *Rom,* 72:2 (1951), 281; K.S. Roberts, *HR,* 17 (1949), 84; H.L.A. van Wijk, *Neoph,* 34 (1950), 119–20.

See also 73, 133.

19 La derivación de *rebelde, rebeldía* y las fuentes del grupo de consonantes *-ld-* en iberorrománico, *EDMP,* 1 (1950), 91–124.

[*Rebelde* involves the (presumably, late) transmutation, in a semilearned channel of transmission, of ancestral -LL- into *-ld-,* as against the familiar vernacular shift -LL- > -ʎ. By way of background, the paper offers an inventory of sources converging upon OSp. *-ld-* which, in the company of *-nd-,* at a certain point became a favorite medial cluster in that speech community.]

Cr.: K. Baldinger (b), 41; J.I. Louro, *BF,* 12 (1951), 200–2.

See also 201.

20 Graeco-Latin IŪDAEUS and IŪDAICUS in the Romance Languages, with Special Reference to Ibero-Romance. *Semitic and Oriental Studies: A Volume Presented to William Popper (= UCP in Semitic Philology,* 11 [1951]), 327–38.

[A general overview of the Graeco-Latin ethnonym, traceable to a Hebrew prototype, and to derivatives extracted from it, with attention to the reflexes of these words in the Romance languages: Fr. *juif,* Sp. *judío,* Ptg. *judeu,* It. *giudeo,* etc., and to new offshoots: Sp. *judería,* etc.]

Cr.: B. Migliorini, *AGI,* 36 (1951), 93–5.

See also 3, 22, 30, 53, 99, 115, 245, 277, 373. Topically related is an (unpublished) evening lecture, given before UCB's Colloquium Orientologicum on February 23, 1972, under the title: "Orient and Occident: The Western transmission of the ethnonyms *Jew, Hebrew,* and *Israeli(te)*".

21 Spanish *duende* and *duendo,* Portuguese-Galician-Asturian *dondo,* Leonese *dondio,* Central American *dundo.* In *Estudios hispánicos: Homenaje a Archer M. Huntington,* 361–92. Wellesley, MA, 1952. To be included in 13.

[An attempt to draw a neat line of demarcation between the descendants of DOMINU 'master' and DOMITU 'tame(d)' in Hispano-Romance. *Duende* 'imp' is explained as a coalescence of *dueñ de* 'master of [a household]', with *dueñ* ranking as an apocopated variant of *dueño.*]

See also 34, 92, 224, 271.

22 En torno a las voces *judío* y *judía. Homenaje a J.A. van Praag (1930–1955),* 73–80. Amsterdam, 1957.

[Basically a collection of stray addenda to 20, including either rarer lexical items previously overlooked, or new details on the better-known items alredy touched upon in the earlier venture; as well as a reëxamination of the analysis performed on the preceding occasion.]

See also 3, 20, 30, 53, 99, 115, 245, 277, 373.

23 The Semantic Link between Latin BIS- and Romance *bes-, bis-. Studies Presented to Joshua Whatmough on his Sixtieth Birthday,* ed. E. Pulgram, 165–71. The Hague: Mouton, 1957.

[Culturally noteworthy about Lat. BIS-, BĪ- is the fact that, in addition to meaning 'twice', it developed a number of secondary connotations, almost invariably derogatory. Italian, French (where *bes-* alternated with *mes-*), and Spanish (which has favored the form *biz-*) all three partook of this development).]

Cr.: H. Guiter, *RLaR,* 75 : 2 (1963), 276; F.W. Householder, Jr., *Lg,* 34 (1958), 399.

See also, on the prefix for 'three': 75, 92, 261.

24 Los interfijos hispánicos; problema de lingüística histórica y estructural. *Estructuralismo e historia; miscelánea-homenaje a André Martinet,* 2, 107–99. La Laguna, Canarias, 1958.

[This study, which includes a Supplement of last-minute additions (187–9) and a word-index in three columns (189–99), concerns itself with such issues as: The terminological problem (107–16); certain historical conditions: (a) dual relationship in secondary derivatives (116–9); (b) crystallization of an interfix through lexical attrition (120–2); (c) the interfix as a result of a lexical blend (123–9); (d) the interfix as a residue of a crumbled inflectional system (129–31); (e) stem variants (131–135); (f) suffixal variants (135–6); (g) genesis of an interfix through lexical borrowing (136–9); (h) conflicting interfixes (139–41); (i) false regression (142–3); (j) the interfix compared with the corresponding suffix (144–53); (k) interfixes in deverbals (153–7); (l) issues in lexical stratification (157–9).]

Cr.: H. Guiter, *RLaR,* 74:2 (1961), 230–1; F.H. Jungemann, *Word,* 15 (1959), 482–3. Cf. F. González Ollé, *Los sufijos diminutivos en castellano medieval* (Madrid, 1962), passim; and Fernando Lázaro Carreter, "¿Consonantes antihiáticas en español?" *Homenaje a Antonio Tovar. . .* (Madrid: Gredos, 1973); see M. Lejeune, *BSLP,* 68:2 (1973), 105–6. The concept has recently been further developed by Wolfgang Dressler, e.g., in his paper "Zur Wertung der Interfixe in einer semiotischen Theorie der natürlichen Morphologie", *Wiener slavistischer Almanach,* 13 (1984), 35–45; cf. also, in collaboration with Lavinia Merlini Barbaresi, the two papers (in press): "Interradical interfixes: contact and contrast" and "Interfissi e non-interfissi antesuffissali nell'italiano, spagnolo e inglese".

See also 34, 154, 222, 224, 229, 235–6, 243–4.

25 The Luso-Hispanic Descendants of pōtiō: A Study in Lexical Proliferation. *Hispanic Studies in Honour of I. González-Llubera,* ed. F. Pierce, 193–210. Oxford, 1959. To be included in 13.

[Inquiry into the interplay of forces that have caused the polymorphism of the descendant of parental pōtiō 'drink, potion', re-interpreted as 'poison'. These forces included: reinforcement of the feminine gender through addition of *-a;* vowel dissimilation: *poçoña* > *peçoña;* sporadic agency of the nasal insert: *poçoña* > *ponçoña.*]

Cr.: K. Baldinger (a), 53; O. Gsell, 4.

See also 195, 250, 283.

26 Etimología y cambio fonético débil: Trayectoria iberorrománica de medicus, medicāmen, medicīna. *Homenagem a Marcel Bataillon (= Ibérida,* 6 [1961(-63)]), 127–71.

[The notoriously capricious development of Latin intervocalic -d- in Spanish may in itself have stimulated certain secondary developments: blends with *vedar* 'to forbid' < vetāre in *vedegambre;* blend with mel 'honey' in *melezina;* borrowing from Catalan of *me(t)ge,* later expanded into *menge,* etc. The consistent loss of ancestral -d- in Portuguese may have made for greater stability: *mèzinha,* etc.]

Cr.: O. Gsell, 4, 7, 9.

See also 207, 283.

27 Filología española y lingüística general. *Actas del Primer Congreso de Hispanistas (Oxford 1962),* 107–26. Oxford, 1964.

[An invitational lecture delivered in a plenary session of the Congress, in the presence of Ramón Menéndez Pidal. The paper aims at delineating the credo and at assessing the accomplishments of the Madrid school of Spanish philology, which was not yet extinct a quarter-century ago, at least not in its derivative forms.]

Cr.: S.G. Armistead & J.H. Silverman, *RPh,* 24 (1970), 140–1; Z. Hampejs, *PhP,* 6 (1963), 198; G. Orduna, *BICC,* 18 (1963), 194–5.

See also 172, 179, 206, 217, 239.

28 Distinctive Traits of Romance Linguistics. *Language in Culture and Society: A Reader in Linguistics and Anthropology,* ed. Dell Hymes, 671–86, in 2 cols. New York, Evanston, & London: Harper & Row, 1964. Rpr.: (a) *ELT,* 47–69; (b) *Readings in Romance Linguistics,* ed. James M. Anderson & Jo Ann Creore, 13–38. The Hague: Mouton, 1972. Tr. *LG,* 146–69.

[This paper is based on a 1959 lecture revised in 1960, then again in 1962. It includes a rather elaborate appended Bibliography. Among the distinctive traits or features adduced are: (a) characteristics traceable to the material; (b) those attributable to the stage of the discipline; (c) the matrix of national cultures; and (d) the impact of powerful personalities. Some of these are subject to further subdivision; thus, among the factors subsumed under (a) one can isolate: (α) the available records; (β) overlapping of philology and linguistics; (γ) the changing hierarchy of approaches; (δ) some special implications of historicism; (ε) lexical emphasis, etc.]

Cr.: O. Gsell, 17; K.D. Uitti, *RPh,* 16 (1962–63), 417–9.

See also 197, 203, 205, 208, 233.

29 Initial Points versus Initial Segments of Linguistic Trajectories. *Proceedings of the Ninth International Congress of Linguists at Cambridge, Mass. (1962),* ed. Horace G. Lunt II, 402–5. The Hague: Mouton, 1964.

[Some theoretical conclusions to be drawn from studies of Old Spanish diphthongization presented elsewhere. In response to the general replacement of *ia* by *ie* in Late Old Spanish, the impf. ind. ending *-ía* (from Lat. -ĪBAT beside Class. -IĒBAT) also gave ground to *-ié,* despite the accentual difference, except in the 1st pers. sg., which retained *-ía,* perhaps on account of the advantage this pattern of distribution offered in distinguishing 'I' from '(s)he'.]

Cr.: R. Posner, 446.

See also 199, 204.

30 (With M.R. Lida de Malkiel). The Jew and the Indian: Traces of a Confusion in the Hispanic Tradition. *In Honor of Max Weinreich's Seventieth Birthday: Studies in Jewish Languages, Literature, and Society,* ed. J.A. Fishman et al., 203–8. The Hague: Mouton, 1964.

[The Spanish word for 'Jew', *judío,* appears in medieval and later manuscripts spelled *judio,* which easily lent itself to misinterpretation, by copyists and hasty readers, as *yndio,* i.e., *indio* 'Indian'. Given the ingredient of myth and folk belief surrounding 'Jew' and '(West, East) Indian', all sorts of confusions developed. By the same token, *yndino* 'indi(g)no' was misread 'judino', a ghost-word, also allegedly signifying 'Jew'.]

Cr.: Gold, *LS.* Cf. M.R. Lida de Malkiel, "Túbal, primer poblador de España", *Ábaco,* 3 (1970), 9–48.

See also 3, 20, 22, 30, 53, 99, 115, 245, 277, 373.

31 Économie phonologique et perte lexicale. *Mélanges de linguistique romane et de philologie médiévale offerts à Maurice Delbouille,* 1, 409–16. Gembloux: Duculot, 1964.

[Regular sound change is apt to produce consonant clusters uniquely or but rarely represented in the lexis of the given language. To the familiar remedies available to the speech community–anaptyxis, metathesis, insertion of some homorganic transition consonant, etc.–one may well add lexical loss and subsequent replacement, as when OSp. *orebze* < AURIFICE 'goldsmith' gave way to *orífice* or *platero.*]

See also 318e.

32 Form versus Meaning in Etymological Analysis: Old Spanish *auze* 'luck'. *Estudios dedicados a James Homer Herriott,* 167–83. Madison: Wisconsin UP, 1966. To be included in 13.

[*Auze* (fem.), a relatively infrequent word in medieval Spanish, has provoked a volume of discussion out of all proportion to its limited prominence. Of the two best-remembered etyma proposed, *ave / aucella* 'bird', cited in connection with augury, turns out to be inferior to *A.B.C.,* i.e., *ABECE.* The criterion of form, it appears, is still the safest, but need not be ranked as necessarily standing in opposition to the criterion of meaning.]

Cr.: A.D. Deyermond, *RPh,* 24:1 (1970), 150–1; R. Posner (b), 437.

See also 213.

33 Genetic Analysis of Word Formation. *Current Trends in Linguistics,* ed. Thomas A. Sebeok, 3: *Theoretical Foundations,* 305–64. The Hague, London & Paris: Mouton, 1966.

[Aside from the introductory remarks, bibliographically slanted, this paper, based on several lectures delivered at Indiana University's Linguistic Institute in the summer of 1964, concerns itself with five major issues: (1) the place of affixation in the edifice of language; (2) the genesis of a derivational suffix; (3) diffusion of derivational suffixes; (4) the esthetic dimension of derivation; (5) prospects for future research. Each of these principal sections is subdivided into narrower-meshed problems; thus, under (1), attention is focused, consecutively, on lexicalization of linguistics, connections between inflection and word formation, disproportionate proliferation (derivatives from animal names in English and

Spanish), degrees of elaborateness in inflection and in derivation, parasynthetic formations, tripartite derivational proportions, suffix chains, etc.]

Cr.: A. Capell, D. Hymes, B. Migliorini, R. Posner, *CA,* 9 (1968), 150a-153c; O. Gsell, 13; R. Posner (b), 439–41; P. Zumthor, *Lingua,* 23 (1969), 358–9.

See also 1–3, 7, 16, 24, 42, 45, 48, 56, 59, 63, 87, 162, 165, 170, 174, 184, 196, 198, 202, 221, 230, 235, 243, 305, 377, 401, etc.

34 Multiple Versus Simple Causation in Linguistic Change. *To Honor Roman Jakobson: Essays on the Occasion of his Seventieth Birthday,* 2, 1228–46. The Hague & Paris: Mouton, 1967. Rpr.: *PGL,* 251–68, also 13, 575–7.

[Aside from the introductory remarks and the concluding paragraph, the paper falls into two parts: (1) a circumstantial analysis of the Spanish adjectives in unstressed *-io,* such as *agrio* 'sour', *lacio* 'withered, faded', and *mustio* 'sad, gloomy'; and (2) a briefer discussion of three supporting examples, including such problems as: (a) the alternation of [ð] and [ɾ] in Hispano-Romance; (b) hypercharacterization of gender; and (c) consonantal dissimilation.]

Cr.: O. Gsell, 15; R. Posner (b), 445.

See also 123, 174; 87, 124, 146, 195.

35 Hispanic Philology. *Current Trends in Linguistics,* ed. Thomas A. Sebeok, 4: *Ibero-American and Caribbean Linguistics,* 158–228. The Hague & Paris: Mouton, 1968.

[The use of 'philology' in the title of this paper shows the extent to which, until the mid sixties, literary, folkloristic, anthropological, and straight linguistic studies were interwoven in Spanish America. Aside from the introductory examination of the prelude (158–64), the report concerns itself with such issues as "Attempts at a global view of American Spanish" (164–72), "Linguistic aspects of immigration and settlement" (172–9), and "Lexicography and etymology geared to local needs" (179–208).]

Cr.: P. Boyd-Bowman, *Lg,* 46 (1970), 191; C. Patiño Rossell, *BICC,* 24 (1969), 512–4; P. Russell-Gebbett, *YW,* 30 (1968–69), 311–2.

See also 8, 76, 95, 326, 364, 438, 601, 605, 607, etc.

36 The Inflectional Paradigm as an Occasional Determinant of Sound Change. *Directions for Historical Linguistics* (1968; see 119), 23–64.

[In harmony with the character of the 1966 symposium at which it was originally offered and discussed, this paper presents, in fairly radical formulation, the occasional interference of morphological conditions with smooth phonological developments. At first, a set of seventeen points is established that seem to preside over many sound changes. Then, to exemplify Point 5 ('The paradigm as a stimulus for a sound change'), the seemingly erratic vicissitudes of ancestral *-rǵ-, -lǵ-,* and *-nǵ-* in Paleo-Romance, especially in Old Spanish, are subjected to scrutiny (33–50), with a bird's-eye view of earlier analyses added for good measure

(50–55). By way of a tentative parallel, the sporadic monophthongization of the rising diphthongs *ie* and *ue,* starting with Late Old Spanish, is introduced (55–63). The author's Acknowledgments (64) round out the piece.]

Cr.: K. Baldinger (a), 400; J.R. Craddock, *Lg,* 46 (1970), 688–95; M.B. Fontanella de Weinberg, *Fil,* 15 (1971), 318–27; O. Gsell, 21; G. Lepschy, *JL,* 6 (1976), 136–7; R. Posner, *RPh,* 23:2 (1969), 146–7, 149, 150–1; O. Szemerényi, *GL,* 10:2 (1970), 122–32; K. Togeby, *RevR,* 5:2 (1970), 257–60; K.D. Uitti, *RF,* 81 (1969), 7–9. One late echo: J. Méndez Dosuna & C. Pensado, "Can Phonological Changes Really Have a Morphological Origin?", *Diachronica,* 3 (1986), 185–201.

See also 39, 67, 71, 84, 215, 223–5, 228, 244–5, 253, 262, 264, 267, 271, 292.

37 Latin PEDICA, *PĒNSUM, and PERTICA in Hispano-Romance. *Mélanges de philologie offerts à Alf Lombard à l'occasion de son soixante-cinquième anniversaire. . .,* 130–50. Études romanes de Lund, 18. Lund: Gleerup, 1969.

[This paper deals with a number of etymologically ambiguous or opaque verbs, some of them narrowly confined to certain territories: *apiescar* to Asturias, *apesgar* to Southern Mexico. Its main purpose is to formulate etymological conjectures with appropriate caution, distinguishing probable solutions from mere possibilities.]

Cr.: P. Gardette, *RLiR* (1970), 249–50; O. Gsell, 4; A. Roceric, *SCL,* 20 (1969), 666–8; H. P. Schwake, *ZRPh,* 86 (1970), 647.

See also 4, 135, 167, 169–71, 183, 402.

38 Deux problèmes de linguistique générale illustrés par le parfait fort de l'ancien hispano-roman. *Mélanges offerts à Rita Lejeune. . .,* 1, 471–83. Gembloux: J. Duculot, 1969.

[Of the two points of possible relevancy to generalists the first concerns certain advantages exploited to the hilt by the speech community in regard to the given form's final vowel, the nuclear vowel, and the radical-final consonant. The second point has a bearing on the broader issue of homonymy.]

See also 147, 175, 178; 204.

39 Le nivellement morphologique comme point de départ d'une "loi phonétique"; la monophtongaison occasionnelle de *ie* et *ue* en ancien espagnol. *Mélanges de langue et de littérature du Moyen Age et de la Renaissance offerts à Jean Frappier. . .,* 1, 701–35. Genève: Droz, 1970.

[What was relegated to the background–merely as a close typological parallel–at the Texas Symposium (1966), namely the occasional monophthongization of *-ie-* and *-ue-* in Late Old Spanish, appears here, in an article actually written one year later, placed in the focus of attention. The documentation is designedly heavy, and the theoretical skewing has remained the same. Aside from Preliminary Remarks and from the definition of the problem at issue (701–6), the gradual blurring of Ĕ > *ie* (707–15) and of Ŏ > *ue* (715–21) is examined at length, then the two processes of diphthongization are compared (721–2) and an inventory of the eventual monophthongization is established (722–8). The concatenation of causes and the reconstruction of the course of events (728–34) involve the peak of the analysis, followed by a brief March 1970 post-script.]

Cr.: K. Baldinger (a), 400; R. Posner (b), 442.

See also 215, 223, 225, 228, 231–2, 259, 262.

40 Ernst H. Kantorowicz. *On Four Modern Humanists: Hofmannsthal, Gundolf, Curtius, Kantorowicz,* ed. Arthur R. Evans, Jr., 146–219. Princeton, N.J.: Princeton UP, 1970.

[An invitational essay, designed to place a straight historian (medievalist) of our own times–but one known for his unusual style and persuasions as well as for his ties to a peculiar esthetic and ethic movement, centered around the poet Stefan George–alongside an inspired poet-essayist, a literary scholar, and a literary critic divided in his interests between the Middle Ages and modern times. Of the various periods in the life of E.K. (1895–1963) his Berkeley years, which corresponded to the forties, receive heightened attention, because here E.K.'s and Y.M.'s orbits intersected.]

Cr.: F.G. Cronheim, *MLR,* 67 (1972), 950–1; R. Exner, *BA,* 46 (1972), 115–6; A. Momigliano, *Rivista storica italiana,* 83 (1971), 741–3.

See also 409, with a reference to a recent book-length study.

41 Lexicography. *The Learning of Language,* ed. Carroll E. Reed, Chap. 10, pp. 363–87. N.Y.: Appleton-Century-Crofts (Educational Division: Meredith Corporation), 1971. For the National Council of Teachers of English.

[This invitational chapter has been written with educators, specifically teachers of English, in mind. It places much heavier stress on the didactic or 'mixed' than on the purely informational services of dictionaries; among the genres de-emphasized are historical and etymological dictionaries, as well as concordances. Some of the points discussed are: laymen's expectations in consulting a dictionary; mono- vs. bi-lingual reference works; lexicographic vs. encyclopedic enlightenment; words to be dealt with in 'general' terms: functional items, most of the primary verbs, nouns, and adjectives of extra-broad scope.]

See also 57, 72, 111–3, 197, 208.

42 The Pan-European Suffix *-esco, -esque* in Stratigraphic Projection. *Papers in Linguistics and Phonetics to the Memory of Pierre Delattre,* ed. Albert Valdman, 357–87. Janua linguarum, Series maior, 54. The Hague: Mouton, 1972[–73].

[This suffix basically involves an ancient blend of a Greek (*-ískos*) and a Germanic (*-isk*) element. Its early evolutionary phase is observed in Rumanian, Sardic, Italian, Old Provençal, Medieval Hispano-Romance, and Old French. Of distinctly later date (essentially the Renaissance) is the wave of Italianisms in *-esco,* and of random imitations thereof, observable in Golden-Age and Modern Spanish, Modern French, English, German, and Russian, to cite a few representative 'Western' languages. Wedged in between the paper proper and the References is a short selective guide to Hispanic *-esco* formations (382–4).]

Cf. Sven Björkman, *Étude sur le suffixe français -ESQUE et sur ses équivalents en espagnol, italien et roumain* (Uppsala, 1984).

See also 221, 265.

43 General Diachronic Linguistics. *Current Trends in Linguistics,* ed. T.A. Sebeok, 9:1: *Linguistics in Western Europe,* 81–118. The Hague & Paris: Mouton, 1972.

[By way of first approach to a field still ill-defined at the moment of writing, the piece concerns itself, first, with the pronouncements of Meillet–here contrasted with Brugmann as a leading German-style Neogrammarian–and of Meillet's disciples Benveniste and Kuryłowicz (82–96), then moves on to the Prague Circle (giving full attention to Roman Jakobson), to the Danes (including L. Hjelmslev), and to André Martinet as author of the *Économie des changements phonétiques,* with some additional concern about other European structuralists (97–112). There follows a brief theoretically-slanted segment (113–8).]

Cr.: O. Gsell, 21.

See also 94, 101, 179, 206, 216–7, 238.

44 Comparative Romance Linguistics. *Current Trends in Linguistics,* ed. T.A. Sebeok, 9:2: *Linguistics in Western Europe,* 835–925. The Hague & Paris: Mouton, 1972.

[The bibliographic information is concentrated in the end notes, 869–925. The distinctly shorter text, 835–69, centers about problems rather than colorful personalities or dogmatic schools of thought. Some of the issues treated are: The classical standard of comparatism (836–8); comparative linguistics as a model of broadly cultural analysis; comparatism on a reduced scale (839–40); the comparative model expanded and refined (840–2); the external organization of Romance linguistics (842–55); inner organization of the Romance language family (865–69).]

Cr.: J.N. Green, *YW,* 34 (1972–73), 22; O. Gsell, 18.

See also 27–8, 49, 69, 70, 94, 97, 103, 117, 121, 172–3, 203, 205, 233, 247–8, 254, 256, 263, 268, etc.

45 Two Problems of Hispanic Morpho-Etymology: (1) The Etymology of OSp. *(de)rretir,* OPtg. *(de)rreter* 'to melt, fuse, smelt'; (2) The Derivational Structure of Sp. *hartazgo* ~ *hartazón* 'fill, surfeit'. *Studies in Honor of Tatiana Fotitch,* ed. J.M. Solà-Solé et al., 261–70. Washington, D.C.: The Catholic University of America Press, 1972. Tr. in 11, 35–49.

[OSp. *retir* and OPtg. *reter* display the familiar regional distribution of *-er* vs. *-ir* conjugation classes. The immediately underlying form must have been

*RETTĔRE, from Class. RE-TERERE. The semantic overburdening of OSp. *fundir* (a) 'to sink', (b) 'to (s)melt' may have contributed to the remedial growth of *retir.* Sp. *hart-azgo* ~ *-azón* 'fill, surfeit' (OSp. *fart-adgo*) exhibits an unusual extension of *-adgo* < -ĀTICU, which seems to have overlaid and thus masked the direct outgrowth of -ĀTIŌ (nomin.), flanking *-azón* < -ĀTIŌNE (obl.).]

Cr.: O. Gsell, 4.

See also 91, 100, 106, 139, 186, 188, 192, 237, 274, etc.; 151, 190, 198.

46 Phonological Irregularity vs. Lexical Complexity in Diachronic Projection: The Etymological Substructure of Luso-Hispanic *abarcar* 'To Clasp, Embrace, Contain'. *Issues in Linguistics: Papers in Honor of Henry & Renée Kahane,* 606–35. Urbana, etc.: Illinois UP, 1973.

[The widely-accepted derivation from *BRĀ(C)CHICĀRE 'to grasp' (with one's arms) is open to criticism. It seems wiser to start from the older spelling, *avarcar,* and try to build a bridge to the progeny of VĀRICĀRE 'to straddle, stand with feet apart' (cf. the compounds PRAE-, TRĀNS-VĀRICĀRE), a family exceedingly well represented in Italian (*varco* 'passage', etc.), also in Romaunsch, Friulan, and Sardic. BRĀ(C)CHIU 'arm' could then constitute a secondary focus of influence in Hispano-Romance.]

Cr.: O. Gsell, 9.

See also 4.

47 Quelques avatars romans d'un zoonyme et d'un ornithonyme latins. *Études de langue et de littérature du Moyen Age offertes à Félix Lecoy par ses collègues, ses élèves et ses amis,* 377–84. Paris: H. Champion, 1973.

[Lat. LACERTUS 'lizard' should have produced OSp. **lazierto* rather than *lagarto;* documented protracted wavering, especially in the past-participial endings, between *-ert-* and *-art-* accounts for the rise of **lacartus* as a by-form of Class. LACERTUS. –It is, on balance, simpler to trace OSp. OPtg. *açor* 'falcon' to parental ASTŬRE (with stress shift) than to ACCEPTŌRE; transmission through Arabic would account for the change of *-st-* into *-ç-*.]

See also 18.

48 (With S.N. Dworkin, C.B. Faulhaber & J.K. Walsh) El núcleo del problema etimológico de *pícaro* ~ *picardía;* en torno al proceso del préstamo doble. *Studia Hispanica in Honorem R. Lapesa,* ed. H. López-Morales, 2, 307–42. Madrid: Gredos, 1974.

[Given the importance of *pícaro* 'rogue' and *picardía* 'roguish trick, mischief' for earlier Spanish literature, it is not surprising that more than a dozen etymological conjectures should have been launched over the years, by linguists and literary historians alike (311–28). The corner-stone of any hypothesis must be the fact that, despite the isolability of the suffix *-ía,* it is impossible to extract *picar-d-ía* from *pícaro,* or vice versa. Hence the necessity of assuming dual borrowing, with the Fr. ethnonym *picar(d)* / *Picardie* serving as an acceptable starting point. Secondary influences (e.g., that of *picar* 'to prick') must be reckoned with, and certain implications of facetious words stressed on the antepenult (329–30) invite attention. A systematic survey of derivatives from *picar(d)- / picañ-* (330–7) and a survey of foreign echoes (348) conclude the core of the study.]

Cr.: C.J. Pountain, *YW,* 37 (1975–76), 234.

See also 19, 116, 229.

49 Friedrich Diez's Debt to Pre-1800 Linguistics. *Studies in the History of Linguistics: Traditions and Paradigms*, ed. Dell Hymes, 315–30. Bloomington & London: Indiana UP, 1974.

[For all his close ties to Jakob Grimm and other contemporaries, Diez, in his etymological dictionary (1853) even more than in his historico-comparative grammar (1836–44), never sought to hide the numerous debts he had contracted toward Renaissance scholars and post-Renaissance antiquarians: S. de Covarrubias, B. Aldrete, L.A. Muratori, T.A. Sánchez, J. de S.R. de Viterbo, E. Forcellini, G. Ménage, and others. He was particularly beholden to the old guard of Humanistic Latinists, including Vossius, Marini, and Orelli.]

Cr.: R.H. Robins, *HL,* 2 (1975), 244–9.

See also 248, 530.

50 Old Spanish *bivo, bevir, vida:* A Preliminary Analysis. *Studies in Honor of Lloyd A. Kasten,* ed. T.S. Beardsley, Jr., 165–73. Madison, WI: Hispanic Seminary of Medieval Studies/Wisconsin UP, 1975.

[Granted the considerable margin of wavering between *b-* and *v-,* of whatever provenience, in medieval Spanish, it is nevertheless striking that in the cases of *visque* 'I lived' and *vida* 'life' the *v-* prevails, while *bivo* 'I live' (or adj. 'live') and *bevir* 'to live' are typically spelled with word-initial *b-,* a contrast unknown to the parent language. The simplest solution is to assume consonant dissimilation in the cases of *bivo* and *bevir.*]

See also 318h, 318j.

51 Perspectives d'un renouvellement de l'étymologie romane. *Actes du XIIIe Congrès International de Linguistique et Philologie romanes* (Québec, 29 août–5 sept. 1971) 1, 967–86. Québec: Presses de l'Université Laval, 1976. Tr. in 11, 9–33.

[By way of compensation, as it were, for its long-delayed publication, this plenary-session talk includes certain questions raised by A. Henry, P. Imbs, J. Pohl, and M. Wandruszka, and the speaker's reactions to them. The main thrust of the paper is toward restoration of a wholesome balance between concern with individual word history and the search for underlying patterns. Thus, while (a) OSp. *(de)rretir,* (b) Ptg. *irto* / OSp. *yerto* beside *direito* / *derecho,* (c) *colher* / *coger* in contradistinction to OSp. *esleer,* and (d) *cuntir,* the predecessor of *acontecer,* can all four be treated individually, it is possible, at the price of a certain effort, to recognize in them a common denominator.]

Cr.: F. Helgorsky, *FM,* 46 (1978), 186, 188.

See also 32, 45, 52, 81–3, 93, 109, 111, 144, 181, 187, 191, 194, 206, 234, 238, 240, 313, etc.

52 The Interlocking of Etymology and Historical Grammar (Exemplified with the Analysis of Spanish *desleír*). *Current Progress in Historical Linguistics;* Proceedings of the Second International Conference on Historical Linguistics, Tucson, AZ, 12–16 Jan. 1976, ed. William M. Christie, Jr., 285–312. Amsterdam: North Holland Publishing Co., 1976. Rpr., *PGL,* 513–42, also ibid. 19, 588–90.

[Advanced historical grammar and sophisticated etymology are inextricably interwoven. The particularly intricate biography of the Spanish verb *desleír* 'to dilute' is here invoked to illustrate that point. Equally complicated is the record of explicative etymological conjectures; it turns out that Cuervo, more than a century ago, came distinctly closer to the 'truth' than other meritorious workers before and after him, including Menéndez Pidal. DĒLĒRE 'to destroy', with potentialities for striking semantic changes, emerges as the best-defensible prototype. The paper is followed by a series of critical comments (J.P. Maher, E.F. Tuttle, A.R. Diebold, Jr., I. Lehiste).]

Cr.: G. Hilty, *Kr,* 31 (1986), 144–7.

53 In Search of "Penultimate" Causes of Language Change: Studies in the Avoidance of /ž/ in Proto-Spanish. *Current Studies in Romance Linguistics,* ed. Marta Luján & Fritz Hensey, 27–36. Washington, D.C.: Georgetown UP, 1976.

[Tempting as it has at all times been to engage in a search for the 'ultimate causes' of change, experience teaches us that the more modest goal of ascertaining merely 'penultimate causes' has merits of its own. Thus, the aloofness of speakers of Proto-Spanish from /ž/ (or its earlier stage [ᵈž] can be fruitfully studied without excessive worry about the ultimate reason for this baffling attitude. The phoneme /ž/ does occur in (semi)learnèd words: *gigante, judío, justo, general;* in borrowings from Gallo-Romance: *juglar, argén, viage,* or from Arabic: *alfaja, javalí,* or else from Gothic: *agasajar,* and in lexical units phonosymbolically tinted: *mugir, rugir.* It is exceedingly rare in the native stock (*ageno, foja*); there either /j/ (*yazer*) or /ø/ (*ermano*) prevail instead, in contexts where cognate languages exhibit /ž/; note the documented transition *(y)ermano.* The history of VǵV abounds in complications.]

Cr.: O. Gsell, 16.

See also 105, 107, 117c, 210, 255, 291, 293.

54 Changes in the European Languages under a New Set of Sociolinguistic Circumstances. *First Images of America: The Impact of the New World on the Old,* ed. Fredi Chiappelli, 581–93. 2 vols. Berkeley, Los Angeles, & London: California UP, 1976. (Transactions of a UCLA Symposium.)

[To understand the many dimensions of the chosen problem we must strive to isolate the universals that can be abstracted from the separate records of English, Dutch, Scandinavian, French, Spanish, Portuguese, and Italian speech projected onto the Western Hemisphere. We must further interpret 'impact' very generously, subsuming under it not only the speakers' reactions to the initial shock of finding themselves almost on a different planet, but also their joyful (or anxious) anticipations of this turning-point.]

See also 8, 35.

55 Gender, Sex, and Size, as Reflected in the Romance Languages. *Studies in Romance Linguistics;* Proceedings of the Fifth Linguistic Symposium on Romance Languages, ed. Michio Peter Hagiwara, 254–77. Rowley, MA: Newbury House, 1977. Rpr., *PGL,* 155–75 [with addenda], also ibid. ii, 567–8.

[The paper falls short of aiming at any sensational discovery, having instead been planned as an attempt to piece together the fascinating story of a protracted scholarly dialogue. The discussion started in low gear a century ago, reaching a much higher plateau of intensity from the early 1920s to the late 1950s. The protagonists of the drama are Munthe, Meyer-Lübke, Jaberg, Montoliu, von Wartburg, Renée Toole, the ménage Kahane, Schneider, Hasselrot, Dauzat, Spitzer, and García, to cite just a few names.]

Cf., independently, R. Stefanini, "Il genere come marca d'alterazione. . .", *AGI,* 65 (1980), 41–73.

See also 73, 581.

56 Why *ap-ISH,* but *worm-Y*? *Studies in Descriptive and Historical Linguistics; Festschrift for Winfred P. Lehmann,* ed. Paul J. Hopper et al., 341–64. Amsterdam: Benjamins, 1977.

[Even though the suffixes *-ish* and *-y,* to the near-exclusion of *-ly,* have been traditionally in competition in helping speakers to derive adjectives from animal names, they were not actually interchangeable in most instances: *-ish,* typically, joined designations of larger animals, such as *ape, sheep,* and *wolf,* subject to individuation; in contrast, *-y* combined preferably with names of smaller animals (fish, birds, insects), often seen as a mass (hence *catty, fishy, wormy*). By breaking this dual tendency (cf. *doggy, waspish*) speakers would emphasize a figurative meaning.]

See also 79, 162, 202.

57 The Analysis of Lexical Doublets: The Romanists' Earliest Contribution to General Linguistics. *Homenaje a Robert A. Hall, Jr. Ensayos lingüísticos y filológicos para su sexagésimo aniversario*, ed. David M. Feldman, 191–6. Madrid: Playor, 1977.

[The movement launched by Auguste Brachet in 1862, the year he published his slim *Dictionnaire des doublets,* bade fair to allow Romance linguists to experiment with something really new. For twenty years or so talented historical linguists, especially those stationed in Germany, Portugal, and Italy, tried to refine this method, but overlooked its true potentialities. Afterward, the problem of a given word's channel of transmission began to recede into the background.]

See also 525.

58 Critères pour l'étude de la fragmentation du latin. *Atti del XIV Congresso internazionale di linguistica e filologia romanza (Napoli, 15–20 aprile 1974),* 1, 27–47. Napoli: G. Macchiaroli; Amsterdam: J. Benjamins, 1977.

[No new classificatory schema for the Romance languages is offered here, but, by way of prolegomena to some future venture of this sort, a strong warning is sounded to avoid reliance on a single set of data, be they phonological, morphological, or lexical. The paper also contains critical comments on various modernist schools of thought–classical structuralism, glottochronology, Lausberg's confrontation of 'Paleo-Romance' and 'Neo-Romance', etc.; passes in review W. von Wartburg's "theory" (which, strictly speaking, is merely a bundle of hypotheses), in its successive formulations (1936, 1950); and operates with such selectively new concepts as 'multiple causation'. A special effort is bent toward reconstructing the climate of opinion that made Wartburg's *Ausgliederung* an instantaneous success half a century ago.]

See also 117.

59 Derivational Categories. *Universals of Human Language,* ed. Joseph H. Greenberg et al., 3: *Word Structure,* 125–49. Stanford, CA: Stanford UP, 1978.

[This paper, entering as a chapter into an influential miscellany, aims to accomplish three things: (a) to delimit derivation–with allowance for transitional cases–against inflection and composition; (b) to distinguish, within the domain of derivation, between (α) the variety best developed in Indo-European, namely affixation (which, by definition, involves an increase in the bulk of the given word), and (β) rival varieties devoid of such increase: back-formation, clipping, contextually recognizable shifting to some other form class, rearrangement of vowels, and the like; (c) to analyze the most sharply profiled varieties of affixes: prefixes, suffixes, infixes, interfixes, etc., beside suffixoids and instances of interplay of pre- and suffixation ('parasynthesis'). Illustrations are offered from Latin, the majority of Romance languages, English, German, Russian, and a few other Indo-European tongues, plus Semitic by way of foil.]

Cr.: J.N. Green, *YW,* 40 (1978–79), 9; O. Gsell, 13; R. Hetzron, *Lingua,* 50:3 (1980), 272.

See also 1, 24, 33, 127, 154, 159, 225, 269.

60 Español antiguo *des(de), fa(s)ta, fazia* y *fascas. Homenaje a Julio Caro Baroja,* ed. A. Carreira, J.A. Cid et al., 711–33. Madrid: Centro de Investigaciones Sociológicas, 1978.

[In this slightly earlier of the two consecutive attacks (cf. 258) on a notoriously intricate problem, the emphasis was placed on the mutual rapprochement of

OSp. *des* and *fata,* in terms of lexical polarization, until both prepositions became near-symmetrical, what with the expansion of *des* into disyllabic *desde,* what with the elaboration on *fata* until it exhibited the dyadic cluster *-st-* (similar to *desde*'s *-sd-*) word-medially. Observe the coalescence of *dueñ de* into *duende.*]

Cr.: O. Gsell, 5; R. Wright & M.W. Wheeler, *YW,* 41 (1979–80), 270. Cf. F. Corriente, *ZRPh,* 99 (1983), 29–32.

See also 21, 62, 68, 167, 169, 177.

61 Ancien espagnol *losenja/lisonja* 'flatterie' et *(a)limos(i)na* 'aumône'. En marge du rayonnement transpyrénéen d'un provençalisme littéraire. *Hommage à Jean Séguy,* 2 (= *VD,* 20–21 [1978]), 195–205.

[If the Italianist is satisfied with classing *lusinga* 'praise' and *(l)usign(u)olo* 'nightingale' (the name of the "literary" bird par excellence) as Provençalisms, the Hispanist runs into a more intricate situation, since the medieval forms *losenjar* 'to flatter, praise', *losenja* 'flattery', *losenjero* 'flatterer', etc. have been transmuted into mod. *lisonja, lisonjear, lisonjero,* etc. An appeal to vocalic metathesis lacks conviction, since the expected product, **lesonja,* is absent from the record. The explanation here advanced instead operates with a lexical blend: *limosna* 'alms', the familiar ecclesiastic Hellenism (*eleēmosýna*), is assumed to have influenced the shape of *losenja,* on the theory that publicly begging alms and heaping flattery on the prospective donor went hand in hand in the given milieu.]

See also 4, 46, 87, 131, 143, 147, 150, 189–91, 207, 290.

62 Semantic Universals, Lexical Polarization, Taboo: The Romance Domain of 'Left' and 'Right' Revisited. *Studies in Diachronic, Synchronic, and Typological Linguistics. Festschrift for Oswald Szemerényi on the Occasion of his 65th Birthday,* ed. Bela Brogyanyi, 507–27. Amsterdam: J. Benjamins, 1979.

[The Romance words for 'left' and 'right' offer an inexhaustible supply for illustration of processes relevant to general linguistics. The meaning 'right(-hand)' often overlaps with 'straight', 'deft', and 'fair, correct'. Through the agency of lexical polarization, the word for 'right', as early as Folk Latin, tended to influence its counterpart for 'left', witness SINEXTER, in lieu of Class. SINISTER, under pressure from DEXTER. Under the influence of taboo, SINISTER has here and there been replaced by some word imported from outside (Sp. *izquierdo,* Ptg. *esquerdo*), or internally by some word originally endowed with a different meaning.]

Cr.: Ph. Baldi, *GL,* 21 (1981), 47–62, at 59–60; J.N. Green, *YW,* 42 (1980–81), 38.

See also 60, 71, 177, 246, 303.

63 The Prelude to the Old French 'frequentative action nouns' in *-ëiz. Festschrift Kurt Baldinger zum 60. Geburtstag 17. November 1979,* ed. M. Höfler, H. Vernay & L. Wolf, 361–74. Tübingen: Max Niemeyer, 1979.

[The piece involves a "prelude" in two senses of the word: It concentrates on certain conditions in different layers of Latin which led to the crystallization of simple and composite suffixes such as -EUS/-IUS, -ĪCIUS, -ĬCIUS, -(ĀR)ĪCIUS,

-(ĀT)ĪCIUS, and the like; and it examines the record of early investigations, including those conducted by L. Meyer, C. Paucker, E. Wölfflin, F.T. Cooper, G.N. Olcott, A. Thomas, E. Gamillscheg, and, above all, Manu Leumann. This "prelude" leads directly to No. 305.]

See also 228, 265.

64 La vacilación fonética como causa de una pérdida léxica. En torno al desarrollo de *gaudēre* y *gaudium* en hispanorrománico. *Homenaje a Fernando Antonio Martínez; estudios de lingüística, filología, literatura e historia cultural,* 34–54. Bogotá: Instituto Caro y Cuervo, 1979. Rpr., *Introducción plural a la gramática histórica,* ed. Francisco Marcos-Marín (Madrid: Cincel, 1982 [–83]), pp. 224–38.

[The basic assumption of this paper is that the splitting-up of a once unified family into autonomous fragments as well as the rise of several variants for each or some of its former members may act as a cause, or as one of the causes, of the replacement of the whole by some less unwieldy substitute. Thus, GAUD-EŌ, -ĒRE and GAUD-IUM formed a close-knit unit at the starting-point. Later GAUDIUM cut loose from the verb, giving rise to *goyo* ~ *gozo* in Old Spanish, while the pl. GAUDIA, via Old French, was re-absorbed as *joya* 'gem'. OSp. *goír* fell into desuetude, yielding ground to *gozar,* newly-developed from *gozo;* etc.]

See also 26, 77, 91, 95, 115, 171, 183, 204, 228, 250, 261, 265, 286, etc.

65 Aspirations, Organization, Achievement. *The European Background of American Linguistics.* Papers of the Third Golden Anniversary Symposium of the Linguistic Society of America [Dec. 1974], ed. Henry M. Hoenigswald, 107–19. Disc.: D. Terence Langedoen, ibid. 145. Dordrecht: Foris Publications, 1979.

[The topic, suggested by the planners of the celebratory meeting, dwells on the relative timidity and modesty of early American pioneers (Whitney, Grandgent); identifies, among New World Romanists, the first flashes of originality (Marden, Read); singles out the mediating role played by immigrants (Collitz, Prokosch, Boas, Pietsch, M. Bloomfield); describes the pilgrimages made by American-born linguists to European centers of learning, with L. Bloomfield going to Leipzig and D.S. Blondheim to Paris before World War I; mentions the first Americans who left an impact on the Old World (Whitney, Buck, Ford), and the first Europeans who came to the New World either to collect fresh data (the older Uhlenbeck) or to establish contacts with innovative analysts (Kuryłowicz's first trip, in the early 'thirties). Frictions and, in the end, mutual admiration.]

See also 103, 120, 263, 430, 434.

66 The Decline of Spanish *luengo* 'long'; the Disappearance of Old Spanish *lueñ(e)* 'far'. *Études de philologie romane et d'histoire littéraire offertes à Jules Horrent à l'occasion de son soixantième anniversaire,* ed. J.M. d'Heur & Nicoletta Cherubini, 267–73. Liège, 1980.

[Lat. LONGUS 'long' and the corresponding adv. LONGĒ 'far', on the whole, have fared surprisingly well in Romance: cf. Fr. *long, loin;* It. *lungo, lungi;* Ptg. *longo, longe,* etc. Old Spanish still kept up this tradition: *luengo, lueñ(e);* but at present *largo* and *lejos* are used instead, a shift that has produced a number of secondary repercussions (e.g., the new meaning 'broad' assigned to *ancho,* given the unavailability of *largo* for this service.)]

Cr.: R. Wright & M.W. Wheeler, *YW,* 42 (1980–81), 261.

For an alternative interpretation, see "Survival of the Primitive Controlled by the Derivative", in preparation.

67 The Fluctuating Intensity of a 'Sound Law'. *Papers from the 4th International Conference on Historical Linguistics* [Stanford, 1979], ed. Elizabeth C. Traugott et al., 321–30. Amsterdam: John Benjamins, 1980.

[This paper has been designedly planned as a radically shortened version of No. 262. The ranks of the diphthongs *ie* and *ue,* initially tied to the accented syllables, have thinned out, through interaction of, at least, ten escape routes. Also, the tendential penetration of these diphthongs into other categories of syllables has diluted their original quintessence of stress-defined and stress-controlled sound sequences.]

Cr.: R. Wright & M.W. Wheeler, *YW,* 42 (1980–81), 260.

See also 39, 71, 209, 215, 242, 259, 271, 292, etc.

68 Catalan *per a,* ancien espagnol *pora,* ancien portugais *pera* 'pour'. *Miscel·lània Aramón i Serra: Estudis de llengua i literatura catalanes oferts a R. Aramón i Serra en el seu setantè aniversari,* 2, 299–314. Barcelona: 1980.

[By way of preliminary hypothesis, one is free to assume that OSp. *pora* (through blend of Lat. PER and PRŌ, plus AD) as well as Cat. *per a* and OPtg. *pera* 'for' can all three be explained individually and independently. However, the early change of *pora* into *para* in Late Old Spanish may have produced a pressure on Old Portuguese, even though *pera* > *para* may also have been fostered by native tendencies. As for Catalan, the phraseological coincidences between *per a* and Sp. *para* are too frequent and too striking to allow one to rule out categorically any possibility of osmosis.]

Cr.: R. Wright & M.W. Wheeler, *YW,* 23 (1981–82), 276.

See also 21, 60, 159, 302.

69 August Friedrich Pott as a Pioneer of Romance Linguistics. *American Indian and Indo-European Studies: Papers in Honor of Madison S. Beeler,* ed. Kathryn Klar, Margaret Langdon, Shirley Silver, 409–20. Amsterdam: John Benjamins, 1980.

[Conceivably the least well known side-interest in the long, productive life of Pott was his brief infatuation with Romance linguistics. However, the half-dozen relevant papers from his pen smoothly fill the gap, left after August Fuchs's death, between the bulk of the concluding publications by Friedrich Diez and the revolutionary writings in a new key coming from Hugo Schuchardt and Graziadio Isaia Ascoli, throughout the late sixties and the early seventies.]

Cr.: J.N. Green, *YW,* 42 (1980–81), 35.

See also 49, 70, 248, 380, 512, 530, 554.

70 Franz von Miklosich and the Rise of Romance Linguistics. *Italic and Romance: Linguistic Studies in Honor of Ernst Pulgram,* ed. Herbert J. Izzo, 327–37. Amsterdam: John Benjamins, 1980.

[Franz von Miklosich (1813–91), a Slovene who made a brilliant career in Imperial Vienna, is usually–and deservedly–thought of as an influential pioneer of Slavic studies. Yet, because areal linguistics also attracted him, he developed a secondary interest in Rumanian, a concern which included not only the standard language, but also certain dialects peculiar to scattered splinter groups–with additional curiosity about Albanian and competence in *Balkanphilologie* as a whole. With Pott, Ascoli, Schuchardt, and Coelho, Miklosich shared keen interest in the provenience, migrations, and language of the Gypsies.]

Cr.: J.N. Green, *YW,* 42 (1980–81), 35.

See also 69, 512, 530.

71 Etymology as a Challenge to Phonology: The Case of Romance Linguistics. *Lautgeschichte und Etymologie: Akten der VI. Fachtagung der Indogermanischen Gesellschaft, Wien, 24–29 September 1978,* ed. M. Mayrhofer, M. Peters, O.E. Pfeiffer, 260–86. Wiesbaden: Dr. Ludwig Reichert, 1980.

[Taking its cue from the *leitmotiv* suggested for the 1978 meeting, the paper reviews, one by one, the following issues: (a) the occasional monophthongization of the Spanish rising diphthong *ue* to *e,* as in *fruente* 'forehead' > *frente,* with side-glances at the parallel process *ie* > *i;* (b) the barely recognizable transmutation of ancestral *-éu* into OSp. *-ió,* as in *Iudaeu* > OSp. *judió* (mod. *judío*); (c) the interchange *-r-* ~ *-l-,* with special attention to two Hispano-Gothic words, *espuera* > *espuela* 'spur' and *esquirar* > *esquilar* 'to shear'; (d) in Sp. *izquierdo* 'left(-hand)', its synonym *zurdo,* and *lerdo* 'slow, sluggish, dull' we are, at best, privileged to witness a misbegotten prelude to a sound change.]

See also 39, 62, 141, 215, 243, etc.

72 The Lexicographer as a Mediator between Linguistics and Society. *Theory and Method in Lexicography: Western and Non-Western Perspectives,* ed. Ladislav Zgusta, 43–58. Columbia, S.C.: Hornbeam Press, 1980.

[In several societies, including USA's, lexicographic research–compiling glossaries, vocabularies, and dictionaries–ranks as a soothing, rather than exciting, activity, befitting a scholar's ripe age. It can be shown, again and again, that leading linguists have tended to delay such work, perhaps subconsciously, until the concluding years of their lives. On the other hand, this sort of activity is the one facet of a many-sided linguist's research that society at large understands best. One comes to terms easiest with one's–sometimes impatient–environment by cultivating, qua linguist, the art of manufacturing dictionaries.]

Cr.: J.N. Green, *YW,* 42 (1980–81), 38.

See also 41, 197.

73 Hypercharacterization of Pronominal Gender in Romance. *Language, Meaning, and Style: Essays in Memory of Stephen Ullmann,* ed. T.E. Hope, 91–107. Leeds UP, 1981.

[Planned as a companion piece to a major study in hypercharacterization (195) published previously in a journal under Ullmann's editorial jurisdiction, this paper centers about an ensemble of closely-related problems: (a) the transmutation of OPtg. *esto, esso, . . . todo* into Mod. *isto, isso, . . . tudo;* (b) the third-person personal pronouns; (c) the definite article in Old Spanish: *él* ~ *ell, la, . . .*, with an excursus on *lo (lo mió, lo to, lo ál, a lo largo*); and (d) animate vs. inanimate indefinite pronouns (esp. Fr. *autrui* vs. *autre chose,* OSp. *otri(e)* → *nadi(e)*.]

Cr.: R. Wright & M.W. Wheeler, *YW,* 44 (1982–83), 296–7.

See also 18, 133, 195.

74 Preliminaries to a Study of the Romance Names of the Synagogue. *Jewish Tradition in the Diaspora: Studies in Memory of Walter J. Fischel,* ed. Mishael Maswari Caspi, 113–22. Berkeley: Judah L. Magnes Memorial Museum, 1981.

[This sketch, superseded before long by a full-fledged inquiry, deals with a scattering of such OSp. and OPtg. forms as *sinoga, senoga, (la) snoga, esnoga*. Bolder modifications include: OSp. *sinoa,* OPtg. *cinun(h)a,* Hisp.-Ar. *xonóga / xenóga, xonõa, xunuga,* ONav. *siaoga*.]

See also 277.

75 Problems Surrounding the Romance Numerals 'one' through 'ten'. *Proceedings of the Tenth Anniversary Linguistic Symposium on Romance Languages,* ed. Helas Contreras & Jürgen Klausenburger (= *Papers in Romance,* Suppl. 2, Vol. 3 [Dec. 1981]), 1–23. Seattle: Univ. of Washington.

[While the wording of the title was, in part, suggested by the occasion on which the paper was orally presented, the problems selected for discussion pertain as much to the realm of kinship terms as they do to the domain of lower numerals (1–10). Patterns that come up for discussion include: Fr. *bisaïeul,* Sp. *biznieto* vs. *Urgroßvater, arrière-grand-père, praded;* the progeny of *prīmus* 'first' (Ptg. *primo* 'cousin'); Sp. *ta(r)taranieto* viewed in relation to Cl. *trinepōs, tritavus* (substitution of *ter-* for *tri-*?); OSp. *tresavuelo* in its relation to dial. *trasnieto* (interference of *tras-* ~ *tres-*).]

Cr.: R. Wright & M.W. Wheeler, *YW,* 44 (1982–83), 309. The talk was repeated on the Berkeley Campus on Oct. 13, 1981, under the title: "Kinship terms and numerals".

See also 23, 75, 86, 92, 272.

76 Dos voces hispanoamericanas, *zonzo* y *secante*. [*Actas del*] *Simposio internacional de lengua y literaturas hispánicas,* ed. Dinko Cvitanovic & M.B. Fontanella de Weinberg, 229–35. Bahía Blanca: Universidad Nacional del Sur [1982].

[The two adjectives have been selected for discussion in tribute to their extraordinary currency in Platense Spanish. *Zonzo* 'stupid' is related to *(en)soso* 'tasteless, dull, silly', from parental ĪNSULSU, lit. 'unsalted'. The apheresis of *en-*, which no longer served any useful purpose, gave the word a more expressive "cut", reminiscent of *loco* and *tonto*. The epenthetic nasal and the change *s-* > *ç* contributed to its enhanced effectiveness. –*Secante* is a straight Italianism, imported by immigrants to the La Plata area.]

Cr.: Anon., *La Nación* (Buenos Aires), Sept. 13, 1981.

See also 35, 79, 81, 105, 107, 210.

77 Los dos núcleos de *almuerzo* / *almorzar:* el latino y el prelatino. *Beiträge zur allgemeinen, indogermanischen und romanischen Sprachwissenschaft; Festschrift für Johannes Hubschmid zum 65. Geburtstag,* ed. Otto Winkelmann & Maria Brasch, 961–84. Bern & München: Francke Verlag, 1982.

[Almost every investigator over the last century and a half has been willing to grant a genetic connection between MORDĒRE 'to bite' (past ptc. and verbal noun MORSU), on the one hand, and, on the other, Sp. *almuerzo,* Ptg. *almoço* 'lunch'. Nevertheless, there has emerged no perfect fit between assumed base and products. Some interference that has been at work must be identified, if the residual discrepancies are to be explained away. Once we recall that *almuerzo,* basically, designated the light snack which the goatherd or sheepherder could comfortably carry in his hands ("en el hueco de las manos"), an appeal to *almueza* "lo que cabe en las manos", a word of Keltic ancestry, becomes plausible.]

See also 88, 137, 394.

78 Between Monogenesis and Polygenesis. *Papers from the Third International Conference on Historical Linguistics,* ed. J. Peter Maher et al., 235–72. Amsterdam: John Benjamins, 1982.

[Explorations in the gray zone stretching between these two categories of genesis. The specific issues focused upon include: (a) *mono- (uni-)* vs. *poly- (multi-)* as used in current scientific terminology; (b) Fr. *désirer* vs. Sp. *desear,* Ptg. *desejar* 'to wish'; cognates or mere victims of chance resemblance?; (c) Fr. *gagner,* It. *guadagnare,* Ptg. *ganhar* as against Sp. *ganar* (and *ganas),* with side-glances at *ingannare, engañar,* and at Sp. *guadañar* 'to mow'; (d) It. *senno,* OProv. *sen* vs. Fr. *sens,* Sp. *seso(s),* Ptg. *siso;* (e) (O)Fr. *égarer, garir, guérir, (re)garder* beside Sp. *guarecer, guardar;* (f) OFr. *ez,* Sp. *he (aquí),* OSp. *(a)fēvos,* Ptg. *eis aqui,* against the background of ancestral *habēt-e, -is* and of *eccum* / *ecce.*]

See also 318b.

79 Semantically-Marked Root Morphemes in Diachronic Morphology. *Perspectives on Historical Linguistics,* ed. Winfred P. Lehmann & Y.M., 133–243. Amsterdam: John Benjamins, 1982.

[Semantic marking of root morphemes, through interplay of vowels, lengthening of the consonantal pillar, choice of an ideal number of syllables, and the like, is usually viewed as a hallmark of Semitic, rather than Indo-European, languages.

However, traces of this development can be detected in a number of 'Western' languages as well, from Antiquity through the Middle Ages down to modern times. The large-scale examples chosen to illustrate this–all too often latent or dormant–possibility are as follows: (1) physical defects designated by *-a-* in Latin root morphemes (138–45); (2) stages in the crystallization of the dominant type of Spanish primary adjectives (149–61); (3) the Italian adjectival type displaying a lengthened pillar consonant (161–78); plus, above all, (4) a counterpart in English derivation: From *snowy* through *bloody* to *flimsy* (178–233). *Snow-y* stands for a normal adjectival satellite of a given noun; in *blood-y* secondary meanings and functions tend to crowd out the original use; *flimsy* is one of the many fancy words in *-y*.]

Cr.: N.E. Collinge, *CanJL*, 30:1 (1985), 81; D. Disterheft, *RPh*, 41:2 (1987), 181; H.H. Hock, *Lg*, 61 (1985), 189–90; F. Lebsanft, *ZRPh*, 100 (1984), 561–5; D. Messner, *RF*, 98 (1986), 393–4; D.C. Walker, *Diachronica*, 1:2 (1984), 275–6.

See also 56, 76, 81, 141, 271.

80 Alternatives to the Classic Dichotomy: Family Tree / Wave Theory? The Romance Evidence. *Language Change*, ed. Irmengard Rauch & Gerald F. Carr, 192–256. Bloomington: Indiana UP, [1983].

[One of the commonplaces of historical linguistics in the classical key is the realization that members of a language family can be best identified either through a family-tree projection (a legacy of A. Schleicher) or by assuming a raying-out process (wave theory). This split leaves out such possibilities as the gradual migration of a given language from one corner to another of the "tree". Thus, Hispano-Romance is usually attributed to the Western branch of the family, in large part on the strength of voicing (and eventual spirantization) of the intervocalic surds; however, in the Pyrenees, in the Balearic Islands and along the Mediterranean coast, the /t/, as has now been established on the strength of toponymic evidence, did not originally tend to give way to /d/, let alone to [δ], etc. The paper also examines the vicissitudes of *ĭ* and *ŭ*, leaning toward the hypothesis that the latter phoneme was originally absorbed as *u*, as in Rumanian and in the Latin lexical ingredients of Albanian, rather than as *o*. Included among the many side-issues discussed are the conflicting developments of *-ĭtia*, *-ĭtie* in Spanish and Portuguese; and the two layers in the transmission of the clusters *pl-*, *fl-*, *kl-*. Result: The family-tree model, whatever the wisdom of its use in other contexts, plainly does not apply to the Iberian Peninsula.]

Cr.: P. Beade, *Lingua*, 63:3 (1984), 327; W.G. Moulton, *Lg*, 61 (1985), 686–7; R. Wright & M. W. Wheeler, *YW*, 48 (1986–87), 295.

See also 58, 86, 117, 210, 254, 311.

81 Etymology: New Thoughts about Possibilities for its Rejuvenation. *Scritti linguistici in onore di Giovan Battista Pellegrini*, ed. Paola Benincà et al., 589–624. Pisa: Pacini [1983].

[The article is basically programmatic: It aims to show in what directions etymological research can be most advantageously pursued if staleness is to be avoided–through rapid discussion of concrete problems still left in abeyance. Some of these issues have thenceforth been taken up elsewhere in more searching detail. The problems here briefly outlined and surveyed include: (a) the relation of Sp. *-én* to Lat. *-ēdine* and *-āgine;* (b) the etymology of OSp. *combl(u)eza,* Ptg. *comborça* 'concubine (of a married man)'; (c) Sp. Ptg. *tomar* 'to take'; (d) *condīre* vs. *condĕre* as the most suitable base (of OSp. *cundir,* etc.); (e) OFr. *dancier* 'to dance': Latin or Germanic?; (f) the adjectival type *tondo, sonso / zonzo, loco, tolo; terco.*]

See also 76, 79, 93, 145, 156, 186, 243, 246, 251, 261, etc.

82 Spanish *estribillo* 'refrain': Its Proximal and Distal Etymologies. *"Florilegium Hispanicum": Medieval and Golden Age Studies Presented to Dorothy Clotelle Clarke,* ed. Charles B. Faulhaber, Dwayne E. Carpenter & John S. Geary, 29–43. Madison, WI: Hispanic Seminary of Medieval Studies, 1983.

[Affirming that Sp. *estribillo* 'refrain' is a diminutive of *estribo* 'stirrup' is merely stating the obvious, i.e., supplying the proximal etymology. Beneath it lie entombed possibilities for, at least, two distal etyma. Arabic *marqaz* could be a distant prototype ("semantic calque"), but the situation is obscured by an embarrassing chronological gap. OGal.-Ptg. *trebelho,* traceable to a Latin verb for ritualistic dancing, at one time established a contact with *estribilho;* was it on the giving or on the receiving side? Then again, although Sp. *estribo*'s Germanic provenience is well established at present, almost all particulars of the transmission remain dubious.]

See also 234, 261, 289.

83 Models of Etymological Dictionaries: Abandoned, Thriving, or Worthy of an Experiment (Exemplified Chiefly with Romance). *Das etymologische Wörterbuch: Fragen der Konzeption und Gestaltung,* ed. Alfred Bammesberger, 117–45. Regensburg: Verlag Fr. Pustet, 1983.

[This paper contains both a critique of earlier etymological practices in the Romance field: Diez, Gröber, Meyer-Lübke, etc. and a few recommendations for future experiments. One category of dictionary never tried out yet, e.g., would be confined to Latin lexical items not transmitted to any daughter language, with comments on the substitute words seized upon by speakers to fill the gaps. Readers will find some thoughts here on improved marking of lexical blends, and on the respective advantages of verbalization and symbolization of messages.]

Cr.: E.A. Ebbinghaus, *GL,* 26 (1986), 68; C.J. Justus, *Diachronica,* 2 (1985), 90; L. Zgusta, *Lg,* 61 (1985), 216.

See also 9, 97, 112, 197, 208.

84 The Discovery in Old French Phonology of the *niece, piece, tierç, cierge* Type. *Medieval French Textual Studies in Memory of T.B.W. Reid,* ed. Ian Short, 99–118. Occasional Publications Series, 1. London: Anglo-Norman Text Society, 1984.

[It took 19th-century Romanists a considerable effort to piece together the extraction of Old French *niece* from NĔPTIA (Class. NEPTIS) 'niece'; also of *piece* from Kelt.-Lat. **pĕttia;* of *tierç* (mod. *tiers*) from *tĕrtiu* 'third'; and of *cierge* 'hind' from **cĕrvia,* because in these words Latin stressed Ĕ diphthongized in a checked syllable, counter to one's usual experience, the recurrent distinctive feature being a following /j/. This paper, a contribution to the history of linguistic scholarship, weighs the rôles played by Ascoli, Förster, Tobler, Mussafia, Gröber, Neumann, Horning, Mall, and G. Paris in gradually achieving a break-through.]

See also 67.

85 A Linguist's View of the Standardization of a Dialect. *The Emergence of National Languages,* ed. Aldo Scaglione, 51–73. Speculum Artium, No. 11. Ravenna: Longo Editore, 1984 (= *Transactions of the Fifth Burdick-Vary Symposium,* April 1–3, 1982, Madison WI).

[For a national language to come into existence there must be a certain predisposition (call it fermentation) in the given speech community; the raw material may be some rural or urban dialect. Contrast between social and regional dialects; also, between social dialects and "registers". B.L. Whorf's concept of Standard Average European (or Western). Examples of literary languages carved from dialect speech: Albanian, Hebrew, Old Provençal (Occitan), Old French; G.I. Ascoli's construct of Franco-Provençal. Examples of clusters of dialect speech, from pre-Columbian *lenguas generales* to oral varieties of Late Imperial Latin (Lyon / Toulouse–Cologne–Milan). Issues in periodization, exemplified with German. Relation between emergent national language and protected prestige language. Thwarted or stunted developments. Possibilities altogether overlooked by potential beneficiaries: Low German. Complicated relationships: Classical Spanish and Portuguese. Three defensible masterplans?]

Cr.: S.M. Embleton, *Lg,* 61 (1985), 732–3; Ž. Muljačić, *AGI,* 69 (1984), 160–2; G. Soldano, *Le lingue del mondo,* June 1985, 279–80.

86 La etimología de *choto* y *chozno*. *Homenaje a Ana María Barrenechea,* ed. L.S. & I. Lerner, 105–17. Madrid: Castalia, 1984.

[While Sp. *choto* 'sucking lamb' seems to descend from *sūctu* 'sucking' (cf. OSp. *enxuto,* OPtg. *enxuito* 'dry' < *ex-sūctu,* lit. 'sucked out')–the change of *s-* into *ch-* is understandable only in terms of phonosymbolism. Obs. *chozno, -a* (vars. *chuznieto, chorlo, chorno*), at present a dialectal kinship term variously defined (e.g., 'grandchild'), could be bracketed with ancestral *ploxĕnu, -ĭnu,* a rare word used by Catullus, described by Quintilian as a unit of Cisalpine Gaulish ancestry, and defined as 'wagon'. Could *ploxenōs* have meant 'baggage, luggage' > (facetiously) 'kids, babies'?]

Cr.: R. Wright & M.W. Wheeler, *YW,* 47 (1985), 282.

See also 75, 80, 105, 107, 291, 293.

87 Las fuentes del sufijo luso-hispánico *-én:* -ĀGINE y -ĒDINE. *Philologica Hispaniensia in Honorem Manuel Alvar,* ed. J. Fernández-Sevilla et al., 2, 407–15. Madrid: Gredos, 1985.

[The fact that, in a few characteristic words, Sp. *-én* reflects ancestral *-āgine*–e.g., *sartén* 'pan' < *sartāgine*–has long been known; in such instances Portuguese wavers between *-ã* and *-ãe*. Another source of *-én,* less prominently displayed in our manuals, is *-ēdine,* a suffix transmitted through vernacular channels only on the level of dialect speech; witness W.Ast. *clarén* (*crarén*) 'clarity, splendor', Gal. *mourén* 'blackness', *rouquén* 'hoarseness', *rubién* 'red color of the sky'.]

Observe that -ĒDINE was identified for the first time as one source of *-én* by J.M. Piel; cf. *Portugiesische Forschungen der Görresgesellschaft*, First Series 14 (1976–77), 299–302.

Cr.: J.N. Green, *YW*, 47 (1985), 35.

See also 81, 145.

88 Para el marco histórico de *comborça*/*combrueça* 'concubina'. *Homenaje a Álvaro Galmés de Fuentes,* 1, 191–211. Madrid: Gredos, 1985.

[While obs. Sp. *combleza* 'concubine' can smoothly be traced to older *comblueça,* it is less easy to reconcile the latter with Ptg. *comborça* despite the commonness of the loss of *r* before /ts/. There exists an overabundance of explicative conjectures, most of them unworthy of further discussion. The hypothesis here advanced starts from **con-vŏrt-ia,* assumed to have been used in the legionaries' crude parlance. For the preference given to *-vŏrt-* over *-vert-,* cf. *dī-vort-ium;* for the use of *-ia* see the names of females, including females of animals, and of maid servants: *av-ia, nūtric-ia, *cania,* etc.]

Cr.: J.N. Green, *YW*, 47 (1985), 34; R. Wright & M.W. Wheeler, ibid., 282.

See also 4, 71, 77, 81, 215, 259, 292.

89 Sound Correspondences and Levels of Transmission: Problems in the Fluctuating Representation of Medial /kt(j)/, /pt(j)/ in Hispano-Romance. *In Honor of Ilse Lehiste,* ed. Robert Channon & Linda Shockey, 451–63. Dordrecht: Foris Publications, 1987.

[The ancestral medial clusters /kt/, /pt/ developed differently in Spanish and Portuguese; as regards the former, sharp contrasts among vernacular, semi-learnèd, and learnèd channels of transmission made themselves felt, with additional complications, due to instances of false regression, as when /kt/ alternates with a /wt/ rather than with /jt/. As if to complicate matters, /ktj/ yielded either *-eiç-* or *-iç-: eleição ~ lição,* and /ptj/ tended to be pressed into the same mould: cf. *descrição* < DĒSCRĪPTIŌNE, in Portuguese.]

See also 193, 210, 241, 247, 251.

90 The Differentiation of Two Hispanic Zoonyms Based on Latin CURTUS 'short'. *Studi linguistici e filologici per Carlo Alberto Mastrelli,* ed. L. Agostiniani, V. Grazi, A. Nocentini, 233–46. Pisa: Pacini, 1985.

[It is argued that Sp. *corzo* (OSp., Ptg. *corço*) 'roe-deer' and its feminine counterpart *corza* / *corça,* on the one hand, and, on the other, Sp. *escuerzo* (older spelling: *escuerço*) 'toad', the arch-rival of *sapo,* may eventually go back to the type *(EX-)CURT-IĀRE, cf. It. *scorciare* 'to shorten, curtail', involving a de-adjectival -IĀRE verb flanking, as happens not infrequently, one in -ĀRE, cf. Sp. *a-, entre-, recortar.*]

See also 47, 54–5, 84, 86, 138, 147, 162, 166, 169, 202, 306.

91 Etimología y trayectoria del verbo ant. esp. *deçir,* port. *descer* 'bajarse'. *Josef Maria Solà-Solé: Homage, homenaje, homenatge* (miscelánea de estudios de amigos y discípulos), ed. A. Torres-Alcalá et al., 341–54. Barcelona: Puvill, 1984.

[OSp. *deçir,* Ptg. *descer* (orig. spelling: *deçer*) seem to be, basically, offshoots of DIS-CĒDĔRE, eventually influenced by DĒ-SCINDĔRE (a member of the *scandĕre* family) and, on a minor scale, by CADĔRE/CAEDĔRE and SCINDĔRE as well. There surely was also some rivalry between the prefixes *dis-* and *dē-*. What in the end sealed the fate of OSp. *deçir* was the devoicing of the /ᵈz/, conducive to harmful homonymy with *dezir* > *decir* 'to say', from DĪCĔRE; the substitute words after this clash were *baxar* and *descender.*]

Cr.: R. Wright & W. Webster, *YW,* 47 (1985), 282.

See also 45, 52, 93, 107, 147, 158, 175, 178, 192, 211, 237, 258, 269, 274–5, 279, etc.

92 The Etymology of Spanish *tras-[h]egar* 'to decant', Italian *trafficare* 'to trade': A Balance Sheet. *Mélanges [Petar] Skok,* ed. R. Filipović, 291–300. Zagreb: Yugoslavenska Akademija Znanosti i Umjetnosti, 1985.

[In this, the more succinct by far of two parallel versions of the analysis (cf. 299), Sp. *tras[h]egar* 'to decant' (lit. 'to purify, cleanse'), based on *faecēs, -um* and entering into a cluster of *-faecāre* verbs, is genetically linked to It. *trafficare* 'to trade' (focal point: Genoa), which eventually percolated into a variety of languages, undergoing noteworthy semantic changes in the process, cf. E. *traffic* and *trafficking.*]

See also 227, 274, 315.

93 The Old Spanish Verbs *contir / cuntir* and *cundir.* To appear in *Miscellanea Aurelio Roncaglia,* ed. Anna Ferrari & Roberto Antonelli.

[The etymology of *contir / cuntir* has been solved, and the relation of this descendant of *conti(n)gĕre* to *(a)contecer* has been definitively established; what continues to be of interest is the transmutation of a prefix into the new radical, as in the cases of *comer,* also *exir, perecer,* and *sobir/subir.* Noteworthy, too, is the light this word history casts on the spread of inchoatives. –As regards *condir / cundir,* we know for sure that any appeal to Gmc. **kundjan* is supererogatory; but the exact shares of *condĕre* and *condīre* remain to be determined.]

See also 81, 186.

94 Linguistique générale et linguistique romane (des deux côtés de l'Atlantique). *Actes du XVII*ᵉ *Congrès de la Société de Linguistique et Philologie Romanes,* Vol. 1, ed. J.-C. Bouvier, 15–32. Aix-en-Provence: Université de Provence, 1986.

[The delicate balance between general diachronic linguistics, Indo-European studies, and advanced research in Romance–in Europe and in the New World. Analysis of the writings of a few scholars who have succeeded in bridging the gap: Grammont, Bally, Brøndal, Lenz. Generalists and Indo-Europeanists rooted in French culture have found it easier to develop a side-interest in Romance: Meillet, Benveniste.]

See also 10, 57, 69, 70, 205–6, 256, 268, 278, 334, etc.

95 La teoría de las sibilantes propuesta por Rufino José Cuervo: noventa años de discusiones. Originally scheduled to appear in *Actas del 1 Congreso Internacional sobre el español de América (Río Piedras, P.R., Oct. 1982),* the piece has now been published in *NRFH,* 35:1 (1987 [–88]), 5–36.

[The discussion of the respective ranges and sources of the OSp. phonemes *ç* and *z* in Cuervo's *Disquisiciones* (1895) ranks as one of the masterpieces from the pen of the Colombian pioneer. The present essay aims at finding a niche for it both in the successive layers of Cuervo's many-faceted *œuvre* and in the early phase of the great debate about the Old Spanish sibilants, which started shortly after 1870.]

See also 163, 175, 182–3, 196, 198, 228, 265, 326.

96 Spontaneous Speech Versus Academic Constraints in Medieval and Renaissance Europe. Presented at "The Fairest Flower: The Emergence of Linguistic National Consciousness in Renaissance Europe", UCLA-sponsored conference, dir. Fredi Chiappelli, Dec. 12–13, 1983. Firenze: Accademia della Crusca and UCLA: Center for Medieval and Renaissance Studies, 1985, pp. 9–17.

[A succinct typology of *Sprachakademien*—as distinct from genuine academies of sciences and the specific place to be assigned in this context to the celebrated Florentine La Crusca Academy. Relation of the Renaissance academies to those of Classical Antiquity in Greece and Rome; assessment of the prospects of academies revived in the 20th century, and of modern normative linguistics: Bruno Migliorini, Tomás Navarro.]

See also 425, 436.

97 Tobler, Gröber und der junge Meyer-Lübke. *Ehrenpromotion Yakov Malkiel am Fachbereich Neuere Fremdsprachliche Philologien der Freien Universität Berlin am 6. Oktober 1983,* 58–91. Universitätsreden, Heft 6. Berlin: Duncker & Humblot, 1984.

[Organized teaching and research in Romance Philology, with a heavy emphasis on Old French, started at Berlin University in 1867, with the appointment of 32-year-old Adolf Tobler, a German-Swiss by background, to an associate professorship. The Tobler régime lasted ca. 40 years and left a profound imprint. Gröber, on the other hand, leaning on a strong Leipzig background, came, via Breslau, to the newly-created University of Straßburg, where he started a vigorous program, mainly as editor-in-chief of a tone-setting journal and an influential encyclopedia. Meyer-Lübke, trained as an Indo-Europeanist in Zürich, and, briefly, in Berlin, reached Vienna in 1890, after a short interlude in Jena. The friendly collaboration among these three scholars, despite profound ideological and temperamental differences, ensured the meteoric rise of Romance philology and linguistics in Central Europe.]

Cr.: O. Gsell, *ZRPh,* 101 (1985), 465–6.

See also 83, 340–1.

98 Carolina Michaëlis de Vasconcelos. To appear in *Woman Scholars in Nineteenth- and Twentieth-Century Linguistics,* ed. Jane H. Hill. Amsterdam Studies in the Theory and History of Linguistic Science, ed. Konrad Koerner. Amsterdam: Benjamins.

[An attempt to reconstruct the life as well as the linguistic and philological gropings of Karoline Michaëlis (1851–1925), later known as Carolina Michaëlis de Vasconcelos—at first in her native Berlin; then, after her marriage to a Portuguese art historian, in Oporto. Although born into a professorial family, she was, fundamentally, self-taught, having been denied the privilege of formal study at university level. In the end, she did teach at the University of Coimbra and earned two honorary doctorates (Freiburg, Hamburg) in Germany. The paper includes a rather elaborate bibliography.]

See also 121, 416.

99 The Designation of Jews in the Luso-Hispanic Tradition. To appear in *Litterae Iudaeorum in Terra Hispanica,* ed. Isaac Benabu, to be sponsored jointly by the Hebrew University of Jerusalem and Misgav Yerushalayim.

[The paper studies, in varying degrees of detail, both designations of Jews and derivatives therefrom: *jud-iego, -engo, -igüelo ~ -ihuelo, -(i)ezno, -ío / -eu, -iaga,* etc., bringing up to date, in the process, some earlier papers by the author as well as certain writings from the pen of M.R. Lida de Malkiel, and casting side-glances at near-parallel developments, in German, English, Russian, and several Romance languages.]

See also 20, 22, 30, 243, 321, 373, etc.

100 Italian *parere / apparire. Romania et Slavia Adriatica, Festschrift für Žarko Muljačić,* ed. J. Kramer & G. Holtus, 401–16. Hamburg: Helmut Buske Verlag, 1987.

[Italian shows an, at first glance, baffling split between the simplex *parere* 'to seem, appear' and the compounds *ap-, com-, (di)s-parire; trasparire,* a relative newcomer, has joined the majority subgroup. At the Latin stage there was no such division: PĀRĒRE matched AP-, COM-, DIS-PĀRĒRE, etc. Could there have occurred some confusion with the PĂRIŌ, -ĔRE family, which included several members endowed with -ĪRE infinitives? If so, it would have involved solely a confusion of forms, not one of meanings.]

See also 282, 290, 314, 318.

101 Sapir as a Student of Linguistic Diachrony. *New Perspectives on Edward Sapir in Language, Culture, and Personality. Transactions of the Edward Sapir Centenary Conference, Held in Ottawa, Ont., October 1–3, 1984,* 315–40. Amsterdam & Philadelphia: John Benjamins, 1986.

[As a graduate student of Germanics at Columbia, Sapir, before he opted for specialization in Amerindian languages under Boas, received a standard training in Indo-European: In his first attempt at a synthesis (*The History and Varieties of Human Speech,* 1911), he still, conventionally enough, placed diachrony in the center of attention. The book *Language* (1921) displayed a momentous shift of emphasis, never abandoned thenceforth. The attempted reconstruction of "superstocks", the newly-awakened interest in the "laryngeal theory", and the last years' intensive concern with Semitics all three marked a partial return to diachronic preoccupations, which only Sapir's early death abruptly cut short.]

The volume also contains a photograph of Y.M., taken at Ottawa (p. 340), plus his share in the discussion of papers read by other participants, including Michael M. Silverstein (107–8), Ives Goddard (211–2), and Richard Handler (451–3).

See also 65, 102, 265, 398, 427, 532, 544, 616, 619, 675.

102 Sapir's Panoramic View (1926) of Recent Advances in Linguistics. To enter into the *Stanley Newman Memorial* (provisional title), ed. Mary Ritchie Key & Henry M. Hoenigswald, to be published by Mouton / de Gruyter.

[The paper is based almost in its entirety on close examination of one of the least frequently consulted writings by Sapir—his progress report on linguistics, for the *Britannica,* traceable to the years 1925/26, which coincides with his dramatic transfer from an, all told, modest position as a staff member of an Ottawa museum to an influential professorial chair at the University of Chicago. Sapir here reports, in a critical vein, on the writings of over twenty fellow workers, including Boas, Cassirer, Delafosse, Jespersen, Kroeber, Malinowski, Marr, and Meillet.]

See also 101, 265, 398, 427.

103 Geschichte des Faches Romanistik an den Hochschulen (Amerika) (45 typescript pages). To enter into *Lexikon der romanistischen Linguistik,* ed. G. Holtus, M. Metzeltin, & C. Schmitt. Tübingen: M. Niemeyer Verlag.

[Apart from its rather full bibliography (appended), this encyclopedia article falls into two parts: a shorter one, highlighting the mutual relation between teaching and research in reference to Romance studies as pursued in the U.S.A.; and a longer one, distinguishing between three successive phases of academic growth: 1875–1915, 1915–40, and 1940-.]

104 Bibliotheken (Amerika) (11 typescript pages). To enter into the same reference volume as the preceding item.

[The basic types of research libraries available to scholars residing in, or visiting, the U.S.A.: (a) the Library of Congress as a national institution; (b) a few exceptional municipal libraries; (c) university and collegiate libraries, including (α) main libraries and (β) departmental collections; and (d) distinguished private libraries, to the extent that they are accessible to highly qualified outsiders.]

105 Integration of Phonosymbolism with Other Categories of Language Change. *Papers from the Seventh International Conference on Historical Lin-*

guistics (Pavia, 9–13. Sept. 1985), ed. Anna Giacalone Ramat, Onofrio Carruba & Giuliano Bernini, 373–406. Amsterdam: John Benjamins, 1987.

[After some broad-gauged discussion of such concepts as onomatopoeia, *Lallwörter, Urschöpfung, accidenti generali,* regular sound correspondences beside residues, and the possibility of a separate structure for semi-learnèd words, the paper examines monographically the relation of ancestral *s-* to *ç-* /ᵗs/ and *ch-* /č/ in Old Spanish and Portuguese words marked by a certain iconicity: SŪCIDU 'sappy' > OPtg. *çujo* 'dirty', SARCĪRE 'to patch' > OSp. *çurzir* (mod. *zurcir*) beside Ptg. *serzir,* and the like.]

See also 53, 76, 107, 117c, 210, 255, 291, 293.

106 Le dernier épanouissement des verbes en -ĒRE. *Actes du Premier Colloque International sur le latin vulgaire et tardif* (Pécs, 2–5 septembre 1985), ed. József Herman, 167–79. Tübingen: Max Niemeyer, 1987.

[Although the absolute number of -ĒRE verbs appears to have decreased in colloquial Late Latin, as a result of substitutions of innovative variants (e.g., *STUDIĀRE in lieu of STUDĒRE) and of the pressure exerted by -DĔRE on -DĒRE (witness the fate of ARDĒRE, MORDĒRE, RESPONDĒRE, RĪDĒRE, and TONDĒRE), nevertheless the weight of -ĒRE verbs preserved or newly-coined increased by a considerable margin: observe (a) HABĒRE, SEDĒRE, TENĒRE, and (b) *POTĒRE (in lieu of POSSE), *VOLĒRE (in lieu of VELLE), also *ESTOPĒRE, newly-carved from the phrase EST OPUS = Class. OPUS EST.

See also 302.

107 Regular Sound Development, Phonosymbolic Orchestration, Disambiguation of Homonyms. To appear in the *Transactions of the Berkeley Sound Symbolism Conference (February 1986)*, ed. Leanne Hinton, Johanna Nichols, & John Ohala.

[A brief discussion of certain key terms: *sound symbolism, expressivity, Affekt, sound imitation, morphosymbolism,* and the like, leads to a shift of emphasis on concrete situations. The first sample examined involves the substitutes for Class. CLAUDĔRE 'to close, shut': Ptg. *fechar,* Ast. *pechar* / *pesllar,* Sp. *cerrar,* Fr. *fermer.* Dividing lines are drawn next between anticipatory *s-* > *ç-*, as in Sp. *cedazo* 'sieve', from SAETĀCEU, and *ç-* from Ar. *sīn,* as in OSp. *çanahoria* 'carrot', *çaranda* 'sieve'; both categories differ, in turn, from genuinely phonosymbolic OSp. *çampoña* 'shepherd's flute', from Gr.-Lat. SUMPŌNIA, i.e., *symphony.*]

See also 53, 105, 117c, 210, 255, 291, 293.

108 Old Spanish Language. To appear in Vol. 11 (June 1988) of the *Dictionary of the Middle Ages.* New York: Charles Scribner & Sons. Published with the support of the National Endowment of Humanities.

[An encyclopedia-style survey of basic facts, already established elsewhere, followed by a rather circumstantial list of references.]

See also 27, 44, 172–3, 239, etc.

109 Pure or Integrated Etymology? (22 typescript pages). To enter into a volume of selected etymological essays, prefaced by Edward F. Tuttle, edited by Carol D. Lanham, and sponsored by UCLA's Center for Medieval and Renaissance Studies. Tentative title: *Theory and Practice of Romance Etymology: Studies in Language, Culture, and History (1947–1987)*. See 13, above.

[While using existing knowledge to good advantage (and occasionally bending it to their needs), devotees of "pure etymology" give the impression of so thoroughly enjoying "etymologizing for its own sake" as not to bother to fill those gaps and to plug those leaks in the reservoirs of the more formally organized disciplines, on whose help they constantly depend. There occurs no recycling of intellectual resources. The reverse approach deserves to be called "integrated etymology".]

See also 32, 45–6, 51–2, 71, 78, 81–2, 159, 181, 184, 187, 191, 194, 206, 218–9, 222, 234, 240, 288–9, 295, 325, 328, 331–2, 336, 354, etc.

110 The Hypothetical Base in Romance Etymology. Expanded version (160 typescript pages) of No. 164. To appear in the same miscellany as the preceding item.

[Since Romance linguistics, basically, operates with a directly or obliquely documented rather than purely conjectural ('reconstructed') parent language, the so-called starred forms deserve to be appealed to only at rare intervals. Each successful replacement of a hypothetical form by an authentic ancestral form, consequently, represents one step in the right direction. The flooding of Romance historical grammars and etymological dictionaries with starred bases is a direct consequence of the vogue of the neogrammatical postulates and practices, when unrealistic bases could be freely invented as long as the "sound laws" were, or rather seemed to be, respected.]

111 How English Dictionaries Present the Etymology of Words of Romance Origin. Chap. 10 of *Oxford Studies in Lexicography*, ed. Robert Burchfield, 178–95. Oxford: Clarendon Press, 1987.

[Differences between a historical and an etymological dictionary; bridges between lexicology and lexicography; transparent source languages (as with *bouquet* and *gondola*); cases of complex transmission (as with *bayadere,* a word of Portuguese ancestry, but one passed on through French); instances of compromise forms (*contraband*); some differences between the British and the Continental traditions of Romance scholarship are also a factor to be reckoned with; critique of methods and techniques favored by W.W. Skeat, Ernest Weekley, the *American Heritage Dictionary,* Webster's Third, and the Onions team; appropriate quota of grammatical information; compression of complicated word histories (as with *apricot*) into compactly-worded dictionary entries.]

Cr.: John A.C. Greppin, "Etymological Excursuses", *TLS,* July 17, 1987.

See also 72, 83.

112 Etymologische Wörterbücher von Informanten- und Corpussprachen. To appear in *Wörterbücher,* ed. Oskar Reichmann, HSK. 3 vols. (1989–90). Berlin: Walter de Gruyter.

[Section 1, aside from preliminary remarks, covers the definition of an etymological dictionary; its typical title; the contrast between a genuine reference work so slanted and one merely providing incidental information on word origins. Another dichotomy pits languages known through a corpus of texts or through data elicited from informants, against reconstructed (hypothetical) tongues; the three examples of the former category here chosen are French, Italian, and English. Section 2 takes up such issues as the varying styles of presentation; the need now felt to avoid discussing one world language in terms of another; the wisdom of a pithy statement, as against circumstantial advocacy; the explicit mention of sources, as against the sweeping use of qualifying adverbs (e.g., 'probably'); mutually complementary, polarized dictionaries; explicative hints of semantic leaps; inclusion of relevant variants; bare data collections vs. demonstrations of felicity of conjectures. Section 3 concerns itself with temporal, spatial, social dimensions; Section 4 takes up noteworthy deviations from the standard, e.g., the comparative etymological dictionary, or one endowed with a peculiar structure of lemmata.]

See also 9, 83, 208, 328.

113 Ausprägungen von Normativität in verschiedenen Wörterbuchtypen. To appear *ibid.* (No. 7a)

[The record of normative dictionaries lends itself to chronological or typological subdivision. The category includes ventures offering only samples of 'correct' phrasing, or singling out for rejection only samples of phrasing deemed inadvisable. The judge may be a single individual of major prestige, or a body of authoritative individuals, or a group of 'classics' appealed to. Overlap of didactic, descriptive, and historical information. The educational influence of a dictionary so skewed may depend on the author's reputation, or on the context, reaching its peak where a dormant or extinct language is to be revived (Pompeu Fabra and Catalan). Dictionaries polemically colored, castigating a motley mixture of peccadillos, or bent on eradicating a single pervasive flaw (e.g., foreignisms). Allusions to 'faux amis'.]

See also 208.

114 Divergent Developments of "inchoatives" in Late Old Spanish and Old Portuguese. To appear in *Studia linguistica et orientalia memoriae Ḥaim Blanc dedicata,* ed. Paul Wexler, Alexander Borg & Sasson Somekh. Wiesbaden: Otto Harrassowitz, 1988.

[While the paradigms of Spanish inchoative verbs offer nothing startlingly erratic (OSp. *par-esco, -eces,* . . .; *paresca,* . . .), late medieval Portuguese underwent a baffling change from *-esco, -eces,* . . . *-esca,* . . . to *-eço, -eces,* . . . *-eça,* . . .), usually explained as an instance of conjugational leveling. The argument gains in strength and explicitness of timing if one interprets the process as a case of overreaction against Sp. *-ngo, -lgo, -rgo, -çco,* and the like, i.e., as an instance of excessive self-assertion in a concrete historical context.]

See also 115, 117d, 242, 296.

115 Español *juez,* portugués *juiz.* ¿Otro caso de auto-afirmación excesiva? To appear in the *Jorge Suárez Memorial Volume* [tentative title], ed. Paulette Levy & Beatriz Garza Cuarón, México, D.F.: El Colegio de México.

[The voc.-nomin. *iūdex* 'judge' yielded in Old Spanish *júez,* which easily became *juéz* in the wake of the powerful spread of the *ue* [we] diphthong. Precisely this is what contemporary Lusophones were eager to avoid; so they substituted *ui* for *ue,* no doubt feeling that *ui,* sparingly represented in both languages (*muyt* / *muito, Ruy*), fell short of contributing to the Castilianization of their mother tongue.]

See also 114, 117d, 242, 296.

116 Romance Counterparts of the Rumanian Plural Ending *-uri.* To appear in *The Importance of Romanian for Romance Linguistics,* ed. M. Manoliu-Manea & L.M. Price.

[The familiar Rumanian plural suffix *-uri,* usually explained as a blend of Lat. *-ora* (as in *corp-ora,* orig. *corpos-a* 'bodies') and *-ī,* serves as a sharp reminder of the spread of *-ora* in late Colloquial Latin. P. Aebischer independently discovered traces of the extended use of *-ora* in early medieval Italo-Latin. It now becomes possible to argue that the celebrated Spanish "sufijos átonos", under the statistically demonstrable leadership of *´ara, ´aro,* may also be traced, at least in part, to Lat. *-ora.*]

See also 229.

117 Old and New Thoughts on the Configuration of the Romance Language Family [tentative title]. Presented at the Austin, TX Symposium on Indo-European linguistics (Nov. 4–6, 1986) and to appear, in expanded form, in its forthcoming Transactions; ed. E. Polomé.

[Critique of some older classificatory theories, including W. von Wartburg's celebrated *Ausgliederung;* and an initial attempt to bracket certain characteristic Luso-Sardic isoglosses, with some attention to Spanish and South Italian as well, in the hope of gradually piecing together scattered lexical remnants of a very archaic Latinity.]

See also 80, 254, 380.

117a Migrations, Settlements, Visits: Their Varying Impacts on Language History. The outgrowth of a paper originally delivered at a Modern Language Assn. convention (Los Angeles, 1982), before a section geared to "Pragmatic and Sociolinguistic Factors in Language Change", this piece is now to appear in a semiotically-oriented miscellany edited by Irmengard Rauch & Gerald F. Carr: *The Semiotic Bridge: Trends from California* (to be included in T.A. Sebeok's *Approaches to Semiotics* series).

[Survey of proposed typologies of lexical borrowings. Varying roles of speakers as donors, beneficiaries, and mediators. Principal varieties of "visits" assumed to have played a role in language history: emigrants, immigrants, and "remigrants" (*Rückwanderer*). The newly-proposed concept of *Unterwanderung.* Relevance of the chosen mode of transportation. Patterns of settlement: city vs. flat country, and coast-line vs. hinterland. Implications of the choice of mountainous territory for (re)settlement. The xenoglottic sea-port. Two models: ancient Massalia/Marseille and pre-modern Seville. Maritime zones; the two acceptations of the ambiguous label "Mediterranean word".]

See also 8.

117b The Etymology, Transmission, and Derivational Structure of Spanish *torbellino:* Studies in an Outgrowth of Western Tyrrhenian Latinity. Written for the opening volume of a new series, *Etymology and Linguistic Principles,* edited and published by Gerald Cohen, Vol. 1: *Pursuit of Linguistic Insight,* 45–66. With an abstract and a Retrospective Statement. 1988.

[Analysis of the medieval and modern record of *torbellino* 'whirlwind' and of its cognates in Occitan, Sardic, Catalan, Spanish, Galician-Portuguese, and French shows that we have before us a lexical unit once moored to TURBŌ, -INIS; marked by a clear focus in the Western half of circum-Tyrrhenian countries; and endowed with two prongs, one leading north all through France; the other, in the Iberian peninsula, thrusting from the Mediterranean all the way to the Atlantic coast. The immediate prototype is likely to have been *TŬRBELLIŌ, -ŌNIS, from recorded TURBELLAE, -ĀRUM, with *TURBELLĪNU prevailing, alternatively, in Spanish-Portuguese territory. The tell-tale vicissitudes of the Hispanic reflexes of Lat. medial -RB- are also surveyed.]

See also 318d, 318g, 318h, 318j.

117c Phonosymbolism in Diachrony: The Case of /r/ > /R/ in Hispano-Romance. To appear in a Testimonial Volume for C.-J. Bailey, ed. Peter Mühlhäuser, Crawford Feagin & Jerold Edmondson.

[An attempt to draw a fine line between (a) instances of straight contamination of certain root morphemes and affixes (e.g., the suffixes *-orio* × *-orro* > *-orrio*) and (b) those that have required a dosage of phonosymbolism to come into existence (e.g., the interfixes *-ar-* and *-arr-*). The semantic domains at issue are: (1) sounds and noises; (2) objects inspiring contempt and/or revulsion.]

See also 53, 105, 107, 210, 255, 291, 293.

117d New Problems in Excessive Self-Assertion vs. Hypercorrection. To be included in *Papers from the Eighth International Conference on Historical Linguistics, Lille, Aug.-Sept. 1987* (tentative title). Previous version offered as an evening lecture on the Berkeley campus on March 10, 1987: "Diachronic Problems in Excessive Self-Assertion (in the Context of Bilingualism)".

[Definition of the phenomenon, as the logical converse of "hypercorrection". Illustrations taken from the stormy relationship between Spanish and Portuguese, chiefly in the 1450–1600 period, marked by self-contradictory reaction of the Portuguese society to the lure (or pressure) of the Spanish language. The biographies discussed in detail are those of *Diogo, sofrer, juiz,* and the present-tense paradigm of the *-ecer* verbs.]

See also 114–5, 242, 296.

117e Los contactos entre las familias de NŌDUS y NŪDUS en gascón, catalán y castellano. To be included in *La Corona d'Aragó i les llengües romàniques; miscel·lania d'homenatge per a Germà Colon,* ed. Günter Holtus, Georges Lüdi & M. Metzeltin; Tübingen: Gunter Narr, ca. 1989.

[The words for 'knot' and 'bare, naked' were sharply distinguished in Classical Latin through contrast between their stressed vowels, while other devices are used in modern Spanish and modern Catalan to maintain a visibly desirable distance between them: *nudo* vs. *desnudo, nu* vs. *nus*. However, there is a fair chance that in the crude language of Roman legionaries stationed in Central and Eastern Hispania and in Aquitania (Gascony), *dēnūdātus* 'stripped' and *dēnōdātus* 'unstrung' were deliberately confused, by way of a vulgar joke, and that thereafter the *ū* variant wormed its way into the entire family of *nōdus* as preserved in Castilian, Catalan, and Gascon.]

See also 117f, 318k-l.

117f Old French *nöer* (var. *näer*) 'to swim' and its Congeners. To appear in a memorial volume for John L. Grigsby, ed. Norris J. Lacy & Gloria Torrini-Roblin.

[The traditional hypothesis of a homonymic conflict between *nöer*$_1$ 'to swim' and *nöer*$_2$ 'to tie' (mod. *nouer*) is defensible, provided one can explain why one of the two rivals surpassed the other in strength. Two circumstances are here adduced which make this course of events understandable. No unanimity of opinion prevails on the factor behind the anomalous transmutation of Class. *nătāre* into **nŏtāre* in the Latinity of France (to the exclusion of Provence) and of Italy (to the exclusion of the South, of most of the North, and of the core territory of Sardinia), with the Iberian peninsula solidly behind the Classical variant. It is here argued that in the sections of the Republic of Rome annexed at an early date, the respect for vowel quantity prevented any annoying confusion of *năt-* 'to swim' and *nāt-* 'born', a barrier which later collapsed, producing a need for some alternative differentiation.]

See also 117e, 318k-l.

117g Some Problems of (A)typicality in Literature, as Seen by a Generalist. To appear in *The Treasurehouse of Memory: A Celebration in Honor of Arthur R. Evans, Jr.*, ed. Erasmo Leiva-Merikakis.

[Of various categories of anomaly encountered in literary history (including those bearing on certain accidents in textual transmission), only one, connected with genres, has here been selected for discussion. It involves definitional analysis, with the generalist being more likely to raise questions than to answer them. The definition of genres is made complicated by use of three overlapping criteria: formal, topical, and communicational (from author to reader or auditor). Further sources of complication: (a) The original title given by author (copyist, translator, reviser, or early printer) may be arbitrary or, worse, misleading; and (b) the key term used to set off a genre need not mean the same thing in different cultures (*cantar, tragicomedia, sirventés, romance*, sonnet). The beholder's basic choice between a static and a dynamic (evolutionary) perspective. In dynamic terms, atypicality may mean vestigial preservation of an otherwise doomed genre or its transformation, by way of exception, in an unexpected direction.]

IV. Books Edited

118 (With Jerry R. Craddock) Emanuel S. Georges, *Studies in Romance Nouns Extracted from Past Participles*. UCPL, 63 (1970); pp. ix, 180; based on 1965 UCB dissertation.

Cr.: J. Dubský, *PhP,* 15 (1972), 45; J.N. Green, *YW,* 32 (1970–71), 22; W.H. Haverkate, *Er,* 24 (1972), 588–90; R.G. Keightley, *BHS,* 49 (1972), 289–90 and *YW,* 33 (1971–72), 236; A.K. Levy, *RPh,* 26:2 (1972), 412–9; V. Pisani, *Paid,* 28 (1973), 126–7; W. Rothe, *ZRPh,* 89 (1973), 310–3.

See also 1, 169, 198.

119 (With W.P. Lehmann) *Directions for Historical Linguistics: A Symposium*. Austin: Texas UP, 1968. Hard-cover and pocket book edns. Pp. ix, 199. (Includes co-signing of Preface.)

Cr.: Anon., *Choice: Language and Literature,* Nov. 1969, p. 95; J.R. Craddock, *Lg,* 46 (1970), 688–93; M.B. Fontanella de Weinberg, *Fil,* 15 (1972), 318–27; G.C. Lepschy, *JL,* 6 (1970), 136–8; R. Posner, *RPh,* 23:2 (1969), 143–53; E. Rodón, *REL,* 1 (1971), 424–6; O. Szemerényi, *GL,* 10 (1970), 121–32; K. Togeby, *RevR,* 5 (1970), 257–60; F. Villar, *Em,* 40 (1972), 222–4.

See also 122, 244, 267.

Tr. R. Stefanini: *Nuove tendenze della linguistica storica,* a cura di W.P.Lehmann & Y.M. Prefatory Note ("presentazione") by Luigi Heilmann (5–7). Bologna: il Mulino, 1977. Pp. 208. A Japanese tr. is in preparation.

Cr.: A. Uguzzoni, *SIL,* 5 (1977[–78]), 694–6.

120 (With Braj B. Kachru, Robert B. Lees, Angelina Pietrangeli & Sol Saporta) *Issues in Linguistics: Papers in Honor of Henry & Renée Kahane*. Urbana: Illinois UP, 1973. Pp. [xii], 933.

Cr.: E.L. Blansitt, *Lgs,* 180 (1976), 71–80; R. Ködderitzsch, *IF,* 80 (1975–76), 192–6; Y. Malkiel, *RPh,* 34 (1981), *122-*135; P. Nieuwenhuijsen, *Spek-*

tator, 4 (1974–75), 372–3; G. Rebuschi, *BSLP,* 70:2 (1975), 125–30; E. Ternes, *Kr,* 18 (1973–75), 110–5.

See also 349, 351.

121 Elise Richter, *Kleinere Schriften zur allgemeinen und romanischen Sprachwissenschaft.* Ausgewählt, eingeleitet und kommentiert von. . . . Preface by Wolfgang Meid. Innsbrucker Beiträge zur Sprachwissenschaft, 21. Innsbruck: Institut für Sprachwissenschaft der Universität Innsbruck, 1977. Pp. 599.

Cr.: K. Baldinger, *ZRPh,* 94 (1980), 573–4; H.H. Christmann, *RF,* 92 (1980), 134–42; J.N. Green, *YW,* 42 (1980–81), 35; H. Kahane, *Lg,* 55 (1979), 701–3; E. Pulgram, *RPh,* 33:2 (1979), 284–99 ("*In Pluribus Prima:* Elise Richter, 1865–1943").

Cf. Hans Helmut Christmann, *Frau und "Jüdin" an der Universität: Elise Richter (Wien 1865–Theresienstadt 1943),* Mainz Akad. der Wissenschaften, Geistes- und Sozialwiss. Kl., 1980:2, 3–46. Cr.: M. Mayrhofer, *ZRPh,* 97 (1983), 531–2.

See also 44.

122 (With Winfred P. Lehmann) *Perspectives on Historical Linguistics.* Amsterdam Studies in the Theory and History of Linguistic Science, 4:24. Amsterdam: John Benjamins, 1982. Pp. xii, 379.

Cr.: W. Bennett, *Lore and Language,* 3:10 (1985), 106; N.E. Collinge, *CanJL,* 30:1 (1985), 79–82; D. Disterheft, *RPh,* 41:2 (1987), 179–86; H.H. Hock, *Lg,* 61 (1985), 187–93; F. Lebsanft, *ZRPh,* 100 (1984), 561–5; D. Messner, *RF,* 98 (1986), 393–4; D.C. Walker, *Diachronica,* 1:2 (1984), 273–9.

See also 56, 119, 271.

V. Journal Articles

123 The Development of [the Suffix] *-īvu* in Latin and Romance, *Lg,* 17 (1941), 99–118.

See also 1, 126–7.

124 The *amulatado* Type in Spanish, *RR,* 32 (1941), 278–95.

Cr.: A. Kuhn, 371.

See also 1, 140, 318i, 651.

125 *Atristar–entristecer:* Adjectival Verbs in Spanish, Portuguese, and Catalan. *StPh,* 38 (1941), 429–61.

See also 114, 124, 223.

126 Old French *soutif* 'Solitary', *MLQ,* 3 (1942), 621–46.

Cr.: L. Spitzer, ibid., 4 (1943), 389.

See also 123, 127.

127 Zur Substantivierung der Adjektiva im Romanischen: Über den Ursprung des Typus ATTRACTIVU, INITIATIVA, *CM,* 5 (1943), 238–56.

Cr.: A. Kuhn, 67; E. Lerch, *ZRPh,* 64 (1944), 405–20.

See also 1, 123, 126.

128 The Latin Base of the Spanish Suffix *-eño, AJPh,* 65 (1944), 372–81.

Cr.: L. Flórez, *BICC,* 1 (1945), 189–90; F. Lecoy, *Ro,* 69 (1946–47), 553, and 70 (1948–49), 285. Cf. Jonathan L. Butler's Berkeley doct. diss. (1969): *Latin*

-ĪNUS, -ĪNA, -ĬNUS, and -ĬNEUS: From Proto-Indo-European to the Romance Languages, UCPL, 68 (1971), passim, and the critical reactions thereto.

See also 26, 152, 369.

129 The Etymology of Portuguese *iguaria, Lg,* 20 (1944), 108–30.

Cr.: A. Kuhn, 434, with references to Wagner, Piel, and Spitzer; F. Lecoy, *Ro,* 70 (1948–49), 140–1; M. Rodrigues Lapa, *BÉP,* 14 (1950), 316–8; L. Spitzer, *Lg,* 21 (1943), 98–9. Cf. É. Veríssimo, *A volta do gato preto,* Porto Alegre & Rio de Janeiro: Globo, 1947 (4th edn., 1957), separate chapter: "O Senhor *iguaria*". Also, Baldinger (a), 29–30.

See also 183, 359.

130 The Etymology of Spanish *sosiego, PhQ,* 23 (1944), 297–306.

Cr.: W.E. Geiger/P. Smith, The Etymology of Hispanic *sosegar,* ibid., 43 (1964), 112–22; A. Kuhn, 383.

See also 201, 251.

131 Three Spanish-Portuguese Etymologies: *pendencia, primencia, fimencia, RR,* 35 (1944), 307–23.

See also 2, 185.

132 The Development of VERĒCUNDIA in Ibero-Romance, *StPh,* 41 (1944), 501–20.

Cr.: K. Baldinger (a), 1986; J.M. Piel, *RPF,* 2 (1949), 283–5.

See also 236, 286.

133 Old Spanish *nadi(e), otri(e), HR,* 13 (1945), 204–30.

Cr.: S. Fernández, *Gramática española* (1951), 385–457; A. Kuhn, 374; F. Lecoy, *Ro,* 69 (1946–47), 553, and 70 (1948–49), 285; L. Mourin, *RB,* 27 (1949), 1091; A. Pardo, *BICC,* 1 (1945), 614–7.

See also 18, 73.

134 The Etymology of Hispanic *que(i)xar, Lg,* 21 (1945), 142–83.

Cr.: V. Buben, *Čas,* 31 (1948), 322; M. Rodrigues Lapa, *BÉP,* 14 (1950), 319–20; F. Lecoy, *Ro,* 70 (1948–49), 137–8; L. Mourin, *RB,* 26 (1948), 841; J.M. Piel, *RF,* 63 (1951), 428–9; H. Sten, *RLiR,* 17 (1950), 208–12.

135 The Etymology of Old Spanish *apesgar, MLQ,* 6 (1945), 149–60.

Cr.: F. Lecoy, *Ro,* 70 (1948–49), 139–40; J.M. Piel, *RPF,* 2 (1949), 286–8.

See also 37, 137, 394.

136 Probleme des spanischen Adjektivabstraktums, *NM,* 46 (1945), 171–91; 47 (1946), 13–45 [submitted in 1939].

Cr.: A. Kuhn, 371–2.

See also 2, 7, 16, 19, 33, 41, 142, 176, 260.

137 Hispanic Reflexes of Latin MORSICĀRE, *PhQ,* 24 (1945), 233–54.

Cr.: A. Kuhn, 372–3; F. Lecoy, *Ro,* 71 (1950), 551–2; L. Mourin, *RB,* 27 (1949), 1091; J.M. Piel, *RPF,* 2 (1949), 288–9.

See also 135, 394.

138 Relics of MERGUS, MERGULUS, and MŪCRŌ in Ibero-Romance, *AJPh,* 67 (1946), 151–67.

Cr.: J.M. Piel, *RPF,* 2 (1949), 300–1.

See also 329, 361.

139 The Word-Family of Old Spanish *recudir, HR,* 14 (1946), 104–59.

Cr.: E. Amaya Valencia, *BICC,* 2 (1946), 403–5; F. Lecoy, *Ro,* 70 (1948–49), 138; L. Mourin, *RB,* 27 (1949), 1091–2; M. Muñoz Cortés, *RFE,* 30 (1946), 239.

See also 45, 52, 91, 93, 100, 106, 186, 192, 215, 274, 290.

140 The Etymology of Hispanic *vel(l)ido* and *melindre, Lg,* 22 (1946), 284–316.

Cr.: E. Amaya Valencia, *BICC,* 3 (1947), 342–3; F. Lecoy, *Ro,* 70 (1948–49), 135–6; H. Meier, *RF,* 63 (1951), 329–30; L. Mourin, *RB,* 27 (1949), 1092; J.M. Piel, *RPF,* 2 (1949), 298–300, and *RF,* 63 (1951), 429. Cf. Steven N. Dworkin, "The Etymology of Hispanic *vel(l)ido:* A New Approach to an Old Problem", *RPh,* 40:3 (1987), 328–33, as well as Id., *Etymology and Derivational Morphology: The Genesis of Old Spanish Denominal Adjectives in -IDO.* Suppl. 206 to *ZRPh* (Tübingen: Niemeyer, 1985).

See also 249, 269, 318i.

141 The Etymology of Spanish *lerdo, PhQ,* 25 (1946), 289–302.

Cr.: F. Lecoy, *Ro,* 71 (1950), 551; L. Mourin, *RB,* 27 (1949), 1092; L. Spitzer, *NRFH,* 1 (1947), 79–80.

See also 21, 66, 71, 76, 122, 156, 189, 190, 264, 271.

142 Castilian *albricias* and its Ibero-Romance Congeners, *StPh,* 43 (1946), 498–521.

Cr.: F. Lecoy, *Ro,* 70 (1948–49), 136–7; L. Mourin, *RB,* 27 (1949), 1092.

See also 136, 311.

143 A Latin-Hebrew Blend: Hispanic *desmazalado, HR,* 15 (1947), 272–301.

Cr.: J.M. Piel, *RPF,* 2 (1949), 297–8; L. Spitzer, *NRFH,* 1 (1947), 78–9.

See also 17, 147.

144 Sp. *cosecha* and its Congeners, *Lg,* 23 (1947), 389–98.

Cr.: L. Mourin, *RB,* 27 (1949), 1903; J.M. Piel, *RF,* 63 (1951), 429–30.

See also 313.

145 The Romance Word-Family of Latin AMBĀGŌ, *Word,* 3 (1947), 59–72.

Cr.: E. Amaya Valencia, *BICC,* 4 (1948), 626; A. Dauzat, *FM,* 17 (1949), 317; M. García Blanco, *RFE,* 35 (1951), 374–5; L. Mourin, *RB,* 27 (1949), 1092–3; J.M. Piel, *RF,* 63 (1951), 429; B. Pottier, *Ro,* 71 (1950), 549–50.

See also 87, 243, 269, 357, 363.

146 The Etymology of Spanish *maraña, BH,* 50 (1948), 147–71.

Cr.: A. Carballo Picazo, *RFE,* 34 (1950), 332–5; V. García de Diego, ibid., 36 (1952), 257–86.

See also 148, 170.

147 Hispano-Arabic *marrano* and its Hispano-Latin Homophone, *JAOS,* 68 (1948), 175–84. To be included in 13.

Cr.: B. Migliorini, *LN,* 10 (1949), 50; L. Mourin, *RB,* 27 (1949), 1095; I.-S. Révah, *BÉP,* 14 (1950), 346–7. Tr. Fanny Rubin, *Davar,* N. 26 (Buenos Aires, 1950), 46–69.

See also 207.

148 The Etymology of Spanish *calaño, PhQ,* 27 (1948), 112–22.

Cr.: L. Mourin, *RB,* 27 (1949), 1093.

See also 161, 237.

149 The Word-Family of Spanish *desmoronar,* Portuguese *esb(o)roar* 'Crumble', *PMLA,* 63 (1948), 785–802.

Cr.: M. Rodrigues Lapa, *BÉP,* 14 (1950), 318–9; L. Mourin, *RB,* 27 (1949), 1094; B. Pottier, *Ro,* 71 (1950), 285.

See also 158.

150 The Etymology of Hispanic *restolho, rastrojo, rostoll, RPh,* 1:3 (1948), 209–34.

Cr.: M. García Blanco, *RFE,* 35 (1951), 343–4; F. Lecoy, *Ro,* 72 (1951), 279; L. Mourin, *RB,* 27 (1949), 1093.

151 Italian *guazzo* and its Hispanic and Gallo-Romance Cognates, *RPh,* 2:1 (1948), 63–82. To be included in 13.

Cr.: M. García Blanco, *RFE,* 35 (1951), 188–9; B. Migliorini, *LN,* 10 (1949), 74; L. Mourin, *RB,* 27 (1949), 1093–4.

See also 45, 190.

152 The Etymology of Spanish *cenceño, StPh,* 14 (1948), 37–49.

Cr.: E. Amaya Valencia, *BICC,* 4 (1948), 435–6; F. Lecoy, *Ro,* 62 (1951), 279–80.

See also 95, 128, 228.

153 Old Spanish *assechur* and its Variants, *HR,* 17 (1949), 183–232.

Cr.: A. Kuhn, 383; B. Pottier, *Ro,* 71 (1950), 550.

See also 158, 182, 228.

154 Studies in the Hispanic In[ter]fix *-eg-, Lg,* 25 (1949), 139–81.

Cr.: F. Lecoy, *Ro,* 72 (1951), 140–2; L. Mourin, *RB,* 29 (1951), 864–5.

See also 3, 24, 59.

155 The Etymology of Spanish *asperiega, esperiega, PhQ,* 28 (1949), 294–311. To be included in 13.

See also 3, 20, 22, 368.

156 The Etymology of Spanish *terco, PMLA,* 64 (1949), 570–84.

Cr.: J.M. Piel, *RF,* 63 (1951), 430; B. Pottier, *Ro,* 71 (1950), 552.

See also 13, 76, 141, 190, 264, 271.

157 Italian *ciarlatano* and its Romance Offshoots, *RPh,* 2:4 (1949), 317–26.

Cr.: M. García Blanco, *RFE,* 35 (1951), 192–3; H. and R. Kahane, *RPh,* 5:2–3 (1951–2), 177–8; B. Migliorini ("I *cerretani* e *Cerreto*"), *RPh,* 7:1 (1953), 60–4, also *Saggi linguistici* (Firenze, 1957), 272–7. Cf. Karl H. Menges, *RPh,* 2:2–3 (1948–49), 229–31.

See also 24, 372.

158 Latin IACTĀRE, DĒIECTĀRE, and ĒIECTĀRE in Ibero-Romance, *BF*, 10 (1949), 201–14 (=*Miscelânea de Filologia, Literatura e História Cultural à Memória de Francisco Adolfo Coelho*).

See also 52, 153, 211, 358.

159 The Ancient Hispanic Verbs *posfaçar, porfaçar, profaçar:* A Study in Etymology and Word-Formation, *RPh,* 3:1 (1949), 27–72.

Cr.: J.G.C. Herculano de Carvalho, *VR,* 15 (1956), 264–5; M. García Blanco, *RFE,* 35 (1951), 379–80; B. Pottier, *Ro,* 72 (1951), 132–3.

See also 60, 68, 95, 150, 183, 196, 198, 228.

160 Romance Descendants of Latin NOCTURNUS, NOCTURNĀLIS, *StPh,* 46 (1949), 497–513. To be included in 13.

See also 3, 20, 22, 368.

161 Old Spanish *fazaña, pa(s)traña,* and *past(r)ija, HR,* 18 (1950), 135–57, 244–59.

See also 95, 228.

162 The Latin Background of the Spanish Suffix *-uno;* Studies in the Genesis of a Romance Formative, *RPh,* 4:1 (1950), 17–45.

See also 202.

163 The Etymology of Hispanic *destroçar* and *troço, PhQ,* 29 (1950), 151–71.

Cr.: J. Hubschmid, *RPF,* 5 (1952), 1–29.

See also 95, 183, 196, 198, 228.

164 The Hypothetical Base in Romance Etymology, *Word,* 6 (1950), 42–69.

Cr.: O. Gsell, 4; L. Spitzer, *RF,* 62 (1950), 227–34. A revised, expanded version has been prepared (see 13, 110).

165 Old Spanish *paladino, palaciano, palanciano, palaciego, PMLA,* 65 (1950), 955–74.

Cr.: M. Garcí-Gómez, "Relación semántica y etimológica entre *latinado (latino, ladino)* y *paladino*", *BRAE,* 53 (1973), 535–42 [*palam* + *Latīnu*].

See also 3, 20, 22, 166.

166 Some Names of the 'Bat' in Ibero-Romance, *HR,* 19 (1951), 238–63, 323–40.

Cr.: I. González-Llubera, *YW,* 13 (1951–52), 119; I.-S. Révah, *BÉP,* 15 (1951), 233.

See also 47, 56, 86, 90, 329.

167 Lexical Polarization in Romance, *Lg,* 27 (1951), 485–518.

Cr.: G. Rohlfs, *ASNS,* 190 (1953–54), 154–5; S. Ullmann, *YW,* 13 (1951–52), 15. Cf. William Safire, "Under Covert", *New York Times Magazine,* July 10, 1983; rpr. as "The War of Words: A 'Covert' Look at Secrets of Language", *Chicago Tribune,* July 24, 1983 (and elsewhere).

See also 60, 62, 177, 222, 246, 303, 382.

168 Cervantes in Nineteenth-Century Russia, *CL,* 3 (1951), 310–29.

Based in part on Ludmilla B. Turkevich, *Cervantes in Russia* (Princeton UP, 1950).

169 Estudios de léxico pastoril: *piara* y *manada, BH,* 53 (1951), 41–80.

Cr.: I. González-Llubera, *YW,* 13 (1951–52), 118–9; I.-S. Révah, *BÉP,* 15 (1951), 231.

See also 4, 37, 161, 177.

170 The Romance Progeny of Latin *pedāneus, AGI,* 36 (1951), 49–74.

See also 4, 37, 169.

171 La historia lingüística de *peón, BICC,* 7 (1951), 3–46.

Cr.: G. Gougenheim, *BSLP,* 48:2 (1952), 82–3.

See also 4, 37, 169–70.

172 Old and New Trends in Spanish Linguistics, *StPh,* 49 (1952), 437–58.

Cr.: K. Baldinger (a), 196, 272–3.

See also 27, 35, 239.

173 The Pattern of Progress in Romance Linguistics, *RPh,* 5:4 (1952), 278–95.

Cr.: A. Ewert, *FS,* 7 (1953), 194; G. Gougenheim, *FM,* 21 (1953), 76–7.

See also 28, 44, 80, 94, 103, 121, 179, 205–6, 216, 233, 247–8, 268, 278, 342, 346.

174 Los derivados hispánicos de TEPIDUS, *Ro,* 74 (1952), 145–76. (Partial list of errata: ibid., 76 [1954], 556.)

Cr.: H. Meier, *RF,* 63 (1951–52), 332–3.

See also 16.

175 Studies in Hispano-Latin Homonymics: PESSULUS, PĀCTUS, PECTUS, DĒSPECTUS, SUSPECTUS, FISTULA in Ibero-Romance, *Lg,* 28 (1952), 299–338.

Cr.: K. Baldinger (a), 28.

See also 37, 318c.

176 La familia *lazerar, laz(d)rar, lazeria:* Estudios de paleontología lingüística, *NRFH,* 6 (1952), 209–76.

Cr.: H. Guiter, *RLaR,* 72 (1955), 79–80; J.M. Piel, *RF,* 57 (1955–56), 144.

See also 182.

177 Ancient Hispanic *vera(s)* and *mentira(s):* A Study in Lexical Polarization, *RPh,* 6:2–3 (1952–53), 121–72.

See also 60, 62, 167.

178 A Cluster of Four Homophones in Ibero-Romance, *HR,* 21 (1953), 20–36, 120–34. To be included in 13.

See also 30, 37, 91, 93, 107, 143, 147, 150, 180, 198, 227, 258, 279, etc.

179 Language History and Historical Linguistics, *RPh,* 7:1 (1953), 65–76.

[An invitational lecture at UCB before a group of history undergraduates.]

See also 808.

180 The Luso-Hispanic Triad *pente(m), pende(jo), (em)peine:* The Comb as a Focus of Linguistic Imagery, *BF,* 14 (1953), 27–79.

See also 332, 336.

181 The Place of Etymology in Linguistic Research, *BHS,* 30 (1954), 78–90.

[Text of an invitational lecture given at Indiana University.]

See also 26, 32, 46, 48, 51–2, 81–3, 222, 234, 238, 240.

182 Old Spanish *maznar* 'Knead' and the Progeny of Latin MĀCERĀRE, *MLR,* 49 (1954), 322–30.

See also 176, 358.

183 From 'Bay-Colored' to 'Spleen': The Romance Phase of Latin BADIUS, *AGI,* 39 (1954), 166–87 (= *Misc. Vittorio Bertoldi*).

Cf. A. Alegre Heitzmann, "En torno a *baça, embaçar* y *embaraçar*", *AF,* 5 (1979), 239–56.

See also 61.

184 Etymology and the Structure of Word-Families, *Word,* 10 (1954), 265–74 (= *Linguistics Today,* ed. A. Martinet & U. Weinreich). Tr., *LG,* 132–45.

[Text of an invitational lecture delivered at Indiana University.]

See also 26, 32, 46, 48, 51–2, 222, 234, 238, 240.

185 La *F* inicial adventicia en español antiguo (*femençia, finchar, fenchir, fallar, finojo*), *RLiR,* 18 (1954), 161–91.

Cr.: K. Baldinger (a), 27, 399.

See also 131.

186 *Cundir:* Historia de una palabra y de un problema etimológico, *BFUCh,* 8 (1954–55), 247–64 (= *Hom. a Rodolfo Oroz*).

See also 91, 93, 100, 106, 188, 237, 274–5.

187 Etymology and Historical Grammar, *RPh,* 8:3 (1955), 187–208. Tr., *LG,* 67–98.

[Amalgam of two invitational lectures delivered at Indiana University.]

Cr.: O. Gsell, 5.

See also 26, 32, 46, 48, 51–2, 206, 222, 234, 238, 240.

188 Español *morir,* portugués *morrer* (con un examen de *esmirriado, morriña, murria* y *modorra*), *BH,* 57 (1955), 84–128.

See also 91, 93, 100, 106, 188, 237, 274–5, 296.

189 *Apretar, pr(i)eto, perto:* historia de un cruce hispanolatino, *BICC,* 9 (1953[–55]), 1–139.

Cr.: G. Gougenheim, *BSLP,* 53:2 (1957–58), 147–8; H. Guiter, *RLaR,* 72 (1955–58), 374–6; M. Leroy, *Lat,* 16 (1957), 378–80; N.P. Sacks, *HR,* 26 (1958), 160–2; H.L.A. van Wijk, *Neoph,* 43 (1959), 156–7.

See also 60, 68, 134.

190 En torno a la etimología y evolución de *cansar, canso, cansa(n)cio* (1), *NRFH,* 9 (1955), 225–76. [The promised sequel has not yet appeared.]

See also 198.

191 The Uniqueness and Complexity of Etymological Solutions, *Lingua,* 5 (1956), 225–52. Rpr., *ELT,* 229–50. Tr., *LG,* 99–131.

See also 26, 32, 46, 48, 51–2, 206, 222, 234, 238, 240.

192 Antiguo español y gallegoportugués *trocir* 'pasar', *NRFH,* 10 (1956), 385–95.

Cr.: K. Baldinger (a), 152–3; I. González-Llubera, *YW,* 19 (1957–58), 183.

See also 91, 93, 100, 106, 237, 274–5.

193 Préstamos y cultismos, *RLiR,* 21 (1957), 1–61. [The network of transmissions of PRETIUM.]

Cr.: J.A. Cremona and I. González-Llubera, *YW,* 19 (1957–58), 23, 182–3; O. Gsell, 8; H. Guiter, *RLaR,* 74:1 (1960), 116–7. Cf. Roger Wright, "Semicultismo", *ArL* (N.S.), 7 (1976), 13–28.

See also 48, 241, 243.

194 A Tentative Typology of Etymological Studies, *IJAL,* 23 (1957), 1–17. Rpr., *ELT,* 199–228, with a Bibl. Suppl. brought up to date. Tr., *LG,* 10–38.

Cr.: G. Gougenheim, *BSLP,* 58:2 (1963), 96–7.

See also 9, 26, 32, 46, 51–2, 191, 197, 203, 206, 222, 234, 238, 240.

195 Diachronic Hypercharacterization in Romance, *ArL,* 9 (1957), 79–113; 10 (1958), 1–36. Tr. (and rev.), *LG,* 170–239.

Cr.: O. Gsell, 5.

See also 25.

196 Español antiguo *cuer* y *coraçón, BH,* 60 (1958), 180–207, 327–63.

Cr.: I. González-Llubera, *YW,* 20 (1958–60), 184–5; J.J. Montes G., *BICC,* 15 (1960), 345–7; N.P. Sacks, *HR,* 30 (1962), 343.

197 Distinctive Features in Lexicography: A Typological Approach to Dictionaries Exemplified with Spanish, *RPh,* 12:4 (1959), 366–99; 13:2 (1959), 111–55.

Cr.: I. González-Llubera, *YW,* 21 (1959–60), 155; G. Gougenheim, *BSLP,* 58:2 (1963), 96–7; O. Gsell, 11; J.J. Montes, *BICC,* 16 (1961), 259–60;

R. Posner, 443; T.A. Sebeok, *Lingua,* 11 (1962), 363–74 ("Materials for a Typology of Dictionaries"); K.D. Uitti, *RPh,* 16:4 (1963), 418.

See also 194, 203.

198 The Two Sources of the Hispanic Suffix *-azo, -aço, Lg,* 35 (1959), 193–258.

Cr.: K. Baldinger (a), 53–4, 293.

See also 190.

199 Toward a Reconsideration of the Old Spanish Imperfect in *-ía* ~ *-ié, HR,* 26 (1959), 435–81 (= *Joseph E. Gillet Memorial Volume).*

See also 270.

200 Studies in Irreversible Binomials, *Lingua,* 8 (1959), 113–60. Rpr., *ELT,* 311–55; tr., *LG,* 240–88 [with R. Stefanini's addenda].

Cr.: K. Baldinger (b), 44–5; P.M. Lloyd, *RPh,* 17 (1963–64), 762–3; N.P. Sacks, *HR,* 30 (1962), 343–4; J.A. van Praag, *Lingua,* 10 (1962), 235–6.

201 Fuentes indígenas y exóticas de los sustantivos y adjetivos verbales en *-e* (I–II), *RLiR,* 23 (1959), 80–111; 24 (1960), 201–53.

Cr.: J. Martin Baldonado, "Affixation and Gender Desinence in the Old Spanish Postverbal Noun," *RPh,* 35:1 (1981), 64–79.

See also 19, 251.

202 Nuevas aportaciones para el estudio del sufijo *-uno, NRFH,* 13 (1959[–60]), 241–90.

Cr.: H. Guiter, *RLaR,* 75:2 (1963), 275; H.L.A. van Wijk, *Lingua,* 16 (1966), 322–4.

See also 56, 128, 162, 318g.

203 A Tentative Typology of Romance Historical Grammars, *Lingua,* 9 (1960), 321–416. Rpr., *ELT,* 71–164 [= with a rev. Bibl. Suppl.].

Cr.: O. Gsell, 14; W.P. Lehmann, *Lg,* 39 (1963), 286–90; R. Posner, 443–4; K. Togeby, "Comment écrire une grammaire historique des langues romanes?", *SN,* 34 (1962), 315–20.

See also 9, 194, 197.

204 Paradigmatic Resistance to Sound Change: The Old Spanish Preterite Forms *vide, vido* against the Background of the Recession of Primary *-d-, Lg,* 36 (1960), 281–346. Rpr., *Readings in Romance Linguistics,* ed. James M. Anderson & Jo Ann Creore, pp. 335–413, with a post-script. The Hague, 1972.

Cr.: O. Gsell, 16; H. Guiter, *RLaR,* 75:1 (1962), 111–2.

See also 4, 16, 36, 38, 64, 117e, 117f.

205 Three Definitions of Romance Linguistics, *RPh,* 15:1 (1960), 1–7. Tr., *LG,* 1–9.

See also 44, 94, 233, 278.

206 Etymology and General Linguistics, *Word,* 18 (1962), 198–219 (= *Linguistic Essays on the Occasion of the 9th Intern. Congress of Linguists,* also published as a separate book). Rpr. in the Bobbs-Merrill Reprint Ser. in Language and Linguistics; *ELT,* 175–198; tr., *LG,* 39–66.

Cr.: O. Gsell, 10; R. Posner, 438.

See also 9, 26, 32, 45–6, 48, 51–2, 71, 81–3, 91–2, 109–12, 129, 131, 134, 140, 146, 150, 155, 181, 184, 186–7, 190–1, 194, 218, 222, 234, 238, 240, 274, 288–9, 293, 295, 325, etc.

207 Weak Phonetic Change, Spontaneous Sound Shift, Lexical Contamination, *Lingua,* 11 (1962), 263–75 (= *Studia Gratulatoria, Dedicated to Albert Willem de Groot. . .*). Rpr., *ELT,* 33–45; tr. ("Cambiamento fonetico debole, mutamento di suoni spontaneo, contaminazione lessicale") in *Linguistica generale, strutturalismo, linguistica storica; testi, note introduttive, indici,* ed. Tristano Bolelli, 247–60. Pisa: Nistri-Lischi, 1971.

Cr.: O. Gsell, 7, 15; R. Posner, 441.

See also 43.

208 A Typological Classification of Dictionaries on the Basis of Distinctive Features, *IJAL,* 38:2 (1962), Part 4 (*Problems in Lexicology,* ed. F.W. Householder & S. Saporta), 3–24. Included in rev. 2d ed. (1967). Rpr., *ELT,* 257–79.

Cr.: K.D. Uitti, *RPh,* 16:4 (1963), 417–9.

See also 83, 112–3, 197, 203.

209 Toward a Unified System of Classification of Latin-Spanish Vowel Correspondences, *RPh,* 16:2 (1962), 153–69.

Cr.: H. Guiter, *RLaR,* 75:2 (1963), 274; J.A. Cremona, R. Posner, & P. Russell-Gebbett, *YW,* 24 (1962–63), 21, 170.

See also 67, 215, 262, 292.

210 The Interlocking of Narrow Sound Change, Broad Phonological Pattern, Level of Transmission, Areal Configuration, Sound Symbolism: Diachronic Studies in the Hispano-Latin Consonant Clusters *CL-, FL-, PL-*, *ArL,* 15 (1963), 144–73; 16 (1964), 1–33.

Cr.: K. Baldinger (a), 27, 44, 218–9, 221–2 and *ZRPh,* 85 (1969), 512–6; O. Gsell, 15; H. Meier, *ASNS,* 204 (1969), 385–90; T. Montgomery, *HR,* 36 (1968), 54–9; R. Posner (b), 441; J. Simon, *ZPh,* 22 (1969), 412–5; K. Togeby, *ALH,* 11 (1969), 227–8; H.G. Tuchel, *RF,* 81 (1969), 617–21.

See also 105, 107, 241, 255, 291, 293.

211 Sobre el núcleo etimológico de esp. ant. *desman(d)ar, desman(o):* lat. *dē-, dī-mānāre, Fil,* 8 (1962[–64]), 185–211 (= *Hom. a María Rosa Lida de Malkiel,* 1).

212 Some Diachronic Implications of Fluid Speech Communities, *AA,* 66:6 (1964), Suppl.: *On the Ethnography of Communication,* ed. Dell H. Hymes & John J. Gumperz, 177–86. Rpr., *ELT,* 19–31.

Cr.: R. Posner (b), 447.

213 Secondary Uses of Letters in Language, *RPh,* 19:1 (1965), 1–27 (= *Howard Rollin Patch Mem.*). Rpr., *The Journal of Typographic Research* (Cleveland), 1 (1967), 96–110, 169–90; exp. *ELT,* 357–98.

See also 32.

214 Quelques fausses applications de la 'Loi de Verner' aux faits romans, *CFS,* 23 (1966), 75–87 (= *Mél. A. Burger*).

See also 43, 80, 268.

215 Diphthongization, Monophthongization, Metaphony: Studies in their Interaction in the Paradigm of the Old Spanish *-ir* Verbs, *Lg,* 42 (1966), 430–72.

Cr.: K. Baldinger (a), 30–1, 116; J.W. Harris, "Diphthongization, Monophthongization, Metaphony Revisited", in: *Diachronic Studies in Romance Linguistics,* ed. M. Saltarelli & D. Wanner, pp. 85–97 (The Hague: Mouton, 1975); also C.J. Pountain, *YW,* 38 (1976–77), 230, plus typescript, pp. 207–53, of Jesús Martín Samoyo's Madrid diss. (1986).

See also 4, 45, 91, 93, 139, 186, 188, 288, 352.

216 Linguistics as a Genetic Science, *Lg,* 43 (1967), 223–45. Rpr., *PGL,* 23–45; cf. 10, 559–60.

[Presidential address, LSA, delivered in Chicago on Dec. 28, 1965.]

Cr.: O. Gsell, 21; R. Posner (b), 445.

See also 27, 43–4, 46, 57, 78, 101–2, 179, 206, 334.

217 Is There Room for 'General Philology'?, *PCPh,* 1 (1966), 3–11.

[Presidential address, Philological Assn. of the Pacific Coast]

See also 27, 57, 94, 206, 247.

218 Each Word has a History of its Own, *Glossa,* 1 (1967), 137–49. Rpr., *PGL,* 217–26; see further ibid. 568–70.

[Prepared originally as a research paper for the 25th Coll. sponsored by the Wenner-Gren Foundation for Anthropological Research: "Revolution vs. continuity in the study of language", which met at Burg Wartenstein (Austria) on Aug. 15–25, 1964.]

Cr.: W. Labov, *Lg,* 57 (1981), 267–308, at 273; R. Posner (b), 444–5.

See also 43, 46, 66, 194.

219 Theory Versus Practice as a Starting Point for Discoveries in Linguistic Research, *AGI,* 53 (1968[–69]), 43–58 (= *Misc. B. Terracini,* 1).

[Originally presented at a 1968 Chicago Symposium on the history of linguistics.]

Cr.: R. Posner (b), 444.

See also 84.

220 Range of Variation as a Clue to Dating, 1, *RPh,* 21:4 (1968), 463–501 (= *Emanuel S. Georges Mem.*). Rpr., *PGL,* 87–125; see further ibid. 1, 563–4).

[Part 2 has not yet appeared.]

Cr.: O. Gsell, 17; R. Posner (b), 446–7.

See also 64, 89.

221 (With Karl D. Uitti) L'ancien français *gab-ois, ir-ois, jargon-ois* et leurs contreparties dans l'anglais d'Amérique, *RLiR,* 32 (1968), 126–74 (= *Homm. à la mémoire de John Orr*).

See also 42, 266.

222 Identification of Origin and Justification of Spread in Etymological Analysis: Studies in Sp. *s(ol)ombra, en-sueño,* dial. *em-berano, RPh,* 22:3 (1969), 259–80. Rpr., *PGL,* 451–72; see also 16–7, 585–6.

[In memory of Ramón Menéndez Pidal.]

See also 44, 210, 224.

223 Sound Changes Rooted in Morphological Conditions: The Case of Old Spanish /sk/ Changing to /θk/, *RPh,* 23:2 (1969), 188–200.

Cr.: M.B. Fontanella de Weinberg, "Interpretaciones teóricas y estudios documentales sobre la evolución de las sibilantes españolas", *RPh,* 31:2 (1977), 298–308, at 305–7.

224 The Five Sources of Epenthetic /j/ in Western Hispano-Romance: A Study in Multiple Causation, *HR,* 37 (1969), 239–75. ("At the Fresh Grave of Ramón Menéndez Pidal".) Rpr., *PGL,* 269–95; also ibid. 13–4, 577–8.

Cr.: K. Baldinger (a), 408–9.

See also 34, 207, 210, 222.

225 Morphological Analogy as a Stimulus for Sound Change, *LS,* 4 (1969), 305–27.

[Special issue dedicated to diachronic structuralism.]

Cr.: O. Gsell, 14.

See also 36, 39, 45, 207, 223, 244, 389.

226 Un paradoxe dans le développement du groupe latin *-sk'-* en ancien portugais, *TLL,* 8:1 (1970), 141–53 (= *Mél. Albert Henry*).

Cr.: R.J. Penny, *YW,* 33 (1971–72), 318.

See also 67, 223.

227 Polysémie, homonymie et dérivation verbale en paléo-roman; autour de la reconstruction de **traginãre, *tragicãre, *traxinãre, ER,* 13 (1963–68[–70]), 1–12 (= *Misc. Pompeu Fabra*).

Cr.: O. Gsell, 3.

See also 107, 175, 178, 250, 279.

228 Derivational Transparency as an Occasional Co-determinant of Sound Change: A New Causal Ingredient in the Distribution of *-ç-* and *-z-* in Ancient Hispano-Romance (1), *RPh,* 25:1 (1971), 1–52.

[Part 2 has remained unpublished.]

Cr.: J.N. Green, *YW,* 33 (1971–2), 17; R.J. Penny, ibid., 318–9; O. Gsell, 13.

See also 45, 59, 95, 193, 196, 198, 265.

229 The Rise of Nominal Augments in Romance; Graeco-Latin and Tuscan Clues to the Prehistory of Hispano-Romance, *RPh,* 26:2 (1972), 306–34. Rpr., *PGL,* 419–47; see further ibid. 16, 548–5.

Cr.: O. Gsell, 12. Cf. Anita Katz Levy, *RPh,* 28:4 (1975), 684–6.

See also 48, 116, 288, 294.

230 Ancien français *faü, feü, malostru.* A la recherche de *-ūcus,* suffixe latin et paléo-roman rare de la 'mauvaise fortune', *TLL,* 11:1 (1973), 177–89 (= *Mél. Paul Imbs*).

Cr.: J.N. Green, *YW,* 35 (1973–4), 29; T.J. Walsh, *RPh,* 35:1 (1981), 99–104 ("Affixation as a Clue to Etymology: The Case of OProv. *faduc,* OFr. *mal-, dur-feü*").

See also 250.

231–2 Deux frontières entre la phonologie et la morphologie en diachronie, *Langages* (Paris: Didier-Larousse), 8:32 (1973), num. spécial: *Le changement linguistique,* pp. 79–87.

Cr.: O. Gsell, 9.

See also 233, 267, 269.

233 Summits of Romance Linguistics, *CJRL,* 1 (1973), 33–48.

[The single issue ever published of this short-lived journal]

See also 44, 49, 69, 70, 203, 205, 237, 248, 278, 280, 380.

234 Primary, Secondary, and Tertiary Etymologies: The Three Lexical Kernels of Hispanic *saña, ensañar, sañudo, HR,* 42 (1974), 1–32. Rpr., *PGL,* 473–96, also 17–8, 587.

Cr.: O. Gsell, 3, 9; C.J. Pountain, *YW,* 36 (1974–75), 242.

See also 159, 187, 191, 194, 206.

235 New Problems in Romance Interfixation (1): The Velar Insert in the Present Tense (with an exc. on *-zer* / *-zir* Verbs), *RPh,* 27:3 (1974), 304–55.

[Part 2 has not yet appeared.]

Cr.: J.N. Green, *YW,* 36 (1974–75), 29; R.J. Penny, ibid., 358.

See also 114, 185.

236 Etiological Studies in Romance Diachronic Phonology, *ALH,* 14:2 (1973[–4]), pp. 201–42. Rpr., *PGL,* 361–95; see further ibid. 14–5, 581–2.

[1. The change of *a, o* into *e* before *r* in Florentine; 2. An Elusive Pattern of Consonant Dissimilation in Italian (*r . . . r* > *d . . . r, r . . . d*); 3. Choice of a Niche in a Sound System and Search for Causation (Illustrated with Old Spanish); 4. Proliferation of Variants as a Co-Determinant of Sound Change? The Case of Old Spanish -*ç*- < -DJ-]

Cr.: J.N. Green, *YW,* 36 (1974–75), 29.

See also 4, 132, 286.

237 Conflicting Prosodic Inferences from Ascoli's and Darmesteter's Laws? *RPh,* 28:4 (1975), 483–520 (= *Jonathan L. Butler Mem.*). Exc. A: Genesis and Spread of the Segments *ens-, enx-* (505–12); Exc. B: From Old Spanish *eñader* to Mod. *añadir,* and Related Problems (512–20). Rpr., *PGL,* 323–6.

See also 14, 233, 579–81.

238 Etymology and Modern Linguistics, *Lingua,* 36 (1975), 101–20. Rpr., *PGL,* 497–511. Tr. in 11, 51–76, and addenda: 133–6.

Cr.: O. Gsell, 11.

See also 18–9, 51–2, 71, 81–3, 164, 181, 187, 191, 194, 206, 240, 257, 295, 347, 354, 434, 587–8.

239 Some Late-Twentieth-Century Options Open to Hispanic Philology and Linguistics, *BHS,* 52 (1975), 1–11.

Cr.: C.J. Pountain, *YW,* 37 (1975–76), 226–7; D.J. Gifford, ibid., 342–3.

See also 172, 206, 295, 342, 350.

240 Deux catégories d'étymologies "intéressantes", *RLiR,* 39 (1975), 255–95. Tr. in 11, 77–123, and addenda: 136–7.

Cr.: J.N. Green, *YW,* 37 (1975–76), 28; O. Gsell, 11.

See also 51–2, 71, 81–3, 164, 187, 191, 194, 206, 238, 288–9, 295, 340.

241 En torno al cultismo medieval: los descendientes hispánicos de DULCIS, *NRFH,* 24 (1975), 24–45 (= *Homenaje a Raimundo Lida,* 1).

Cr.: C.J. Pountain, *YW,* 37 (1975–76), 234; S.L. Hartman, "La etimología de *dulce:* ¿realmente una excepción?", *NRFH,* 29 (1980), 115–27; R. Wright & M.W. Wheeler, *YW,* 43 (1981–82), 276–7.

See also 193, 210, 284.

242 Español y portugués antiguos *Diago, Diego* y *Diogo:* En torno a la hipercaracterización interna y externa, *MR,* 2:2 (1975), 177–92.

See also 114–5, 117d, 296.

243 One Characteristic Derivational Suffix of Literary Italian: *-(t)aggine, AGI,* 61 (1976), 130–45 (= *Misc. Bruno Migliorini*). Rpr., *PGL,* 399–409; see further 15, 582–3.

See also 87, 193, 210, 357, 425.

244 Multi-Conditioned Sound-Change and the Impact of Morphology on Phonology, *Lg,* 52 (1976), 757–78. Rpr., *PGL,* 229–50; see further 12–13, 570–5.

Cr.: J.N. Green, *YW,* 38 (1976–77), 5; C.J. Pountain, ibid., 231. Cf. Leo Pap, *Lg,* 32 (1956), 738–43 (book review); R.W. Wescott, *Lacus Forum,* 5 (1979), 81–92; L. Pap, "The Etymology of E. *tip* 'Gratuity'", to appear in *Forum;* W. Labov, "Resolving the Neogrammarian Controversy", *Lg,* 57 (1981), 267–308.

See also 32, 36, 39, 58, 253.

245 From Falling to Rising Diphthongs: The Case of Old Spanish *ió* < **éu* (with Excursuses on the Weak Preterite; on the Possessives; and on *judío, sandío,* and *romero*), *RPh,* 29:4 (1976), 435–500.

Cr.: J.C. Pountain, *YW,* 38 (1976–77), 231; J.R. Craddock, "Portugués antiguo *sandeu,* castellano antiguo *sandío*. . . .", *FS Hubschmid* (Bern, 1982), 955–9; Id., "Descending Diphthongs and the Regular Preterite in Hispano-Romance", *BHS,* 60 (1983), 1–14.

246 Contacts between BLASPHĒMĀRE and AESTIMĀRE (with an exc. on the Etymology of Hisp. *tomar*); *RPh,* 30:1 (1976), 102–117 (= *Jean Frappier Mem.*). Rpr., *PGL,* 543–58; see further ibid. 19 and 590–1.

See also 81, 167, 276, 303.

247 From Romance Philology through Dialect Geography to Sociolinguistics, *IJSL,* 9 (1976), 59–84 (= *Linguistics,* No. 177).

[Special issue, titled "The Social Dimension of Dialectology", ed. José Pedro Rona & Wolfgang Woelck. Absorbed into this paper have been sections of a lecture delivered at the Univ. of Illinois to commemorate Henry Kahane's retirement: "Urbana et ruralia".]

See also 172–3, 205.

248 Friedrich Diez and the Birth Pangs of Romance Linguistics, *Friedrich Diez Centennial Lectures,* ed. Edward F. Tuttle, 1–15 (= Suppl. to *RPh,* 30:2 [1976] = Center for Medieval and Renaissance Studies, Contr. 9).

See also 49, 97, 530.

249 Studies in Luso-Hispanic Lexical Osmosis: Old Spanish *famn-, fambriento, (des)fambrido,* Portuguese *faminto, es-fom-eado* 'Hungry' and the Growth of the Suffix *-(i)ento* < -(UL)ENTU, *HR,* 45 (1977), 235–67.

See also 318a.

250 La fragmentación de FĪDŪCIA en hispanorrománico, *NRFH,* 26 (1977[–79]), 1–55.

Cr.: O. Gsell, 4.

See also 16, 230.

251 The Social Matrix of Palaeo-Romance Postverbal Nouns, *RPh,* 31:1 (1977), 55–90. Rpr., *PGL,* 179–213; see further 11–12, 568.

Cr.: O. Gsell, 8. Cf. J.M. Baldonado, *RPh,* 35:1 (1981), 64–79 ("Affixation and Gender Desinence in the Old Spanish Postverbal Noun").

See also 4, 130.

252 Ernst G. Wahlgren—et les perspectives d'une réhabilitation de la morphologie, *SN,* 49 (1977), 69–85.

See also 32, 36, 39, 244, 253, 255, 304.

253 On Hierarchizing the Components of Multiple Causation, *StL,* 1 (1977), 81–107. Rpr., *PGL,* 297–319; see further 14, 579.

Cr.: O. Gsell, 9.

See also 32, 244.

254 The Classification of [the] Romance Languages, *RPh,* 31:3 (1978), 467–500.

Cr.: J.N. Green, *YW,* 41 (1979–80), 31.

See also 80, 117.

255 From Phonosymbolism to Morphosymbolism, *Lacus Forum,* 4 (1978), 511–29. Cf. R. Jakobson & Linda R. Waugh, *The Sound Shape of Language,* 182 (Bloomington & London: Indiana UP, 1979).

See also 105, 107, 211.

256 Between Heymann Steinthal and Adolf Tobler: Georg Cohn in Turn-of-the-Century Berlin, *HL,* 5 (1978), 237–51.

See also 263.

257 (With S.N. Dworkin, C.B. Faulhaber, J.F. Levy & J.K. Walsh) AEQUUS Versus (IN)GENUUS: Etymological Studies in Old Spanish *(y)engo* 'Free', *(y)e(n)guedad* 'Freedom', *RPh,* 32:1 (1978), 49–64.

Cr.: O. Gsell, 4.

See also 129, 148.

258 Problems in the Diachronic Differentiation of Near-Homophones, *Lg,* 55 (1979), 1–36.

Cr.: W. Cowan, *CanJL,* 26 (1981), 223–6 ("On the Origin of *-s-* in Spanish *hasta*"); O. Gsell, 7; J.N. Green, *YW,* 41 (1979–80), 34; R. Wright & M.W. Wheeler, ibid., 270 (see further 43, 276).

See also 107, 175, 178, 198.

259 The Abandonment of the Root Diphthong in the Paradigms of Certain Spanish Verbs, *IL,* 5 (1979 [1980]), 123–38 (= *Vittore Pisani Testimonial*).

See also 67.

260 Medieval Roots of the Spanish Derivational Model *sabid-or* ~ *sabid-uría, RPh,* 33:1 (1979), 102–16.

Cr.: R. Wright & M.W. Wheeler, *YW,* 41 (1979–80), 270.

See also 19, 48, 136.

261 Du latin TRIPODĀRE/TRIPUDIĀRE 'danser' à l'anc. esp. *trebejar,* anc. port. *trebelhar* 'gambader' (avec un coup d'œil sur *trépigner*), *RLiR,* 44 (1980), 1–56.

Cr.: J.N. Green, *YW,* 42 (1980–81), 38; R. Wright & M.W. Wheeler, ibid., 262.

See also 23, 75.

262 The Fluctuating Intensity of a 'Sound Law': Some Vicissitudes of Latin Ĕ and Ŏ in Spanish, *RPh,* 34:1 (1980), 48–63.

[For a shorter version see 67.]

263 Federico Hanssen y Henry R. Lang, *BFUCh,* 31 (1980–81[–82]), 275–84 (= *Hom. a Ambrosio Rabanales*).

See also 256.

264 The Old Spanish and Old Galician-Portuguese Adjective *ledo,* Archaic Spanish *liedo, Cor,* 9:2 (1981), 95–106. Cf. Geoffrey Stagg, "A Note on the Persistence of Old Spanish *ledo*", ibid., 11:1 (1982), 46–48.

Cr.: R. Wright & M.W. Wheeler, *YW,* 43 (1981–82), 276, and 44 (1982–83), 297.

See also 131–2.

265 A Hidden Morphological Factor behind Instances of Erratic Distribution of *ç* and *z* in Old Spanish?, *RPh,* 35:1 (1981), 105–29.

Cr.: R. Wright & M.W. Wheeler, *YW,* 43 (1981–82), 275.

See also 183, 196, 198, 223, 225.

266 Drift, Slope, and Slant: Background of, and Variations upon, a Sapirian Theme, *Lg*, 67 (1981), 535–70.

Cr.: R. Wright & M.W. Wheeler, *YW*, 43 (1981–82), 275.

See also 101–2, 221.

267 Interplay of Sounds and Forms in the Shaping of Three Old Spanish Medial Consonant Clusters, *HR*, 50:3 (1982), 247–66.

Cr.: R. Wright & M.W. Wheeler, *YW*, 44 (1982–83), 296.

See also 53.

268 Romance and Indo-European Linguistics in Italy, *HL*, 9:3 (1982), 471–93.

See also 322, 341, 425.

269 Infinitive Endings, Conjugation Classes, Nominal Derivational Suffixes, and Vocalic Gamuts in Romance, *ALH*, 17:1 (1982), 15–48.

[For a list of errata see Vol. 20.]

Cr.: O. Gsell, 13.

See also 7, 33, 52, 59, 91, 139, 186, 188.

270 In Search of Coefficients in Diachronic Morphological Analysis: /i/ as an Increasingly Dominant Vowel in Spanish Inflectional Morphemes, *PBLS*, 8 (1982), 36–78.

Cr.: J.N. Green, *YW*, 44 (1982–83), 16; R. Wright & M.W. Wheeler, ibid., 296.

271 Morpho-semantic Conditioning of Spanish Diphthongization: The Case of *teso* ~ *tieso*, *RPh*, 36:2 (1982), 154–84.

Cr.: R. Wright & M.W. Wheeler, *YW*, 44 (1982–83), 296.

See also 281, 284, 291–3.

272 Los prototipos latinos de (esp. ant.) *avuelo* ~ *avuela*, *ayo* ~ *aya*, (port. ant.) *avoo* ~ *avoa*, (francés) *aïeul(e)*, *MR*, 8:2 (1981–83), 161–74.

See also 84, 88.

273 The Founding Editor's "White Paper", *RPh*, 37:1 (1983), 1–19.

Cr.: J.N. Green, *YW*, 45 (1983), 16.

See also 494–5, 501, 505, 508, 511, 516–7, 537, 542, 561, 567–8, 572, 574–5.

274 A Revisionist View of the Etymology of OSp., OGal.-Ptg. *trocir* 'Pass', *Cor,* 12:1 (1983), 92–106.

See also 52, 100, 106, 114, 139, 192, 275.

275 Croisement, empiètement, bousculade de verbes latins en hispano-roman (SPLENDĒRE, EXPANDĔRE, EXPĔNDĔRE), *RLiR,* 47 (1982), 271–97.

Cr.: J.H. Green, *YW,* 45 (1983), 20.

See also 64, 91, 93, 100, 106, 114, 139, 274.

276 Trois exemples nouveaux de la «polarisation lexicale» en roman, 1 [: 'Perdre' et 'trouver' en ancien portugais], *Ro,* 104:3 (1983), 289–315.

See also 62, 167, 177, 246, 303.

277 Las peripecias luso-españolas de la voz *synagōga.* En la encrucijada de helenismos y hebraísmos, *NRFH,* 32:1 (1983[–84]), 1–40.

See also 74.

278 Lingüística románica, *CS,* 16 (1983[–84]), 5–15.

See also 28, 44, 205, 233.

279 Prevention of Highly-Objectionable Homonymy in Luso- and Hispano-Romance, *BF,* 28 (1983 [1984–85]), 179–93 (= *Hom. Manuel Rodrigues Lapa*).

Cr.: J.N. Green, *YW,* 47 (1985), 30; R. Wright & M.W. Wheeler, ibid., 282.

See also 107, 116, 178, 227, 258.

280 The Place Assigned to Rumanian by 19th-Century Comparatists, *SEE,* 10:1 (1983–84), 1–24.

[Revision of a talk delivered at the 8th Convention of the American Rumanian Academy of Arts & Sciences, Davis, CA, April 21–23, 1982.]

See also 297.

281 Old Spanish Resistance to Diphthongization, or Previous Vowel Lengthening?, *Lg,* 60 (1984), 70–114.

See also 67, 71, 215, 259.

282 The Overlap of CŬRRĔRE, -CŬTERE, and COR-RĬGĔRE in Hispano-Romance, *RPh,* 38:2 (1984), 127–70.

Cr.: R. Wright & M.W. Wheeler, *YW,* 47 (1985), 281.

See also 139, 290, 318.

283 Six Categories of Nasal Epenthesis: Their Place in the Evolution from Latin into Romance, *PBLS,* 10 (1984), 27–46.

Cr.: J.N. Green, *YW,* 47 (1985), 30.

See also 17, 165, 190, 237, 291, 293.

284 Rising Diphthongs in the Paradigms of Spanish Learnèd *-ir* Verbs, *HR,* 52 (1984), 303–33.

See also 241, 259, 262, 290.

285 La aversión al monosilabismo en los adjetivos del español antiguo y moderno, *LEA,* 6 (1984), 5–27.

See also 241.

286 The Development of Three Late Latin Consonant Clusters in Old Spanish and Old Portuguese. AUDEŌ, ˣPERDIŌ, HORDEOLU, VIR(I)DIA; GRUNDIŌ, ĪRĀ-, VERĒ-CUNDIA; AUDIŌ, GAUDIU, *NM,* 85 (1984), 7–18.

See also 64, 132, 183.

287 CRUMĒNA, a Latin Lexical Isolate, and its Survival in Hispano-Romance (Sp. *colmena,* dial. *cormena* 'Beehive'), *Glotta,* 62 (1984), 106–23.

288 Ramón Menéndez Pidal as Etymologist, *HL,* 11 (1984), 325–47.

See also 294, 307.

289 (With Charlotte Stern) The Etymology of Spanish *villancico* 'Carol'; Certain Literary Implications of this Etymology, *BHS,* 61 (1984), 137–50.

290 El engranaje de las peripecias románicas de FERRE y FERĪRE (con particular atención a *reyerta* y *zaherir*), *MR,* 9 (1984), 161–81.

Cr.: J.N. Green, *YW,* 47 (1985), 34.

See also 282, 284.

291 Language-Universal vs. Language-Specific Phonosymbolism: /t/ as the Carrier of the Idea of 'Stubborn Resistance', *Zb,* 27 (1984–85), 423–30 (= *Hom. Milka & Pavle Ivić*).

Cr.: J.N. Green, *YW,* 47 (1985), 30.

See also 105, 107, 210, 255, 283, 293.

292 Spanish Diphthongization and Accentual Structure (in Diachronic Perspective), *Diachronica,* 1:1 (Fall 1984), 217–41.

Cr.: R. Wright & M.W. Wheeler, *YW,* 47 (1985), 30–36.

See also 189, 199, 215, 262, 293.

293 Studies in Secondary Phonosymbolism, *AGI,* 69:1–2 (1984[–85]), 1–25.

[Dedicated to the memory of Giacomo Devoto.]

Cr.: J.N. Green, *YW,* 47 (1985), 30; R. Wright & M. W. Wheeler, *YW,* 48 (1986–87), 295.

See also 53, 105, 107, 189, 199, 205, 262, 292.

294 La última fase (1939–1969) de la labor lingüística de Ramón Menéndez Pidal, *AL,* 23 (1985), 5–68.

See also 288, 307.

295 Toward Higher Formalization in Etymology: The Spanish Culinary Term *ciliérveda* and its Variants, *Neoph,* 69 (1985), 204–15.

[Given as keynote address at the Tenth California Convocation in Romance Philology, Berkeley, November 19, 1983.]

Cr.: J.N. Green, *YW,* 47 (1985), 34; R. Wright & M.W. Wheeler, ibid., 281–2.

See also 318h, 318j.

296 Excessive Self-Assertion in Glottodiachrony: Portuguese *sofrer* and its Latin and Spanish Counterparts, *Lingua,* 65 (1985), 29–50.

Cr.: J.N. Green, *YW,* 47 (1985), 35.

See also 114–5, 117d, 242.

297 Old and New Problems in the Latinity of the Lower Danube, *JARA,* 6–7 (1985), 90–103.

Cr.: J.N. Green, *YW,* 47 (1985), 35.

See also 280.

298 (With Raquel F. Alessandri Teixeira) Latin Word-Medial Consonants Lost in Portuguese: Early and Delayed Conjugational Reverberations, *PBLS,* 11 (1985), 226–44.

See also 296, 298.

299 La etimología de esp. *tras-[h]egar* 'trasvasar', it. *trafficare* 'comerciar': un nuevo balance, *MR,* 10 (1985), 305–38.

Cr.: R. Wright & M.W. Wheeler, *YW,* 47 (1985), 282.

See also 92.

300 From Old Portuguese *caer* 'Fall' to Modern *cair:* Three Explanations, *(K)RQ,* 33:1 (1986), 5–10.

See also 296, 298.

301 A la recherche des désignations latines de femmes et de femelles en *-ia, BSLP,* 80:1 (1985), 145–63.

See also 88, 306.

302 The Romance Vicissitudes of Latin *opus est*: Jakob Jud's Reconstruction Reconsidered, *CM,* 38 (1987), 189–202.

See also 106.

303 Trois exemples nouveaux de la "polarisation lexicale" en roman: *nourrir* et *pourrir, Ro,* 105:4 (1984[–86]), 411–61.

See also 62, 167, 177, 276, 312.

304 (With Keith E. Karlsson) Erik Staaff (1867–1936)—portrait rétrospectif, *SN,* 59(1987), 81–98.

See also 252, 412, 422, 597.

305 The Old French Verbal Abstracts in *-ëiz, ZRPh,* 102: 1–2 (1986), 1–39.

See also 63.

306 Trois modèles latino-romans pour la désignation d'une femme, d'une servante ou d'une femelle, *RLiR,* 50 (1986), 317–50.

See also 88, 301.

307 El brillo y el calor. En torno a la última etimología (*re-focilar*) de Ramón Menéndez Pidal. To appear in *Archivum.*

See also 288, 294.

308 The Designations of the Cupbearer in Medieval Hispano-Romance, *StPh,* 83 (1986), 286–302.

See also 318e.

309 A Spanish Conjugational Model Superimposed on Portuguese, *MeLR,* 2 (1984), 51–66.

See also 114, 313.

310 Carolina Michaëlis de Vasconcelos' Forgotten Sketch of an Unfinished Monograph on *e(n)-zebra* 'wild donkey'. To appear in *BF.*

See also 47, 90, 98, 166.

311 A Cluster of (Old) Portuguese Derivational Suffixes: *-ece, -ice, -ez(a),* Viewed in Relation to their Spanish Counterparts, *BHS,* 65 : 1 (1988), 1–19.

See also 33, 59, 136, 142, 228, 249, 264.

312 Romance Reflexes of Latin *nūtrīcia* and *nūtrīciō, Glotta,* 63 (1985), 326–40.

See also 88, 272, 301, 306.

313 Diachronic Phonology as a Clue to the Transmission of Etyma, Exemplified with Old Portuguese Verbs, *GL,* 26 : 3 (1986), 149–81.

See also 114, 144, 309.

314 Spanish *pudiente, pudiendo*—A Case of Lexical Aberrancy, *(K)RQ,* 34 : 1 (1987), 5–13.

See also 91, 93, 106, 131, 188, 207, 215, 237, 269, 274–5, 282, 290, 303.

315 The Etymology of Portuguese *ofegar, RN,* 26 : 2 (1986), 177–84.

See also 92, 299.

316 The Spanish Nominal Augments Reconsidered. To appear in *RPh,* 43 : 1 (1989) ("Alison Goddard Elliott Memorial Issue").

See also 229.

317 La linguistica diacronica e i suoi tre legami con la storia generale. *Fondamenti, rivista trimestrale di cultura,* ed. Massimiliano Pavan, 7 (1987), 89–111.

See also 27–8, 40, 43, 179, 216–8.

318 Español *correrse, corrido* en dos perspectivas: la sincrónica y la diacrónica, *LEA,* 9 (1987), 315–31.

See also 282.

318a El sardo como guía por los matorrales léxicos del gallegoportugués: la derivación de *faminto* 'hambriento', *MR,* 11 (1986), 337–44.

See also 249.

318b Why Spanish *seso,* but Portuguese *siso,* from Ancestral SĒ(N)SU? *Neoph,* 72 (1988), 44–55.

See also 174, 215.

318c Un breve retorno a la prole románica de PESSULUS, FISTULA y FERRUM. *RevR,* 22(1987), 182–93.

See also 175.

318d French *courber* and *corbeau:* From Classical CURVĀRE to Gallo-Latin *CURBĀRE. To appear in *RF.*

See also 47, 138, 404b.

318e (With Kathryn Klingebiel) Studies in the Names of the Goldsmith in Romance (and in Some Other Languages), *GL,* 27.1 (1987), 1–33.

See also K.K.'s Berkeley doctoral dissertation, *Romance Reflexes of the Latin Compositional Type* MANŪTENĒRE, to be published by the University of California Press; and 308.

318f *Belesa* y *belleza:* en torno al verbo portugués *embelezar, MR* ("Limentani Memorial"), 12 (1987), 13–27.

See also 25.

318g Apocope: Straight; through Contact of Languages; via Suffixal Polarization: The Spanish Derivational Morphemes and Word-Final Segments *-ín* and *-ino*. To appear in *HR*.

See also 33, 59, 128, 147, 152, 157, 162, 165, 171, 202.

318h Latin SUPERBUS/SUPERBIA: Their Reflexes in Spanish and Portuguese (Older and Modern). To appear in *(K)RQ*.

See also 34, 39, 215.

318i Early Old Spanish *desfaç-ido (-ado, -iado), desfaz-ido (-ado), porfaç-ado (-zido), Cor,* 15:2 (1987), 293–301.

See also 60, 140, 159.

318j Una correspondencia fonética latina/luso-española débilmente perfilada: *-RB-* > *-rv-*, *NM,* 88 (1987), 109–25.

See also 50, 207, 210, 318d, 318h.

318k La agonía del verbo *nozir, nuzir* 'dañar' en las postrimerías de la Edad Media española. To appear in *NRFH.*

See also 215, 237, 274, 282, 284, 290, 296, 300, 303, 314, 318.

318l The Transmission into Romance of Latin NŌDUS, NŬPTIAE, NŬRUS, and NŬX: Diachronic Interplay of Phonetic and Semantic Analogies, *GL,* 27:4 (1987), 239–60.

See also 117e, 117f, 318k.

318m La teoría de las sibilantes propuesta por Rufino José Cuervo. (See 95.)

VI. Review Articles, Composite Appraisals, Lengthy Book Reviews

319 Joseph H.D. Allen, Jr., *Portuguese Word-Formation with Suffixes* (Suppl. to *Lg*, 17 [1941]), *Lg*, 18 (1942), 51–62.

Cr.: K. Baldinger (a), 184.

See also 2, 3, 7, 16, 18, 20, 24, 33, 42, 45, 59, 87, 88, 118, 123, 129, 132, 140, 150, 154, 162, 170, 189, 198, 201–2, 381, 627–8, etc.

320 María Concepción Casado Lobato, *El habla de la Cabrera Alta; contribución al estudio del dialecto leonés* (Madrid, 1948), *Lg*, 25 (1949), 291–307.

Cr.: M.L. Wagner. *ZRPh*, 69 (1953). 348–58.

See also 324, 367, 599, 600.

321 The Jewish Heritage of Spain [Américo Castro, *España en su historia: cristianos, moros y judíos*, Buenos Aires, 1948], *HR*, 23 (1950), 328–40.

See also 143, 277, 362, 373, 603.

322 Cultural History through Linguistics [Vittorio Bertoldi, *La parola quale testimone della storia*, Napoli, 1946], *It*, 27 (1950), 330–43.

See also 240, 268, 287, 322, 331–2, 336, 349, 351, 446.

323 Rafael Lapesa, *Historia de la lengua española*$_2$ (Madrid, 1950), *RPh*, 6:1 (1952), 52–63.

Cr.: K. Baldinger (a) 69, 71, 84, 86, 101, 265, 338.

See also 108, 341, 593–5, 605, 643.

324 Lorenzo Rodríguez-Castellano, *La variedad dialectal del Alto Aller* (Oviedo, 1952), *Lg*, 30 (1954), 128–53.

Cr.: K. Baldinger (a), 25, 168.

See also 7, 320, 367, 599, 600.

325 Max L. Wagner, "Etymologische Randbemerkungen zu neueren iberoromanischen Dialektarbeiten und Wörterbüchern" (*ZRPh,* 69 [1953], 347–91), *RPh,* 9:1 (1955), 50–68.

Cr.: M.L. Wagner, *RF,* 68 (1956), 443–50.

See also 320, 324, 408.

326 Amado Alonso, *De la pronunciación medieval a la moderna en español,* ed. Rafael Lapesa, 1 (Madrid, 1955), *RPh,* 9:2 (1955), 237–52.

Cr.: K. Baldinger (a), 267.

See also 95, 228, 354c.

327 Max Gorosch, ed. *El Fuero de Teruel* (Stockholm, 1950), *Lg,* 31 (1955), 261–91.

See also 333.

328 Linguistic Problems in a New Hispanic Etymological Dictionary [Joan Corominas, *Diccionario crítico etimológico de la lengua castellana,* 1, Bern & Madrid, 1954], *Word,* 12 (1956), 35–50.

Cr.: K. Baldinger (a), 268; I. González Llubera, *YW,* 18 (1956–57), 175.

See also 9, 46, 51–2, 83, 112, 164, 181, 187, 191, 194, 347, 354, 636, 638–9, etc.

329 Studies in Spanish and Portuguese Animal Names [Delmira Maçãs, *Os animais na língua portuguesa,* Lisboa, 1950–51], *HR,* 24 (1956), 111–43, 207–31.

See also 47, 86, 90, 147, 162, 166, 202, etc.

330 André Martinet, *Économie des changements phonétiques; traité de phonologie diachronique* (Berne, 1955), *RPh,* 10:4 (1957), 350–62.

See also 24, 31, 43, 65, 99, 236, 334, 346, 374, 604, 621, 625, etc.

331 José Gonçalo C. Herculano de Carvalho, *Coisas e palavras; alguns problemas etnográficos e linguísticos relacionados com os primitivos sistemas de debulha na Península Ibérica* (Coimbra, 1953 = *Biblos,* 19), *Lg,* 33 (1957), 54–76. Rpr. (under the title: "Words, Objects, Images: Shapes, Makes, and Names of the Flail in Portugal"), *ELT,* 281–310.

Cr.: K. Baldinger (a), 173.

See also 287, 332, 336.

332 The Skein-Winding Reel in Gallo-Romance: Studies in Etymology, Dialect Geography, and Material Civilization [Charles H. Livingston, *Skein-Winding Reels; Studies in Word History and Etymology,* Ann Arbor, 1957], *RPh,* 12:3 (1959), 262–82 [= *Charles H. Livingston Testim.*].

Cr.: H. Guiter, *RLaR,* 74:2 (1961), 250.

See also 287, 331, 336.

333 Gunnar Tilander, ed. *"Vidal Mayor": Traducción aragonesa de la obra "In excelsis Dei thesauris" de Vidal de Canellas,* 3 vols. (Lund, 1956), *Lg,* 35 (1959), 670–92.

Cr.: I. González Llubera, *YW,* 21 (1959–60), 156.

See also 318c, 327.

334 From Diachronic Phonology to General Linguistics [André Martinet, *Éléments de linguistique générale,* Paris, 1960–61], *RPh,* 15:2 (1961), 139–53.

Cr.: C.F. Voegelin & A. Valdman, *IJAL,* 29 (1963), 283a.

See also 27, 31, 38, 43–4, 94, 330, 346, 604, 625–6, etc.

335 The Leningrad Circle of Romance Philologists [*Romanskaja filologija = Mélanges B.A. Krževskij,* Leningrad, 1961], *RPh,* 15:2 (1961), 154–62.

See also 420, 447, 488, 593, 617.

336 Johannes Hubschmid, (a) *Schläuche und Fässer; wort- und sachgeschichtliche Untersuchungen mit besonderer Berücksichtigung des romanischen Sprachgutes* (Bern, 1955) and (b) *Substratprobleme; eine neue iberoromanisch-alpinlombardische Wortgleichung. . .* (Bern, 1961), *Lg,* 38 (1962), 149–85.

Cr.: K. Baldinger (a), 349; J.A. Cremona & R. Posner, *YW,* 24 (1962–63), 37; O. Szemerényi, *RPh,* 17 (1963–64), 405.

See also 287, 331–2, 343, 612.

337 Thomas A. Sebeok, ed. *Style in Language* (Cambridge, MA; New York & London, 1960), *IJAL,* 28 (1962), 268–86.

Cr.: J.A. Cremona & R. Posner, *YW,* 24 (1962–63), 35.

338 History of Linguistics [John T. Waterman, *Perspectives in Linguistics,* Chicago, 1963; L. Kukenheim, *Esquisse historique de la linguistique française* *et de ses rapports avec la linguistique générale,* Leiden, 1962; I. Iordan & W. Bahner, *Einführung in die Geschichte und Methoden der romanischen Sprachwissenschaft,* Berlin, 1962], *RPh,* 17:4 (1964), 823–8.

See also 64–5, 70, 84, 97–8, 101–2, 121, 172–3, 203, 214, 233, 247–8, 256, 268, 304, 338, 340–2, 694–5, etc.

339 Nuggets of Linguistic Information in Critical Editions of *Siglo de Oro* Texts [Comments on publications by J.A. Castañeda, V. Černý, A.V. Ebersole, R.R. MacCurdy, R. Marcus, A.G. Reichenberger, B. Wittmann], *RPh,* 18:1 (1964), 137–42.]

See also 598.

340 (With Margaret Langdon, responsible for pp. 566–72) History and Histories of Linguistics [T.A. Sebeok, ed. *Portraits of Linguists. . .,* Bloomington & London, 1966; M. Leroy, *Les grands courants de la linguistique moderne,* Bruxelles & Paris, 1963; M. Ivić, *Trends in Linguistics,* The Hague, 1965; B. Malmberg, *New Trends in Linguistics. . .,* Stockholm & Lund, 1964; G.C. Lepschy, *La linguistica strutturale,* Torino, 1966], *RPh,* 22:4 (1969), 530–66, 573–4 (= *Lucien Foulet Mem.-Alfred Foulet Testim.*) Rpr., *PGL,* 49–83; cf. 10, 560–3.

See also 64–5, 70, 84, 97–8, 101–2, 121, 172–3, 203, 214, 233, 247–8, 256, 268, 304, 338, 341–2, 694–5, etc.

341 Linguistics (Including its History) and the Humanities: Two New Approaches to a Fluid Relationship. [Karl D. Uitti, *Linguistics and Literary Theory: A Structural and Historical Overview of the Relationship,* Englewood Cliffs, 1969; Alberto Vàrvaro, *Storia, problemi e metodi della linguistica romanza,* Napoli, 1968], *RPh,* 23:3 (1970), 323–35.

See also 338, 340, 353.

342 A Straightforward Report on the Latest "Crises" in Romance Linguistics. [R. Posner, *Thirty Years On*; Suppl. to Iordan-Orr, *An Introduction. . .*$_2$] *RPh,* 25:2 (1971), 216–24.

See also 338, 340–1, 611.

343 Johannes Hubschmid, *Thesaurus Prae-Romanicus:* 1. Grundlagen für ein weitverbreitetes mediterranes Substrat, dargestellt an . . . *p-* Suffixen; 2. Probleme der . . . baskisch-vorromanischen Etymologien (Bern, 1963–65), *Lg,* 47 (1971), 465–87.

See also 3, 77, 163, 336, 612.

344 Horst Geckeler, *Zur Wortfelddiskussion: Untersuchungen zur Gliederung des Wortfeldes 'alt'–'jung'–'neu' im heutigen Französisch* (München, 1971), *FL,* 12 (1974), 271–85.

345 T.E. Hope, *Lexical Borrowing in the Romance Languages* . . . (New York, 1971), *Lg,* 51 (1975), 962–76. Rpr., *PGL,* 137–51, cf. 11, 565–6.

Cr.: J.N. Green, *YW,* 37 (1975–6), 28.

See also 48, 57, 61, 76, 131, 193, 264.

346 Bertil Malmberg, *Linguistique générale et romane*. . . (La Haye & Paris, 1973), *GL,* 15 : 4 (1975), 214–26.

See also 27, 94, 173, 334, 340, 604, 625–6.

347 Max Pfister, *Lessico etimologico italiano (= LEI),* 1 : 1–2 and *Supplemento bibliografico,* with Dieter Hauck (Wiesbaden: Dr. Ludwig Reichert, 1979–80), *Kr,* 25 (1980–81), 148–61.

See also 83, 112, 636, 638–39.

348 How to Cook Humble Pie, *TLS,* No. 4,089, Aug. 14, 1981, p. 942a-e. [Barbara Reynolds, ed. *The Cambridge Italian Dictionary,* 2: *English-Italian,* Cambridge UP, 1981.]

Cf. Betty Radice, *TLS,* Aug. 28, 1981, p. 983.

See also 197, 208, 629.

349 *Issues in Linguistics: Papers in Honor of Henry and Renée Kahane,* ed. Braj V. Kachru et al. (Urbana: Illinois UP, 1973), *RPh,* 34 : 3 (1981), *122-*135.

See also 351, 622–3.

350 Revisionist Dialectology and Mainstream Linguistics. [K.M. Petyt, *The Study of Dialect,* London, 1980; J.K. Chambers & Peter Trudgill, *Dialectology,* Cambridge, 1980.] *LiS,* 13 (1984), 29–65.

See also 247.

351 A Double Golden Anniversary in "Mediterranean" Lexicology [Henry & Renée Kahane, *Graeca et Romanica: Scripta Selecta;* 2 vols.; Amsterdam: Adolf M. Hakkert, 1979–80], *RPh,* 38 : 3 (1985), 310–24.

See also 139, 188, 192, 218, 622.

352 Jerzy Kuryłowicz's Analysis of Old Spanish Conjugational Classes [J.K., La conjugaison en *-ir* de l'espagnol, in: *Omagiu lui Alexandru Rosetti* . . ., Bucureşti, 1965(–67), pp. 457–66], *GL,* 25:3 (1985), 141–70.

Cr.: J.N. Green, *YW,* 47 (1985), 30.

See also 139, 188, 192, 215, 269, 274, 290, 303, 430, 642.

353 Frederick B. Agard, *A Course in Romance Linguistics,* Vol. 1: *A Synchronic View* . . ., Vol. 2: *A Diachronic View* (Washington, D.C., 1984), *GL,* 26:1 (1986), 38–54.

See also 71, 205.

354 An Aberrant Style of Etymological Research [Harri Meier, *Notas críticas al "DECH" de Corominas / Pascual,* Santiago de Compostela, 1984], *RPh,* 40:2 (1986), 181–99.

Cr.: R. Wright & M. W. Wheeler, *YW,* 48 (1986–87), 307–8.

See also 51–2, 81–2, 109–10, 194, 197, etc.

354a Steven N. Dworkin, *Etymology and Derivational Morphology: The Genesis of Old Spanish Denominal Adjectives in -IDO*. Suppl. 206 to *ZRPh* (Tübingen, 1985), *GL,* 26:4 (1986), 282–301.

See also 140, 585–6, 588.

354b Gerhard Rohlfs, *Antroponimìa e toponomastica nelle lingue neolatine; aspetti e problemi* (Tübingen, 1985); Id., *Panorama delle lingue neolatine: piccolo atlante linguistico pan-romanzo* (Tübingen, 1985), *It,* 64 (1987), 637–42.

See also 608.

354c An Experimental Connubium between Modernity and Traditionalism in Spanish Phonology [Carmen Pensado Ruiz, *Cronología relativa del castellano* (Salamanca, 1984)]. To appear in *RPh* (May, 1989).

See also 326, 330.

VII. Notes

355 Difficulties in the Simultaneous Study of Spanish and Portuguese, *MLJ,* 25 (1941), 853–8.

356 A Lexicographic Mirage, *MLN,* 56 (1941), 34–42. [Pseudo-participles, i.e., those unaccompanied by finite verbs].

See also 124.

357 The Latin Suffix -ĀGŌ in Astur[o]-Leonese-Galician Dialects, *Lg,* 19 (1943), 256–8.

Cr.: A. Kuhn, 404.

See also 81, 145–6, 243; 318f (Post-Script).

358 Spanish *deleznar* 'Slide', *lezne* 'Smooth, Slippery', *HR,* 12 (1944), 57–65.

Cr.: J. Corominas, *Word,* 3 (1947), 73–76; J.M. Piel, *RPF,* 2 (1949), 285–6; L. Spitzer, *RFH,* 7 (1945), 298.

See also 182, 201.

359 Old Judaeo-Spanish *yegüería* 'Mess, Dish', *Lg,* 21 (1945), 264–5.

Cr.: L. Spitzer, *Lg,* 22 (1946), 358–9.

See also 129, 257.

360 Three Old French Sources of the English *Arriv-al, Withdraw-al* Type, *JEGPh,* 43 (1944), 80–7.

See also 2, 56.

361 Dos problemas de etimología hispánica: *(g)avión–(g)olondrina, BFUCh,* 4 (1944–46), 79–82.

See also 47.

362 Antiguo judeo-aragonés *aladma, alalma* 'excomunión', *RFH,* 8 (1946), 136–41.

See also 74, 277, 407, 603, 757.

363 Relics of Latin MELLĪGŌ in Balkan Romance, *Lg,* 23 (1947), 429–30.

See also 81, 140, 404a.

364 On Analyzing Hispano-Maya Blends, *IJAL,* 14 (1948), 74–6.

See also 8, 35, 76, 207, 601.

365 La etimología de *cansino, NRFH,* 2 (1948), 186–94.

See also 190, 198, 318g.

366 The Contrast *tomáis–tomávades, queréis–queríades* in Classical Spanish, *HR,* 17 (1949), 159–65.

Cr.: C. Blaylock, *HR,* 54 (1986), 279–85; P.M. Boyd-Bowman [and A. Alonso], *NRFH,* 4 (1950), 283–4; A. Kuhn, 373. Steven Dworkin lectured on this topic in 1987.

See also 199.

367 Lexical Notes on the Western Leonese Dialect of La Cabrera Alta, *Lg,* 25 (1949), 437–46.

Cr.: L. Spitzer, *Lg,* 26 (1950), 284–5; M.L. Wagner, *ZRPh,* 59 (1953), 347–91, esp. 348–58.

See also 3, 7, 20, 334, 599.

368 The Etymology of Hispanic *churniego, churriego, chorniega, MLR,* 44 (1949), 378–80.

See also 3, 7, 20, 155, 160, 242.

369 Los derivados ibero-románicos de PĔTRINUS, *Fil,* 3 (1951), 201–6.

See also 318g, 339, 383.

370–1 An Early Formulation of the Linguistic Wave Theory, *RPh,* 9:1 (1955), 31.

See also 80.

372 A Post-Script to It. *ciarlatano,* Sp. *charlatán, RPh,* 11:1 (1957), 39–40.

See also 157, 318g.

373 Old Spanish *judezno, morezno, pecadezno, PhQ,* 37 (1958), 95–9.

Cr.: K. Baldinger (a), 20–1.

See also 20, 22, 74, 99, 243, 762a.

374 [Participation in the Symposium: "La notion de neutralisation dans la morphologie et le lexique".] *Travaux de l'Institut de Linguistique* (Univ. de Paris), 2 (1957[–59]), 70–2. Tr. Geneviève Corréard.

375 Two Diverse Repercussions of the OSp. *-ie-* > *-i-* Shift, *RPh,* 21:1 (1967), 41.

See also 39, 67, 215, 388, 392.

376 Vignettes: Kurt Lewent / Lincoln Constance / William B. Fretter / Murray B. Emeneau, *RPh,* 13:4 (1960), 441; 16:1 (1962), 142; 20:3 (1967), 388; 25:3 (1972), 372.

377 The Double Affixation in Old French *gens-es-or, bel-ez-or,* Old Provençal *bel-az-or, SN,* 45 (1973), 217–25. Rpr., *PGL,* 411–7, also 15–6, 583–4.

Cr.: F. Lecoy, *Rom,* 95 (1974), 426; S.C. Aston, *YW,* 37 (1975–76), 210.

See also 24, 154.

378–9 Typological Affinity of Italian *eglino, elleno* 'they' to the Portuguese Inflected Infinitive, *RN,* 14 (1973), 636–9.

Cr.: R.J. Penny, *YW,* 35 (1973–74), 338.

See also 73, 133, 596.

380 Adelung-Vater's Pioneering Survey of Romance Languages and Dialects (1809), *SCL,* 15:5 (1973), 589–93.

Cr.: J.N. Green, *YW,* 35 (1973), 26.

See also 107, 254.

381 Pre-Classical French *une (~un) image* 'Likeness, Statue', Old Portuguese *um (~uma) viage(m)* 'Journey': A Study of Parallelism in Reverse, *RPh,* 28:1 (1974), 20–7.

Cr.: R.J. Penny, *YW,* 36 (1974–75), 358.

See also 145–6.

382 Diachronic Lexical Polarization Once More: The Case of Spanish *primero*–Old Spanish *postrimero*–Classical Spanish *postrero, RRL,* 20 (1975), 523–6 (= *Mél. A. Rosetti*).

See also 62, 167, 246, 303.

383 The Trajectories of PETRUS and PETRA, *RN,* 16:3 (1975), 770–8.

See also 369.

384 *Santiago, Santander* y *San Diego, MR,* 3 (1976), 161–4.

See also 3, 20, 22, 99, 160, 165, 242.

385 Old Spanish *far, fer, fazer, RPh,* 31:2 (1977), 257–62.

See also 100, 106, 185, 237, 275, 296, 300, 314.

386 Factors in the Unity of "Romania", *RN,* 18:2 (1977), 263–71. Rpr., *PGL,* 129–34; cf. 11, 565.

See also 117, 205, 254, 278, 670.

387 Americana, 2: F.T. Cooper [1864–1937] and G.N. Olcott [1869–1912], Two Pacesetters of Romance Linguistics in Turn-of-the-Century America, *RPh,* 31:3 (1978), 583–4.

See also 65, 94, 103.

388 Old Spanish *maraviella* 'Marvel', Late Old Spanish *Sierta* 'Syrtis', *RPh,* 33:4 (1980), 509–10.

Cr.: R. Wright & M.W. Wheeler, *YW,* 42 (1980–81), 262.

See also 375, 389, 392.

389 Points of Abutment of Morphology on Phonology: The Case of Archaic Spanish *esti(e)do* 'Stood', *RPh,* 34:2 (1980), 206–9.

Cr.: R. Wright & M.W. Wheeler, *YW,* 42 (1980–81), 261.

See also 38–9, 204, 215, 259, 375, 392.

390 Diachronic Implications of Romanian Phonology for General Romance Linguistics, *YRS,* 5 (1980[–82]), 8–13.

See also 116.

391 Language Change in Literature: Three Thoughts on its Voluntaristic Ingredient, *RPh,* 34:3 (1981), 323–8.

See also 689.

392 Contrastive Patterns of Overextension of Diphthongs in Old Spanish, *RPh,* 36:1 (1982), 18–28.

Cr.: R. Wright & M.W. Wheeler, *YW,* 44 (1982–83), 296.

See also 388.

393 Mutual Attraction, Typological Convergence, Multiple Borrowing, Parallel Independent Development, Spiral-Shaped Curve, Periodicity, Advanced State, Slope, Drift, Drag, Slant, *RPh,* 35:3 (1982), 479–84.

See also 48, 80, 266.

394 Some Second and Third Thoughts on Luso-Hispanic *almuerzo/almoço* 'Lunch', with Special Attention to Older Sp. *yantar*/Ptg. *jantar* 'Dinner', *RPh,* 36:3 (1983), 393–403.

Cr.: J.N. Green, *YW,* 45 (1983), 20.

See also 77.

395 Comments by Y.M. [made at the Dec. 1982 Los Angeles convention of the Modern Language Assn. of America], in *Editors' Notes; Bulletin of the Conference of Learned Journals,* 2:1 (Spring 1983), 8–11.

See also 273.

396 The Two Sources of Old French *sergant, FS,* 38:1 (Jan. 1984), 1–5.

Cr.: T. E. Hope, "Old French *ser-gent, -jant*", *French Studies Bull.,* 13 (1984–85), 1–3.

See also 403.

397 Lateral, Marginal, Peripheral Zone: Three Key-Terms of Spatio-Temporal Linguistics, *MeLR,* 1 (1983), 11–4.

See also 210, 610.

398 The Prospects of a Sapir Renaissance in Linguistics [Berkeley Campus talk, May 11, 1959, reconstructed from a tape], *HL,* 11:3 (1984), 389–95.

See also 101–2, 616, 619, 675, 693, 729.

399 Points of Convergence of FLĒBILIS, DĒBILIS, and FĔBRIS/FEBRĪLIS: Old French *feible* > *foible* vs. *fieble, RPh,* 37:4 (1984), 426–33.

See also 84, 404, 597.

400 Reconstruction of Latin *ACCURSĀRE 'Pursue' from Old Spanish and from Italian Dialects, *GL,* 24 (1984), 230–32.

Cr.: R. Wright & M.W. Wheeler, *YW,* 47 (1985), 281.

See also 282, 318g.

401 The Derivation of Old French *servantois,* Old Provençal *sirventes, MAe,* 54:2 (1985), 272–4.

Cr.: G. Price, *YW,* 47 (1985), 50.

See also 42, 222, 266, 734.

402 El desarrollo de PERTICA en español, a la luz de una desconocida «ley fonética», *RevR,* 21 (1985), 36–45.

Cr.: J.N. Green, *YW,* 47 (1985), 30–1; R. Wright & M.W. Wheeler, ibid. 282.

See also 37.

403 The Etymology of French *concierge, FS,* 40 (1986), 26–31.

See also 396.

404 (American) English *perspire, transpire, AS,* 62:1 (1987), 84–9.

See also 42, 399.

404a From Latin MELLĪTUS to Old Spanish *v-, b-ellido* (with Attention Newly Drawn to the Role Played by *bar-va, -ba*). To appear in *RN* (Aug. 1988).

See also 363.

404b (With Olga Grlić) One More Adriatic (or Central Danubian?) Bridge to Daco-Romance CORVUS / *CORBUS 'Raven'. To appear in *RPh* (1989).

See also 318d, 750.

VIII. Necrological and Commemorative Essays

(a) **In *Romance Philology:***

405 Karl Jaberg (1877–1958), 12:3 (1959), 258–61. Rpr., *Portraits of Linguists,* ed. T.A. Sebeok, 2, 454–8. Bloomington & London, 1966.

See also 44.

406 Leo Spitzer (1887–1960), 14:4 (1961), 362–4. Rpr., *Portraits of Linguists,* ed. T.A. Sebeok, 2, 522–6. Bloomington & London, 1966.

Cf. the unpublished lecture given at the University of Kentucky, in Sept. 1986. "Leo Spitzer (1887–1960), the Most Controversial Romance Philologist of his Generation".

407 Ignacio González Llubera (1893–1962), 16:1 (1962), 137–42.

See also 603.

408 Max Leopold Wagner (1880–1962), 16:3 (1963), 281–9. Rpr., *Portraits of Linguists,* ed. T.A. Sebeok, 2, 463–74. Bloomington & London, 1966.

See also 325.

409 Ernst H. Kantorowicz (1895–1963), 18:1 (1964), 1–15.

Cr.: Eckhard Grünewald, *E.K. und Stefan George. . .* (Wiesbaden: Steiner, 1982), passim.

See also 40.

410 Arnald Steiger (1896–1963), 18:3 (1965), 285–96.

411 Uriel Weinreich–Jakob Jud's Last Student (1926–67), 22:1 (1968), 128–32.

See also 350, 441, 467.

412 "...Era omme esencial" [Ramón Menéndez Pidal] (1869–1968), 23:4 (1970), 371–411.

See also 44, 288, 294–5, 612.

413 Hayward Keniston (1883–1970), 24:4 (1971), 677–80; 25:3 (1972), 371–2.

414 Percival B. Fay (with Supplement to Earlier Bibliography) (1890–1972), 26:1 (1972 = Silver Anniversary Issues, Part 1), 135–8.

See also 561.

415 S. Griswold Morley (1878–1970), 26:1 (1972), 211–4 (with Supplement to Earlier Bibliography).

See also Benjamin M. Woodbridge, Jr., 6:4 (1953), 215–30.

416 Elise Richter [1865–1943]: A Retrospective Essay, 26:2 (1972), 337–41.

See also 44, 121, 556, 571, 584.

417 Georges Gougenheim (1900–72), 27:1 (1973), 58–61.

418 Urban Tigner Holmes (1900–72), 27:1 (1973), 62–7.

419 Ernst Gamillscheg (1887–1971) and the Berlin School of Romance Linguistics (1925–45), 27:2 (1973), 172–89. Tr. into German to be included in a miscellany sponsored by the Berlin Free University, ed. Jürgen Trabant.

Cr.: J.N. Green, *YW,* 35 (1973–4), 26.

420 Viktor M. Žirmunskij (1891–1971), 28:1 (1974), 52–6.

See also 335, 447, 488, 617.

421 Archer Taylor (1890–1973), 28:1 (1974), 56–60.

See also 200.

422 Bengt Hasselrot (1910–74), 29:1 (1975), 27–31.
See also 423, 443a, 557.

423 Knud Togeby (1918–74), 29:1 (1975), 31–38.

Cr.: J.N. Green, *YW,* 37 (1974–76), 25.

See also 758.

424 Edwin B. Williams (1891–1975), 29:1 (1975), 140–2.

See also 684.

425 Bruno Migliorini (1896–1975), 29:3 (1976), 398–408.

Cr.: J.N. Green, *YW,* 38 (1976–77), 28.

See also 243, 609, 657, 717, 727.

426 Jean Frappier (1900–74)–Dedication and Necrology, 30:1 (1976), 3–8.

427 Harry Hoijer (1904–76), 30:3 (1977), 475–9.

See also 101, 266, 532, 544, 616, 619, 675.

428 Stephen Ullmann (1914–76), 30:3 (1977), 481–6.

Cr.: J.N. Green, *YW,* 38 (1976–77), 28.

See also 690.

429 Marcel Bataillon (1895–1977), 31:2 (1977), 457–66.

430 Jerzy Kuryłowicz (1895–1978), 31:4 (1978), 711–7.

See also 352.

431 From Rome to New York City. Necrology–Mario Andrew Pei (1901–78), 32:4 (1979), 495–502; 35:3 (1982), 572.

432 Anna (Granville) Hatcher (1905–78), 33:2 (1979), 328–33; 35:3 (1982), 572.

See also 591.

433 Grace Frank (1886–1978), 33:4 (1980), 544–50.

434 Lexis and Grammar–Necrological Essay on Émile Benveniste (1902–76), 34:2 (1980), 160–94.

435 Helmut A. Hatzfeld (1892–1979), 34:3 (1981), *88-*98.

436 A Hispanist Confined to his Inner Castle: Tomás Navarro Tomás (1884–1979), 34:3 (1981), *98-*115; 35:3 (1982), 572.

Cr.: R. Wright & W.M. Wheeler, *YW*, 43 (1981–82), 272.

See also 8, 323, 326, 412, 479, 604.

437 Two Berkeleyans: Manfred Sandmann (1906–80) and George R. Stewart (1895–1980), 35:3 (1982), 515–25.

See also 443.

438 The End of an Era: Raimundo Lida (1908–79) and Frida Weber de Kurlat (1914–81), 35:4 (1982), 617–41.

See also 8, 763.

439 Helaine Newstead (1906–81), Part 1, 36:4 (1983), 564–9.

Cf. Part 2, by Barbara N. Sargent-Baur, ibid., 469–71.

440 Joseph G. Fucilla (1897–1981), 37:4 (1984), 456–8.

440a Ronald N. Walpole (1903–86). To appear in 42:2 (1988).

See also 414, 437.

(b) Elsewhere:

441 Uriel Weinreich, *Lg*, 43 (1967), 605–7 [followed by Marvin I. Herzog's bibliography of U.W.'s writings].

See also 411, 467.

442 (With D.L. Olmsted) Jonathan Lowell Butler (1939–1974). In Memoriam Vol. for 1974, Univ. of California, pp. 31–3.

See also 569.

443 (With B. Guy, H. Penzl & R.N. Walpole) Manfred Sandmann (1906–80). In Memoriam Vol. for 1980, University of California.

See also 437.

IX. Obituary Notices (in Romance Philology*)*

444 Amado Alonso, Milton A. Buchanan, William J. Entwistle, Jakob Jud, Pedro Salinas, 6:1 (1952), 70.

445 Benedetto Croce, Eugen Lerch, 6:4 (1953), 312.

446 Vittorio Bertoldi, 7:2–3 (1953–54), 192.

See also 322.

447 E. Brugger, H.J. Chaytor, María Goyri de Menéndez Pidal, Mixail Lozinskij, 8:4 (1955), 281.

448 Albert Dauzat, Archer M. Huntington, Inez Isabel Macdonald, J.J. Perry, 9:3 (1956), 402.

449 Caroline B. Bourland, Courtney Bruerton, Ernst Robert Curtius, Einar Löfstedt, 10:2 (1956), 92.

450 Ern(e)st Hoepffner, Ettore Li Gotti, 10:3 (1957), 224.

451 William A. Nitze, 11:1 (1957), 40.

452 Erich Auerbach, 11:2 (1957), 162.

453 Joseph E. Gillet, 12:2 (1958), 161–2.

454 Oliver H. Hauptmann, 13:3 (1960), 278.

455 Joseph Vendryes, 14:1 (1960), 27.

456 Henri-F. Muller, 14:2 (1960), 188.

457 Alfred L. Kroeber, 14:3 (1961), 285–6.

458 Leonardo Olschki, 15:3 (1962), 331–2.

459 Howard R. Patch, 17:3 (1964), 632–3.

460 Edward B. Ham, 19:3 (1966), 482.

461 Bernard Bloch, 19:4 (1966), 648.

462 J.U. Hubschmied, Charles H. Livingston, 20:1 (1966), 90.

463 John Orr, 20:2 (1966), 191.

464 Benvenuto (A.) Terracini, 21:4 (1968), 462.

465 Charles E. Kany, 22:1 (1968), 35.

466 Edward H. Wilkins, 20:2 (1968), 217.

467 Anita Krause, Max Weinreich, 23:1 (1969), 142.

468 Pierre Delattre, 23:2 (1969), 227.

469 Alfred Ewert, 23:3 (1970), 311.

470 Antonio Rodríguez-Moñino, 24:1 (1970), 57.

471 Raphael Levy, 24:1 (1970), 107.

472 Jean Misrahi, 24:1 (1970), 137.

472a Samuel Miklos Stern, Cynthia M. Crews, J. Mattoso Câmara, Jr., C. Douglas Chrétien, R. McNulty, 24:2 (1970), 258.

473 Holger Sten, 25:1 (1971), 96.

474 William E. Bull, 26:3 (1973), 556–7.

475 Bernard Weinberg, 26:3 (1973), 557.

476 Hans Rheinfelder, 26:4 (1973), 689–91.

477 Tatiana Fotitch, 26:4 (1973), 691.

478 J.Homer Herriott, 26:4 (1973), 751–2.

479 Américo Castro, 27:1 (1973), 61–2.

480 Reine Cardaillac Kelly, 28:1 (1974), iv.

481 Brenton K. Campbell, 28:1 (1974), 51.

482 Alfred Ernout, 28:1 (1974), 101.

483 Francis Lee Utley, 28:3 (1975), 353.

484 Carlos Clavería, Erhardt Lommatzsch, 28:4 (1975), iv, 554.

485 William Matthews, 29:3 (1976), 310.

486 Thornton Wilder, 29:4 (1976), 521.

487 Charles A. Knudson, 30:3 (1977), 479–81.

488 Mark L. Slonim, 30:4 (1977), 688.

489 E.M. Wilson, Arnold G. Reichenberger, 31:2 (1977), 282.

490 V. Frederic Koenig, 31:4 (1978), 717–8.

491 Lewis Thorpe, 30:2 (1978), 258–9.

492 Otis H. Green, 33:3 (1980), 460.

493 Robert W. Ackerman, Hannah E. Bergman, Yuen R. Chao, T.B.W. Reid, 36:2 (1982), 224–8.

X. Editorial Comments (in Romance Philology*)*

494 [A re-definition of the editorial goals], 6:2–3 (1952–53), 212.

495 [Return to the journal's original scope: historical linguistics and medieval literature], 7:1 (1953), 110.

496 [The West Coast's learnèd journals], 7:2–3 (1953–54), 192.

497 [Library Subscription List], 9:4 (1956), 438.

498 An Apocryphal Book by Charles Bally, 15:1 (1961), 62.

499 New Printing of Milà y Fontanals, 15:2 (1961), 162.

500 Stressed *nós, vós* vs. Weak *nos, vos* in Old Spanish, 16:1 (1962), 137.

Cr.: J. Piccus, *NRFH,* 16 (1962), 16.

See also 503.

501 Circulation Department: Domestic Market, 16:3 (1963), 289.

502 The John Simon Guggenheim Memorial Foundation, 16:3 (1963), 331.

503 Old Spanish *ý, ó* vs. *y, o,* 17:3 (1964), 667.

See also 500.

504 Special Symbols, 17:4 (1964), 784.

505 Expansion of the Editorial Board, 18:2 (1964), 210.

506 Six Media of Communication, 18:3 (1965), 386.

507 Rejuvenation, 18:4 (1965), 528.

508 Scope and Variety of Book Reviewing, 19:1 (1965), 68.

509 Free Market vs. Planned Economy, 19:2 (1965), 285.

510 Typographic Refinement, 20:2 (1966), 190–1.

511 *Romance Philology* Comes of Age, 21:1 (1967), 66.

See also 567.

512 August Fuchs (1818–47), the Founder of Comparative Romance Dialectology, 21:3 (1968), 285.

513 The Portrayal of Philologists and Linguists in Fine Literature, 21:3 (1968), 362.

See also 539.

514 Special Punctuation Marks for Quoted Translations [i.e., Translated Quotations]? 22:1 (1968), 24.

515 Harbingers of the Phonemic and the Generative Approaches, 22:3 (1969), 313.

See also 531.

516 Typographic Experimentation, 24:2 (1970), 328.

See also 510, 521, 537, 553.

517 Latest Trends in Circulation, 24:4 (1971), 633.

See also 497, 501.

518 Philology and Philately, 25:1 (1971), 96.

See also 524, 531–4, 550.

519 Gustav Gröber's Private Library at Urbana, 25:2 (1971), 262.

See also 69, 70, 97–8, 103, 256, 263, 265, 512, 515, 522, 526, 530, 536, 543, 547–9, 551, 554, 556.

520 Dubious Names of Languages (*Costano-an, Occitan-ian*), 25:4 (1972), 420.

521 Selective Reading, Dull Abstracts, Pointed Subheadings, 25:4 (1972), 481–2.

See also 510, 516, 537, 554.

522 K.A.F. Mahn [1802–87], 26:1 (1972), 67.

See also 69, 70, etc. (cf. under 519).

523 Troublesome Names of Scholars, 26:1 (1972), 138.

See also 546.

524 Linguistics–the Name of a Discipline, 26:2 (1973), 508.

See also 518, 531, 533, 550, 552.

525 One Short-Lived Genre of Glotto-Historical Research, 26:4 (1973), 749–51.

See also 57, 527.

526 The Third Schlegel Brother and the Element of Chance in the History of Linguistics, 21:1 (1973), 67–8.

See also 69, 70, 97, etc. (cf. under 519).

527 Old and New Genres of Scholarly Writings, 27:1 (1973), 142.

See also 57, 525.

528 Which Scholars Have Received No *Festschrift?* 27:2 (1973), 211–3.

529 Americana, 1: The Year 1917 as a Turning Point, 27:2 (1973), 213.

[Cf. the unpublished lecture given at the University of Kentucky on Oct. 28, 1986, and previously at Austin, TX: "The First Cycle of Romance Philology (1880–1935) in America"]

See also 65, 558.

530 Jakob Grimm and Friedrich Diez, 27:3 (1974), 448–50.

See also 69, 70, 97–8, 248, etc. (cf. under 519).

531 'Deep Structure' vs. 'Surface Structure' in Johannes Schmidt (1872)? 27:3 (1974), 450.

See also 515, 518, 524, 533, 550–2, 554, 556, etc. (cf. under 519).

532 A Herder-Humboldt-Sapir-Whorf Hypothesis? 28:2 (1974), 199.

See also 101, 266, 398, 544.

533 Linguistic Paleontology (Geology, Archeology)? 28:4 (1975), 600.

See also 518, 524, 531, 550–2, 554, 556, etc. (cf. under 519).

534 Late-20th-Century "Vulgar Latin", 28:4 (1975), 763–4.

See also 518.

535 Scholar, Philologist, Critic, Analyst, Essayist, 29:1 (1975), 38–9.

536 Madrid Linguistics in the Mid '90s, 29:2 (1975), 214.

Cr.: C.J. Pountain, *YW,* 37 (1975–76), 227.

537 Typographic Experiments, 29:2 (1975), 280.

See also 510, 516, 521, 553.

538 Further Thoughts on Archaisms, 29:3 (1976), 398.

539 The Portrayal of a Philologist by Henrik Ibsen, 30:1 (1976), iv.

See also 513, 540, 548–9.

540 Hugo von Hofmannsthal's Quarrel with Romance Philology, 30:2 (1976), 390–1.

See also 513, 539, 548–9.

541 Followers, Successors, Counterparts, Admirers, Imitators, 30:3 (1977), 486.

See also 546.

542 Grotesquerie in Philology? 30:3 (1977), 561–4.

543 New Light on Meyer-Lübke? 30:4 (1977), iii–iv.

See also 540, 548–9.

544 What did Edward Sapir Mean by "Drift"? 30:4 (1977), 622.

See also 101, 266, 532, 544, 675.

545 Odessa as an Outpost of Romance Culture, 31:1 (1977), 127.

See also 168.

546 Love, Marriage, Divorce, Widow(er)hood, Escapism, Quest for "Ethnic Purity", and the Continuity of Advanced Research, 31:1 (1977), 187–90.

See also 523, 541.

547 Gaston Paris' Severest Disappointment, 31:2 (1977), iii–iv.

548–9 Vienna, 1900, 31:2 (1977), 466.

See also 540.

550 Semiborrowings? 32:2 (1978), 259–60.

See also 518, 524, 531, 533, 552.

551 A Partial Return to Bernardino Biondelli [1804–86]? 32:4 (1979), 502–4.

552 Another Ambiguous Linguistic Term: 'Thematic Vowel', 33:2 (1979), 333–5.

See also 518, 524, 531, 533, 550.

553 Three Isolated Ideograms–the Ampersand, the Dagger, and the Asterisk, 33:2 (1979), 356.

See also 510, 516, 521, 537.

554 Was Hugo Schuchardt Ever a Neo-Grammarian?, 34:1 (1980), 93–4.

See also 69, 70, 97–8, 103, etc. (cf. under 519).

555 Three Preludes to Inquiries into Romance Augments, 34:1 (1980), 94.

See also 48, 116, 229, 288, 294.

556 Two Houses, Once Homes, in Austria [Elise Richter's and Hugo Schuchardt's], 34:1 (1980), 141–2.

See also 44, 121, 416, 548–9, 554, 571, 584.

557 Romance Philology and a 'Full' Life [J. Vising's], 34:4 (1981), 437–41.

See also 252, 304.

558 (Prae-) Americana, 3: Two Splinters from the 'Group of 77', 35:2 (1981), 347.

See also 65, 529.

XI. Dedications and Prefaces

559 Antonio García Solalinde, *RPh,* 5:2–3 (1951–52), v–vi (= *A.G.S. Memorial*).

560 Edward C. Armstrong, *RPh,* 10:2 (1956), 142–4 (= *E.C.A. Memorial*).

561 Percival B. Fay, *RPh,* 11:3 (1958), 191–3 (= *P.B.F. Testimonial,* I).

See also 414.

562 Kurt Lewent, *RPh,* 20:4 (1967), 389–90 (= *K.L. Memorial*).

See also 376.

563 Emanuel S. Georges, *RPh,* 21:4 (1968), 365–7 (= *E.S.G. Memorial*).

See also 118, 566.

564 (With Winfred P. Lehmann) Prefatory Note, *Directions for Historical Linguistics: A Symposium* (Austin & London: Texas University Press, 1968), pp. vii–ix.

See also 577.

565 (With Karl D. Uitti) Dedication, Lucien and Alfred Foulet, *RPh,* 22:4 (1969), 369–72 (= *L.F. Memorial / A.F. Testimonial*).

See also 573.

566 (With Jerry R. Craddock) Prefatory Note to Emanuel S. Georges, *Studies in Romance Nouns Extracted from Past Participles,* UCPL, 63 (1970), pp. vii–ix.

See also 118, 563.

567 The First Quarter-Century [of *Romance Philology*] (and Some Antecedents), *RPh,* 26:1 (1972: First of two Silver Anniversary Issues), 3–15.

Cr.: O. Gsell, 20.

See also 273, 511, 568, 572, 574.

568 Foreword, *A Bibliographic Index to "Romance Philology", Vols. I–XXV,* comp. Mark G. Littlefield, pp. vii–xiii. Berkeley: University of California Press, 1974.

See also 273, 567.

569–70 Jonathan L. Butler, *RPh,* 28:4 (1975), 427–9 (= *J.L.B. Memorial*).

See also 442.

571 Introduction to Elise Richter, *Kleinere Schriften*. . . (Innsbruck, 1977), pp. 9–12.

See also 44, 121, 416, 556, 584.

572 Prefatory Note, Rejuvenation Issue, *RPh,* 31:2 (1977), 191–2.

See also 567–8, 574–5.

573 (With Karl D. Uitti) *C. Carroll Marden Memorial–Raymond S. Willis Testimonial, RPh,* 33:1 (1981), 1.

See also 565.

574 Prefatory Note to Special Issue, *RPh,* 34:3 (S.I., 1981),*1.

575 Approaching the Second Cycle. Dedication to *Henry R. Lang Memorial* and *Frank M. Chambers Testimonial, RPh,* 35:1 (1981), pp. iii–vi.

See also 567.

576 New Studies in Romance Parasynthetic Derivation [Prefatory Note bracketing two articles, one by Joanne Martin Baldonado, the other by Andrew S. Allen], *RPh,* 35:1 (1981), 63–4.

See also 33, 59.

577 (With Winfred P. Lehmann) Prefatory Note, *Perspectives on Historical Linguistics* (Amsterdam, 1982), pp. v–viii.

See also 564.

XII. Comments and Post-Scripts

578–9 Comments on *Current Trends in Linguistics,* 3: *Theoretical Foundations* (1966), *CA,* 9 (1968), 128*bc,* 174*a-c.*

See also 33.

580 The Evidence of OSp. *erzer* (= OGal.-Ptg.-Leon. *erger), yerto, coherir, apegar, RPh,* 22:4 (1969), 505–8 (= *Lucien Foulet Memorial / Alfred Foulet Testimonial*) [appended to J.H. Marshall, "The Etymology of Old French *aerdre. . .*"], 497–504.

See also 36, 300, 303.

581 Post-Script (55–7) to Érica C. García, "Gender Switch in Spanish Derivation. . .", *RPh,* 24:1 (1970), 39–54.

Cr.: D.J. Gifford, *YW,* 32 (1970–71), 348.

See also 55.

582 Post-Script (303–5) to Dana A. Nelson, "The Domain of the Old Spanish *-er* and *-ir* Verbs: A Clue to the Provenience of the *Alexandre*", *RPh,* 26:2 (1972), 265–303.

See also 4, 45, 50, 52, 64, 91, 93, 100, . . . 580, 588.

583 Comment (244–6) on Martin Joos, "Definition Theory". *Lexicography in English: Papers from International Conference on Lexicography in English. . .* (June 6–7, 1972), ed. Raven I. McDavid, Jr. & Audrey R. Duckert. Annals of the New York Academy of Sciences, 211 (1973).

See also 41.

584 Anmerkungen zu Elise Richter, *Kleinere Schriften*. . . (Innsbruck, 1977), 555–82.

See also 44, 121, 416, 556, 571.

585 Post-Script (205–6) to Steven N. Dworkin, Older Luso-Spanish *garrido* (a) 'Silly, Foolish', (b) 'Handsome, Beautiful': One Source or Two Sources? *RPh,* 34:2 (1980), 195–205.

See also 318a, 318i, 354a, 588.

586 Post-Script (31–4) to Eric P. Hamp, "Old Spanish *sencido* Again", *RPh,* 36:1 (1982), 28–31.

Cr.: R. Wright & M.W. Wheeler, *YW,* 44 (1982–83), 297.

See also 140, 585, 588, 651.

587 Old Provençal *trobar,* Old Spanish *fallar.* Post-Script (148–53) to María Rosa Menocal, "The Etymology of Old Provençal *trobar, trobador*—a Return to the Third Solution", *RPh,* 36:2 (1983), 137–48.

Cr.: R. Wright & M.W. Wheeler, *YW,* 44 (1982–83), 309–10.

See also 185.

588 Post-Script (173–4) to Steven N. Dworkin, "The Fragmentation of the Latin Verb *tollere* . . .", *RPh,* 37:2 (1983), 165–73.

See also 25, 250, 585–6, 588, 651.

XIII. Standard-sized Book Reviews

589–90 Norman P. Sacks, *The Latinity of Dated Documents in the Portuguese Territory* (Philadelphia, 1941) – *Lg*, 18 (1942), 292–7.

See also 319.

591 Anna Granville Hatcher, *Reflexive Verbs: Latin, Old French, Modern French* (Baltimore, 1942) – *Lg*, 19 (1943), 49–53.

See also 432.

592 Hans Nilsson-Ehle, *Les adverbes en "-ment" compléments d'un verbe* (Lund, 1941) – *RR*, 34 (1943), 280–4.

See also 253.

593 V. Šišmarëv, *Očerki po istorii jazykov Ispanii* (Moskva – Leningrad, 1941) – *Lg*, 20 (1944), 155–60.

See also 109, 617, 725.

594 Jaime Oliver Asín, *Historia de la lengua española*$_4$ (Madrid, 1940) – *Lg*, 21 (1945), 113–20.

See also 109, 593, 595.

595 Rafael Lapesa, *Historia de la lengua española* (Madrid, 1942) – *Lg*, 22 (1946), 46–9.

See also 109, 323, 593–4, 606, 643.

596 Gustaf Brandt, *La concurrence entre "soi" et "lui, eux, elle(s)"; étude de syntaxe historique française* (Lund, 1942) – *RR*, 37 (1946), 188–93.

See also 73, 133, 195.

597 Eva Thorné Hammar, *Le développement de sens du suffixe latin -BILIS en français* (Lund, 1942) – *RR*, 37 (1946), 376–83.

See also 33, 59.

598 Margaret J. Bates, *"Discreción" in the Works of Cervantes; a Semantic Study* (Washington, D.C., 1945) – *Word*, 2 (1946), 98–100.

599 María Josefa Canellada, *El bable de Cabranes* (Madrid, 1946) – *Lg*, 23 (1947), 60–6.

See also 7, 320, 324, 367.

600 F. Lázaro Carreter, *El habla de Magallón; notas para el estudio del aragonés vulgar* (Zaragoza, 1945) – *HR*, 16 (1948), 82–3.

See also 327, 333, 646.

601 Víctor M. Suárez, *El español que se habla en Yucatán; apuntamientos filológicos* (Mérida, Yuc., 1945) – *HR*, 16 (1948), 175–83.

See also 8, 364.

602 Felipe Mateu i Llopis, *Glosario hispánico de numismática* (Barcelona, 1946) – *HR*, 16 (1948), 262–8.

See also 9, 322.

603 I. González-Llubera, ed. Santob de Carrión, *Proverbios morales* (Cambridge, 1947) – *HR*, 17 (1949), 79–82.

See also 321, 359, 362, 407.

604 Tomás Navarro [Tomás], *Estudios de fonología española* (Syracuse, N.Y., 1946) – *HR*, 17 (1949), 174–9.

See also 436, 625–6, 765.

605 Berta Elena Vidal de Battini, *El habla rural de San Luis*, 1: *Fonética, morfología, sintaxis* (Buenos Aires, 1949) – *RPh*, 3 (1949–50), 191–201.

See also 8, 665.

606 Rafael Lapesa, *Asturiano y provenzal en el Fuero de Avilés* (Salamanca, 1948) – *HR*, 19 (1951), 81–6.

See also 327, 643.

607 Raymond R. MacCurdy, *The Spanish Dialect in St. Bernard Parish, Louisiana* (Albuquerque, 1950) – *Lg,* 27 (1951), 405–11.

See also 8, 710.

608 Gerhard Rohlfs, *Romanische Philologie,* 1: *Allgemeine Romanistik; französische und provenzalische Philologie* (Heidelberg, 1950) – *RPh,* 5:1 (1951), 65–70.

See also 44, 611, 722.

609 Bruno Migliorini, *Che cos'è un vocabolario?* (Firenze, 1946) – *RPh,* 5:2–3 (1951–52), 252–5.

See also 9, 41, 72, 83, 111–3, 425, 657.

610 Manuel de Paiva Boléo, *Dialectologia e história de língua; isoglossas portuguesas* (Lisboa, 1950; reprinted from *BF*) – *Lg,* 28 (1952), 124–9.

See also 331.

611 Alwin Kuhn, *Romanische Philologie,* 1: *Die romanischen Sprachen* (Bern, 1951) – *Lg,* 28 (1952), 509–24.

See also 44, 608.

612 Ramón Menéndez Pidal, *Toponimia prerrománica hispana* (Madrid, 1952) – *Spec,* 29 (1954), 588–94.

Cr.: K. Baldinger (a), 201.

See also 77, 229, 288, 294, 322, 336, 343, 653.

613 Diego Catalán Menéndez-Pidal, *Poema de Alfonso XI* (Madrid, 1952) – *RPh,* 8:4 (1955), 306–11; preceded by a review of the same book, but from a different angle, by María Rosa Lida de Malkiel, 303–6.

See also 131, 143, 264.

614 P. Perrochat, ed. Pétrone, *"Le festin de Trimalcion": commentaire exégétique et critique*$_2$ (Grenoble & Paris, 1952) – *RPh,* 9:3 (1956), 353–9.

See also 671.

615 Walter Schmid, *Der Wortschatz des "Cancionero de Baena"* (Bern, 1951) – *RPh,* 9:4 (1956), 441–8.

See also 108.

616 Harry Hoijer, ed. *Language in Culture; Conference on the Interrelations of Language and Other Aspects of Culture* (Chicago, 1954) – *IJAL,* 22 (1956), 77–84.

See also 101–2, 266, 393, 398, 427, 532, 619.

617 *Romano-germanskaja filologija. Sbornik statej v čest' akademika V.F. Šišmarëva* (Leningrad, 1957) – *RPh,* 11:4 (1958), 384–9.

See also 168, 335, 420, 545, 593, 725.

618 José María Valverde, *Guillermo de Humboldt y la filosofía del lenguaje* (Madrid, 1955) – *HR,* 26 (1958), 162–7.

See also 338, 340–1, 532, 616, 619.

619 Paul Henle, ed. *Language, Thought, and Culture,* by R.W. Brown, I.M. Copi, D.E. Dulaney, W.K. Frankena, P. Henle, C.L. Stevenson (Ann Arbor, MI, 1958) – *IJAL,* 25 (1959), 122–33.

See also 101–2, 260, 393, 398, 616, 618.

620 Olof Brattö, *"Filipe", "Henrique" e outros nomes próprios em Portugal e na Europa* (Göteborg, 1958) – *Names,* 8 (1960), 96–8.

See also 383–4, 727.

621 T.B.W. Reid, *Historical Philology and Linguistic Science* (Oxford, 1960) – *RPh,* 14:4 (1961), 328–31.

See also 6, 24, 27–8, 31, 38, 43–4, 57, 94, 121, 173, 179, 187, 200, 230, 234, 346, etc.

622 Henry & Renée Kahane and Andreas Tietze, *The "lingua franca" in the Levant: Turkish Nautical Terms of Italian and Greek Origin* (Urbana, 1958) – *RPh,* 15:3 (1962), 346–9.

Cr.: J.A. Cremona & R. Posner, *YW,* 24 (1962–63), 32–3.

See also 120, 247, 322, 331–2, 336, 345, 349, 351, 623, 750.

623 Henry R. Kahane & Angelina Pietrangeli, ed. *Structural Studies on Spanish Themes,* by Sol Saporta, Francine Frank, Robert Rexer, Louise H. Allen (Urbana & Salamanca, 1959) – *Spec,* 37 (1962), 619–24.

See also 349, 351, 622, 750.

624 Leonard Bloomfield & Clarence T. Barnhart, *Let's Read; a Linguistic Approach* (Detroit, 1961) – *RPh,* 16:1 (1962), 83–91. Rpr. (under the title "Leonard Bloomfield in Retrospect") in *ELT,* 165–74.

Cr.: J.A. Cremona & R. Posner, *YW,* 24 (1962–63), 12.

See also 715.

625 Josef Vachek, ed. *A Prague School Reader in Linguistics* (Bloomington, 1964) – *AA,* 68 (1966), 585–8.

See also 65, 626.

626 Roman Jakobson, *Selected Writings,* 1: *Phonological Studies* (The Hague, 1962) – *AA,* 68 (1966), 1405–6.

See also 65, 338, 625.

627 W. Meyer-Lübke, *Historische Grammatik der französischen Sprache,* 2: *Wortbildungslehre,* rev. by J.M. Piel (Heidelberg, 1966) – *RPh,* 22:1 (1968), 49–53.

See also 2, 24, 33, 42, 55, 59, 63, 87, 97, 123, 126, 136, 154, 159, 162, etc.

628 Anthony Gooch, *Diminutive, Augmentative, and Pejorative Suffixes in Modern Spanish; a Guide to Their Use and Meaning* (Oxford & London, 1967) – *Lingua,* 26 (1971), 205–9.

See also 7, 55.

629 Josette Rey-Debove, *Étude linguistique et sémiotique des dictionnaires français contemporains* (The Hague & Paris, 1971; = Approaches to Semiotics, 13) – *LSc,* (Oct. 1975), 29–31.

See also 9, 41, 72, 96, 113, 197, 208.

630 In Memoriam Friedrich Diez: *Akten des Kolloquiums zur Wissenschaftsgeschichte der Romanistik, Trier, 2.-4. Okt*[*ober*] *1975,* ed. H.-J. Niederehe & H. Haarmann (Amsterdam, 1976) – *Lg,* 54 (1978), 426–32.

See also 49, 233, 248.

631 Gianni Mombelli, *Les avatars de* TALENTUM; *recherches sur l'origine et les variations des acceptions romanes et non romanes de ce terme.* Bibl. di *Studi Francesi* (Torino, 1976) – *Spec,* 53 (1978), 170–4.

See also 690.

632 Alfred Foulet & Mary Blakely Speer, *On Editing Old French Texts* (Lawrence, 1978) – *RPh*, 33:1 (1979), 241–6.

633 Jens Lüdtke, *Die romanischen Sprachen im "Mithridates" von Adelung und Vater; Studie und Text* (Tübingen, 1978) – *Kr*, 24 (1979–80), 117–26.

See also 254, 338, 380.

634 Daniel Droixhe, *La linguistique et l'appel de l'histoire (1600–1800): Rationalisme et révolutions positivistes.* Langue et culture, 10 (Genève & Paris, 1978) – *Lg*, 56 (1980), 427–31.

See also 49, 338, 340, 707.

635 Anna Laura & Giulio Lepschy, *The Italian Language Today* (London, 1977) – *RPh*, 34:3 (S.I., 1981), *170-*174.

See also 243, 348, 425, 759.

636 Max Pfister, LEI = *Lessico etimologico italiano*, 1:4 (Wiesbaden, 1981) – *Kr*, 27 (1982–83), 122–6.

See also 81, 83, 111–2, 347, 638–9.

637 Nicholas Brooks, ed. *Latin and the Vernacular Languages in Early Medieval Britain.* Papers Delivered . . . (Leicester, 1982) – *Lg*, 60:3 (1984), 615–8.

See also 117.

638 Max Pfister, *LEI* = *Lessico etimologico italiano*, 1:3, 384–576 (Wiesbaden, 1981) – *Kr*, 28 (1983[–84]), 162–8.

See also 81, 83, 111–2, 347, 636, 639.

639 Id., *LEI* = *Lessico etimologico italiano*, 1:5–6, 769-1152 (Wiesbaden, 1982) – *Kr*, 30 (1985), 140–6.

See also 81, 83, 111–2, 347, 636, 638.

640 Alfredo Stussi, *Avviamento agli studi di filologia italiana* (Bologna, 1983) – *It*, 62:2 (1985), 154–8.

See also 649, 717, 759.

641 Hadumod Bußmann, *Lexikon der Sprachwissenschaft* (Stuttgart, 1983) – *MeLR*, 3 (1987), 125–9.

See also 688.

642 Nelly Andrieux & Emmanuèle Baumgartner, *Systèmes morphologiques de l'ancien français*, A: *Le verbe* (= *Manuel du français de moyen âge*, ed. Y. Lèfevre, Série III; Bordeaux, 1983) – *CCM*, 29:3 (1986), 273–4.

See also 353, 699.

643 Rafael Lapesa, *Estudios de historia lingüística española* (Madrid, 1985) – *RPh*, 40:2 (1986), 253–62.

See also 323, 593–5, 606, 726.

644 Gregorio Salvador, *Semántica y lexicología del español* (Madrid, 1985) – *RPh*, 40:3 (1987), 397–400.

See also 690.

645 *Handbuch der Lexikologie*, ed. Christoph Schwarze & Dieter Wunderlich. –*RPh*, 41:4 (1988), 421–6.

See also 609, 629, 643–4, 742.

646 José María Iribarren, *Vocabulario navarro*$_2$ (rev. by Ricardo Ollaquindia) (Pamplona, 1984) – *RPh*, 40:3 (1987), 391–7.

See also 300, 324, 367, 599, 600.

647 Veikko Väänänen, *Recherches et récréations latino-romanes* (Napoli, 1981) – *RPh*, 40:4 (1987), 493–501.

See also 346, 589–91, 608, 611, 614, 637, 671, 726.

648 G. Gómez de Silva, *Elsevier's Concise Spanish Etymological Dictionary* (Amsterdam, etc., 1985) – *HR*, 54 (1986), 323–6.

See also 657, 684.

649 Mirko Tavoni, *Latino, grammatica, volgare: storia di una questione umanistica*. Medioevo e umanesimo, 53 (Padova, 1984) – *It*, 65 (1988), 46–50.

See also 96, 716–7.

650 Brenda Laca, *Die Wortbildung als Grammatik des Wortschatzes: Untersuchungen zur spanischen Subjektnominalisierung*. Tübinger Beiträge zur Linguistik, 286 (Tübingen, 1986). *Kr*, 32 (1987), 122–5.

651 (With Kathryn Klingebiel) Jean Batany, *Français médiéval; textes choisis, commentaires linguistiques, commentaires littéraires, chronologie phonétique*$_2$ (rev.) (Paris, 1985). To appear in *CCM*.

See also 642, 703.

XIV. Book Notices

651a C.L. Hornaday, *Nature in the German Novel of the Late Eighteenth Century (1770–1800)* – *BA,* 15 (1941), 129.

651b Mario A. Pei, *Languages for War and Peace* – *BA,* 18 (1944), 258–9.

See also 431.

652 *The Year's Work in Modern Language Studies,* 12 (1950–51), 13 (1951–52), 14 (1952–53), ed. S.C. Aston – *RPh,* 8:1 (1954), 67–8.

See also 661, 673, 678, 686, 696, 700, 705, 709, 714, 723, 731, 738, 745.

653 Erwin Gustav Gudde, *California Place Names; a Geographical Dictionary* – *RPh,* 8:1 (1954), 68–9.

See also 612, 711.

654 Lore Terracini, *L'uso dell'articolo davanti al possessivo nel "Libro de buen amor"* – *RPh,* 8:1 (1954), 69–70.

655 Maria Teresa Atzori, *Bibliografia di linguistica sarda* – *RPh,* 8:2 (1954), 168.

See also 682.

656 Herbert H. Golden & Seymour O. Simches, comp. *Modern French Literature and Language; a Bibliography of Homage Studies* – *RPh,* 8:2 (1954), 169.

See also 681–2.

657 Bruno Migliorini & Aldo Duro, *Prontuario etimologico della lingua italiana*$_2$ (rev.) – *RPh,* 8:2 (1954), 169–71.

See also 609, 648, 717.

658 Louis Remacle, *Atlas linguistique de la Wallonie,* 1 – *RPh,* 8:2 (1954), 171–2.

See also 247.

659 Periodicals: *Newsletter of the Comparative Romance Linguistics Group (MLA), Revue de linguistique romane, Romanistisches Jahrbuch, Bollettino: Centro di studi di filologia e linguistica siciliani, Studier i modern språkvetenskap* – *RPh,* 8:3 (1955), 242.

See also 674, 683.

660 Edmund L. King, *Gustavo Adolfo Bécquer: From Painter to Poet* (164–323: "Concordance of the *Rimas*") – *RPh,* 8:4 (1955), 312.

See also 689.

661 *The Year's Work in Modern Language Studies,* 15 (1955), ed. S.C. Aston – *RPh,* 9:1 (1956), 94.

See also 652, 673, 678, 686, 696, 700, 705, 709, 714, 723, 731, 738, 745.

662 *Onoma: Bulletin d'information et de bibliographie,* 4 (1953), ed. H.J. van de Wijer – *RPh,* 9:1 (1955), 94.

See also 653.

663 C.M. Bowra, *Inspiration and Poetry* – *RPh,* 9:2 (1955), 267–8.

See also 689, 703, 712.

664 Alexander H. Schutz, *Vernacular Books in Parisian Private Libraries of the Sixteenth Century, According to the Notarial Inventories* – *RPh,* 9:2 (1955), 268.

665 Berta Elena Vidal de Battini, *El español de la Argentina* – *RPh,* 9:3 (1956), 401–2.

See also 8, 605, 695.

666 Bror Danielsson, ed. *John Hart's Works on English Orthography and Pronunciation,* 1 – *RPh,* 9:4 (1956), 472.

667 C.H. de Rocha Lima, *Uma preposição portuguêsa; aspectos do uso da preposição "a" na língua literária moderna* – *RPh,* 10:1 (1956), 70.

See also 60.

668 A.G. Cunha, "Influências eslávicas na língua portuguesa", *Revista da Academia Fluminense de Letras,* 6 (1953), 159–89 – *RPh,* 10:2 (1956), 139.

669 Florival Seraine, *Ensaios de interpretação linguística.* Cadernos de Cultura, 4 – *RPh,* 10:2 (1956), 139–40.

670 T.H. Maurer, Jr. *A unidade da Romània Ocidental* – *RPh,* 10:2 (1956), 140.

Cr.: K. Baldinger (a), 259.

See also 386.

671 Serafim da Silva Neto, *Fontes do latim vulgar: o "Appendix Probi"*$_3$ – *RPh,* 10:2 (1956), 140.

See also 611, 617.

672 Augusto Magne, ed. *A Demanda do Santo Graal*$_2$ (rev.), 1 – *RPh,* 10:2 (1956), 140.

See also 676.

673 *The Year's Work in Modern Language Studies,* 16 (1954–55), ed. S.C. Aston – *RPh,* 10:3 (1957), 306.

See also 652, 661, 678, 686, 696, 700, 705, 709, 714, 723, 731, 738, 745.

674 *Annual Report of the Dante Society, with Accompanying Papers,* 73 (1955) & 74 (1956) – *RPh,* 10:4 (1957), 408.

See also 659, 683.

675 Edward Sapir, *Culture, Language, and Personality; Selected Essays,* ed. David G. Mandelbaum – *RPh,* 11:1 (1957), 101–2.

See also 101–2, 266, 532, 544, 693, 729.

676 Celso Ferreira da Cunha, ed. *O Cancioneiro de Martin Codax* – *RPh,* 11:2 (1957), 187.

See also 672.

677 Arnold G. Reichenberger, ed. Luis Vélez de Guevara, *El embuste acreditado y el disparate creído* – *RPh,* 11:2 (1957), 188.

See also 339.

678 *The Year's Work in Modern Language Studies,* 17 (1955–56) & 18 (1956–57), ed. L.T. Topsfield – *RPh,* 11:3 (1958), 330.

See also 652, 661, 673, 686, 696, 700, 705, 709, 714, 723, 731, 738, 745.

679 J.J. Salverda de Grave, Variantes du préfixe *re-* (*Mélanges M. Roques,* 2 [1953]) – *RPh,* 12:1 (1958), 75.

See also 627.

680 Mario Wandruszka, *Haltung und Gebärde der Romanen* – *RPh,* 12:1 (1958), 109–10.

See also 697.

681 Herbert M. Golden & Seymour O. Simches, comp. *Modern Iberian Language and Literature: A Bibliography of Homage Studies* – *RPh,* 13:3 (1960), 350.

See also 656, 682.

682 Id., comp. *Modern Italian Language and Literature: A Bibliography of Homage Studies* – *RPh,* 13:3 (1960), 350.

See also 655–6, 681.

683 *Annual Report of the Dante Society with Accompanying Papers,* 66 (1958) & 67 (1959) – *RPh,* 13:4 (1960), 478.

See also 659, 674.

684 Edwin B. Williams, *Diccionario del idioma español* – *RPh,* 13:4 (1960), 478–9.

See also 424, 648, 718.

685 William M. Pepper, Jr. *Dictionary of Newspaper and Printing Terms* – *RPh,* 13:4 (1960), 479.

686 *The Year's Work in Modern Language Studies,* 19 (1957–58), ed. L.T. Topsfield – *RPh,* 13:4 (1960), 479.

See also 652, 661, 673, 678, 696, 700, 705, 709, 714, 723, 731, 738, 745.

687 Werner Beinhauer, *Spanische Umgangssprache*$_2$ (rev.) – *RPh,* 13:4 (1960), 479–80.

688 Eric P. Hamp, *Glossary of American Technical Linguistic Usage 1925–1950* – *RPh,* 14:1 (1960), 106–8.

See also 641, 704.

689 Albert Henry, *Langage et poésie chez Paul Valéry, avec un lexique des œuvres en vers;* & *Les grands poèmes andalous de Federico García Lorca* – *RPh,* 14:1 (1960), 108–9.

See also 660, 663.

690 Stephen Ullmann, *Précis de sémantique française*$_2$ (rev.) – *RPh,* 14:1 (1960), 109.

See also 73, 644.

691 New Printings and Collections (L. Kukenheim & H. Roussel, E. Auerbach, M. Schlauch, F. De Sanctis, G. Tilander, J. Leite de Vasconcelos & S. da Silva Neto, F. Lot, J.F. Montesinos) – *RPh,* 14:1 (1960), 110.

See also 671, 713.

692 Richard W. Emery, *The Jews of Perpignan in the Thirteenth Century* – *RPh,* 14:2 (1960), 186.

See also 736.

693 Alfred L. Kroeber & George William Grace, *The Sparkman Grammar of Luiseño* – *RPh,* 14:2 (1960), 186–7.

See also 544, 675, 698, 729.

694 Santiago Key-Ayala, *Obra inducida de Lisandro Alvarado; piezas de su archivo* – *RPh,* 14:2 (1960), 187.

See also 8, 665, 695.

695 Guillermo Feliú Cruz, *Andrés Bello y la redacción de los documentos oficiales. . . de Chile; Bello, Irisarri y Egaña en Londres* – *RPh,* 14:2 (1960), 187–8.

See also 605, 665, 694.

696 *The Year's Work in Modern Language Studies,* 20 (1958–60), ed. William Henry Barber – *RPh,* 14:3 (1961), 284.

See also 652, 661, 673, 678, 686, 700, 705, 709, 714, 723, 731, 738, 745.

697 Hans Flasche, *Die Sprachen und Literaturen der Romanen im Spiegel der deutschen Universitätsschriften, 1885–1950* – *RPh,* 14:3 (1961), 284–5.

See also 680, 744, 747.

698 William Bright, *Animals of Acculturation in the California Indian Languages* – *RPh,* 14:4 (1961), 360–1.

See also 544, 675, 693, 729.

699 Moritz Regula, *Historische Grammatik des Französischen,* 2 vols. – *RPh,* 14:4 (1961), 361–2.

See also 627.

700 *The Year's Work in Modern Language Studies,* 21 (1959–60), ed. William Henry Barber – *RPh,* 15:1 (1961), 109.

See also 652, 661, 673, 678, 686, 696, 705, 709, 714, 723, 731, 738, 745.

701 Rosalyn Gardner & Marion A. Greene, *A Brief Description of Middle French Syntax* – *RPh,* 15:1 (1961), 110.

702 Gerhard Rohlfs, *Diferenciación léxica de las lenguas románicas,* tr. Manuel Alvar – *RPh,* 15:1 (1961), 110.

See also 117, 729.

703 Geoffrey Brereton, *An Introduction to the French Poets: Villon to the Present Day* – *RPh,* 15:2 (1961), 203–4.

See also 650–1, 689.

704 Martin Joos, ed. *Readings in Linguistics; the Development of Descriptive Linguistics in America since 1925* – *RPh,* 16:3 (1963), 385–6.

See also 583, 688, 719.

705 *The Year's Work in Modern Language Studies,* 22 (1960–62), ed. W.H. Barber – *RPh,* 16:4 (1963), 504.

See also 652, 661, 673, 678, 686, 696, 700, 709, 714, 723, 731, 745.

706 John T. Waterman, *Perspectives in Linguistics: An Account of the Background of Modern Linguistics* – *RPh,* 17:4 (1964), 823–4.

See also 340–1, 707–8.

707 Louis Kukenheim, *Esquisse historique de la linguistique française et de ses rapports avec la linguistique générale* – *RPh,* 17:4 (1964), 824–6.

See also 634, 706.

708 Iorgu Iordan, *Geschichte und Methoden der romanischen Sprachwissenschaft,* tr. Werner Bahner – *RPh,* 17:4 (1964), 826–8.

See also 342, 720.

709 *The Year's Work in Modern Language Studies,* 23 (1961–62) & 24 (1962–63), ed. P.F. Ganz – *RPh,* 18:4 (1965), 522–3.

See also 652, 661, 673, 678, 686, 696, 700, 705, 714, 723, 731, 738, 745.

710 Minna Babington & E. Bagby Atwood, *Lexical Usage in Southern Louisiana* – *RPh,* 18:4 (1965), 524.

See also 607, 711.

711 Clyde T. Hankey, *A Colorado Word Geography* – *RPh,* 18:4 (1965), 524.

See also 710.

712 G.R. Coulthard, *Race and Colour in Caribbean Literature* – *RPh,* 18:4 (1965), 524–5.

See also 753.

713 New Printings (Auerbach, Bombaugh, Foerster, Holt, Mead, Ritchie & Simmons, Smalley, Warnke, Weekley) – *RPh,* 18:4 (1965), 525–6.

See also 691.

714 *The Year's Work in Modern Language Studies,* 25 (1963–64) & 26 (1964–65), ed. Graham Orton – *RPh,* 20:1 (1966), 148–9.

See also 652, 661, 673, 678, 686, 696, 700, 705, 709, 723, 731, 738, 745.

715 Leonard Bloomfield, *"Language History" from "Language",* ed. Harry Hoijer – *RPh,* 20:1 (1966), 149.

See also 624.

716 Hans Baron, *The Crisis of the Early Italian Renaissance* – *RPh,* 20:1 (1966), 150.

See also 717.

717 Bruno Migliorini, *The Italian Language,* tr. (& abridged) by T. Gwynfor Griffith – *RPh,* 20:1 (1966), 150.

See also 96, 609, 657, 716, 727.

718 Dictionaries (J.C. Traupman, E.A. Peers, E.B. Williams, J.S. Crespo Pozo, E.H. Wilkins & T.G. Bergin, B. Kottler & A.M. Markman, A. Juilland & E. Chang-Rodríguez, B. Reynolds) – *RPh,* 20:2 (1966), 259–62.

See also 348, 684.

719 Winfred P. Lehmann, ed. *A Reader in Nineteenth-Century Historical Indo-European Linguistics* – *RPh,* 21:3 (1968), 359–60.

See also 704.

720 Demetrio Găzdaru, ed. *Controversias y documentos lingüísticos* – *RPh,* 21:3 (1968), 360–1.

See also 338, 340, 708.

721 A.R. Fernández y González, *Hispanistas norteamericanos en la vida de Menéndez Pelayo* – *RPh,* 21:3 (1968), 361.

722 Gerhard Rohlfs, *Einführung in das Studium der romanischen Philologie*$_2$ (rev.) – *RPh,* 21:3 (1968), 361–2.

See also 342, 608, 702, 724, 732.

723 *The Year's Work in Modern Language Studies,* 28 (1966–67), ed. Nigel Glendinning – *RPh,* 21:4 (1968), 609–11.

See also 652, 661, 673, 678, 686, 690, 700, 705, 709, 714, 736, 738, 745.

724 Rebecca Posner, *The Romance Languages: A Linguistic Introduction* – *RPh,* 22:3 (1969), 365–6.

See also 342, 346, 722.

725 Vladimir F. Šišmarëv, *Rukopisnoe nasledie v arxive Akademii Nauk* – *RPh,* 24:4 (1971), 676–7.

See also 335, 420, 593, 617, 734.

726 Morton Bloomfield, *Essays and Explorations: Studies in Ideas, Language, and Literature* – *RPh,* 25:1 (1971), 152–5.

See also 341, 728.

727 Bruno Migliorini, *Dal nome proprio al nome comune*$_2$ (rev.) – *RPh,* 25:1 (1971), 155–7.

See also 717.

728 Frederick R. Rebsamen, ed. *"Beowulf is My Name" and Selected Translations of Other Old English Poems* – *RPh,* 25:3 (1972), 369–70.

See also 726.

729 Theodora Kroeber, *Alfred Kroeber, a Personal Configuration* – *RPh,* 25:3 (1972), 370–1.

See also 675, 693.

730 Index to the *Bulletin of Hispanic Studies* (50 [1973], 433–583) – *RPh,* 29:1 (1975), 138–9.

731 *The Year's Work in Modern Language Studies,* 35 (1973–74), ed. Glanville Price – *RPh,* 29:1 (1975), 139–40.

See also 652, 661, 673, 678, 686, 696, 700, 705, 709, 714, 723, 738, 745.

732 New editions: *Das altfranzösische "Rolandslied",* ed. Gerhard Rohlfs; *Zwei altfranzösische "fablels",* ed. Hans Helmut Christmann – *RPh,* 30:4 (1977), 688.

See also 722.

733 Irena Dulewiczowa, *Nomina actionis we współczesnym języku rosyiskim* – *RPh,* 31:4 (1978), 707.

734 M.B. Mejlax, *Jazyk trubadurov* – *RPh,* 31:4 (1978), 707–11.

See also 725.

735 Daniele Gambarara & Paolo Ramat, *Dieci anni di linguistica italiana (1965–1975)* – *Lg,* 55 (1979), 739*b*-741*a*.

See also 635, 759.

736 Herbert H. Paper, ed. *Jewish Languages: Theme and Variations* – *Lg*, 55 (1979), 746*b*-747*b*.

See also 321.

737 Antonio Quilis, ed. Antonio de Nebrija, *Reglas de orthografía en la lengua castellana* – *Inter-American Review of Bibliography*, 29 (1979), 103–4.

738 *The Year's Work in Modern Language Studies*, 37 (1975–76), ed. Glanville Price & David A. Wells – *RPh*, 34:1 (1980), 138–9.

See also 652, 661, 673, 678, 686, 696, 700, 705, 709, 714, 723, 731, 745.

739 Johannes Kramer (with Elisabeth Klein), ed. *Studien zum Ampezzanischen;* Romanica Ænipontana, 11. Innsbruck, 1978 – *Lg*, 56 (1980), 227*a*-228*a*.

740 Gerhard Resch, *Die Weinbauterminologie des Burgenlandes: eine wortgeographische Untersuchung. . .* – *Lg*, 57 (1981), 232*a*-233*b*.

See also 322, 331–2, 336.

741 Mark A. Gabinskij, *Grammatičeskoe var'irovanie v moldavskom jazyke: Nekotorye aspekty* – *Lg*, 57 (1981), 239*a*-240*a*.

742 Ladislav Zgusta, ed. *Theory and Method in Lexicography: Western and Non-Western Perspectives* – *Lg*, 57 (1981), 251*b*-253*a*.

See also 72, 609, 629, 645.

743 P. Sture Ureland, ed. *Standardsprache und Dialekte in mehrsprachigen Gebieten Europas: Akten des 2. Symposions über Sprachkontakt in Europa* — *Lg*, 57 (1981), 228*a*-229*b*.

Cf. Jean-Claude Muller, *Lg*, 58 (1982), 481*b*.

See also 85, 752.

744 K.F. Bach & Glanville Price, *Romance Linguistics and the Romance Languages* – *RPh*, 36:2 (1982), 315–6.

See also 697, 747.

745 *The Year's Work in Modern Language Studies*, 41 (1979–80), ed. G. Price & D.A. Wells – *RPh*, 36:2 (1982), 317–8.

See also 652, 661, 673, 678, 686, 696, 700, 705, 709, 714, 723, 731, 738.

746 Edmund Stengel & Hans-Josef Niederehe, *Chronologisches Verzeichnis französischer Grammatiken* – *RPh,* 36:2 (1982), 318–9.

747 Willy Bal & J. Germain, *Guide bibliographique de linguistique romane* – *RPh,* 36:2 (1982), 319–21.

See also 697, 744.

748 Silvio Pellegrini & Giovanna Marroni, *Nuovo repertorio bibliografico della prima lirica portoghese (1814–1977)* – *RPh,* 36:2 (1982), 321–2.

See also 676.

749 Joseph L. Laurenti, *Ensayo de una bibliografía de la novela picaresca española, 1554–1964* – *RPh,* 36:2 (1982), 322–3.

750 Henry & Renée Kahane, Lucille Bremner, Manlio Cortelazzo, *Glossario degli antichi portolani italiani* – *RPh,* 36:2 (1982), 323–4.

See also 622, 623.

751 Manfred Mayrhofer, *Zur Gestaltung des etymologischen Wörterbuches einer Großcorpus-Sprache* – *RPh,* 36:2 (1982), 324–6.

See also 9, 203, 208.

752 P. Sture Ureland, ed. *Die Leistung der Strataforschung und der Kreolistik. Typologische Aspekte der Sprachkontakte* — *Lg,* 60:3 (1984), 683.

See also 743.

753 John A. Holm & Alison Watt Shilling, *Dictionary of Bahamian English* – *Lg,* 60:3 (1984), 683–4.

See also 712.

754 Gernot U. & Gisela R. Gabel, *La littérature française: Bibliographie des thèses de doctorat soutenues devant les universités autrichiennes et suisses 1885–1975* — *RPh,* 38:4 (1985), 561–2.

See also 697, 744, 747.

755 Henri Cottez, *Dictionnaire des structures du vocabulaire savant: Éléments et modèles de formation* — *RPh,* 38:4 (1985), 562–5.

See also 629.

756 Ralph de Gorog, *Dictionnaire inverse de l'ancien français* – *RPh,* 38:4 (1985), 565–7.

See also 197, 208.

757 Lorenzo Amigo Espada, *El léxico del Pentateuco de Constantinopla y la Biblia medieval romanceada judeo-española* – *RPh,* 38:4 (1985), 567–9.

See also 603, 736.

758 *Hispanismen omkring Sven Skydsgaard. . .,* ed. J.K. Madsen – *RPh,* 38:4 (1985), 569–71.

See also 423.

759 Anna Laura & Giulio Lepschy, *La lingua italiana: storia, varietà dell'uso, grammatica* – *RPh,* 38:4 (1985), 571–3.

See also 635.

760 Hans Helmut Christmann, *Frau und "Jüdin" an der Universität: Die Romanistin Elise Richter (Wien 1865—Theresienstadt 1943)* – *RPh,* 38:4 (1985), 573–6.

See also 121, 416, 556, 584.

761 Aldo Scaglione, *Komponierte Prosa von der Antike bis zur Gegenwart,* 2 vols. – *RPh,* 38:4 (1985), 577–80.

762 Ursula Kilbury-Meißner, *Die portugiesischen Anredeformen in soziolinguistischer Sicht.* Romanistik in Geschichte und Gegenwart, 9. To appear in *MeLR,* 4 (1986–8).

See also 687.

762a Dwayne E. Carpenter, *Alfonso X and the Jews: An Edition and Commentary on "Siete Partidas" 7.24–De los judíos.* To appear in *(K)RQ.*

See also 321.

XV. The Literary Legacy of María Rosa Lida de Malkiel

(a) Critical assessment, biography, bibliography

763 Necrology: María Rosa Lida de Malkiel (1910–62), *RPh,* 17:1 (1963), 9–32.

See also 765, 767, 768, etc.

764 Preliminary Bibliography of the Writings of María Rosa Lida de Malkiel, *RPh,* 17:1 (1963), 33–52; Supplement, 17:2, 523–4.

See also 770, 773

765 Personal Profile of María Rosa Lida de Malkiel, *RPh,* 17:1 (1963), 53–4.

766–7 Cómo trabajaba María Rosa Lida de Malkiel, *Homenaje al Profesor [Antonio] Rodríguez-Moñino; estudios de erudición,* 1, 371–9. Madrid: Editorial Castalia, 1966.

768 María Rosa Lida de Malkiel et la philologie argentine. In: M.R.L. de M., *L'Idée de la gloire dans la tradition occidentale: Antiquité, Moyen Age occidental, Castille,* tr. Sylvia Roubaux, 287–95 ("Postface"). Paris: C. Klincksieck, 1968.

Cr.: Klaus-Jürgen Bremer, *RJb,* 22 (1971[–72]), 278–80; Nicholas G. Round, *MLR,* 64 (1969), 683–5.

769 "El libro infinido" de María Rosa Lida de Malkiel: *Josefo y su influencia en la literatura española, Fil,* 13 (1968–69), 205–26 (= *Homenaje a Ramón Menéndez Pidal*).

Cr.: Lía Schwartz Lerner, *RPh,* 35:2 (1981), 374–88 ("Un vasto proyecto recuperado: Los estudios sobre Josefo de M.R.L. de M."); Derek W. Lomax, *YW,* 33 (1971–72), 240; Gillian Weston, *YW,* 35 (1973–74), 218.

See also 771–2, 779, 782–7, 798.

770 Bibliografía analítica preliminar de los trabajos de M.R.L. de Malkiel. In: M.R.L. de M., *La originalidad artística de "La Celestina"*$_2$ [and thereafter], 753–79. Preceded by Y.M., "Semblanza biográfica" (1–3). Buenos Aires: EUDEBA, 1970. Segment of the book reprinted in Alan Deyermond, *Historia y crítica de la literatura española,* 1, 485–528.

Cr.: Carmen Castro, "M.R.L., una argentina valiente y sabia", *Ya* (Madrid), April 1, 1975; J.L. Gallardo, "Hacia una interpretación *otra* de *La Celestina*", *Bol. Millares Carlo,* 1 (ca. 1980), 167–78, cf. M.J. Woods & A.L. Mackenzie, *YW,* 42 (1980–81), 303; Adrienne Schizzano Mandel, *"La Celestina" Studies: A Thematic Survey and Bibliography, 1824–1970* (Metuchen, N.J.: The Scarecrow Press, 1971), 149–56; J. Villegas, "La estructura dramática de *La Celestina*", *BRAE,* 54 (1974), 439–78; Varii, *YW,* 37 (1975–76), 258.

See also 764, 773, 778a, 798.

771 Las fuentes de los estudios josefinos de María Rosa Lida de Malkiel, *CS,* núm. 11 (1971) (= *Homenaje a Arturo Marasso*), 9–18.

See also 769, 772, 779, 782–7.

772 The Judaic Strain in María Rosa Lida de Malkiel, *Hebrew University Studies in Literature,* N° 2 (1973), 119–31.

See also 781, 789–90.

773 Sobre la cronología interna de algunos trabajos de María Rosa Lida de Malkiel. In: *Homenaje al Instituto de Filología y literaturas hispánicas "Dr. Amado Alonso" en su cincuentenario 1923–1973,* ed. Frida Weber de Kurlat, 243–52. Buenos Aires, 1975.

See also 770, 778a.

774 María Rosa Lida de Malkiel como investigadora de las letras coloniales. In: *Homenaje a Don Agapito Rey,* ed. Josep Roca-Pons, 357–73. Bloomington, Ind.: Dept. of Spanish & Portuguese, Indiana Univ., [1980]. Includes two *inedita* by M.R.L.: "El nombre de la isla *Hispaniola*" (1936) and "Semblanza de San Martín" (1946).

Cr.: Peter T. Bradley, *YW,* 42 (1980–81), 399.

See also 788, 794.

775 A Brief History of M.R. Lida de Malkiel's *Celestina* Studies, *Cel,* 6:2 (1982), 3–13.

Cf. "Carta de M.R.L. de M. a D.W. McPheeters" [Feb. 6, 1957], preceded by Joseph T. Snow's remarks: ibid., 11:1 [1987], 2, 21–3.

Cr.: Ann L. Mackenzie, *YW,* 44 (1982), 343.

See also 777–8, 780, 792, 800.

776 Recognition for María Rosa Lida de Malkiel in her Native Argentina, *RPh,* 36:2 (1982), 221–4.

777 M.R. Lida de Malkiel's *Ur-"Celestina"* (1949), *Cel,* 8:2 (1984), 15–28.

See also 775, 778, 780, 792, 800.

778 "The Earliest Trace of Euripides in Spanish Literature" (ca. 1955), *Cel,* 9:2 (1985), 75–9.

See also 795.

778a Antiquity, Middle Ages, and the Renaissance Seen through the Eyes of an Argentinian Scholar: The Buenos Aires Years of María Rosa Lida de Malkiel (1910–62). To appear in *Transactions of the 20th State University of N.Y. at Binghamton Conference (1986) on "The Classics in the Middle Ages"*, ed. Aldo S. Bernardo & Saul Levin.

(b) Prefaces, epilogues, notes, and indexes to posthumous editions

779 Dos opúsculos inéditos: 1. "Alejandro Magno en Jerusalén según Josefo" (A. Traducción, B. Comentario); 2. "La Universidad de Jerusalén", *Davar,* No. 99 (1963), 70–7. (Y.M.'s Prefatory Note: 70.)

780 El ambiente concreto en *La Celestina.* In: *Estudios dedicados a James Homer Herriott,* 145–64. Madison: University of Wisconsin, 1966.

See also 775, 777–8, 792, 800.

781 Materiales del archivo de María Rosa Lida de Malkiel, 1: Esbozos de las últimas reseñas [Albert A. Sicroff, *Les controverses des statuts de 'pureté de sang' en Espagne du XVe au XVIIe siècle,* Paris, 1960), *RPh,* 21:4 (1968), 611–2.

See also 772.

782 "Las infancias de Moisés" y otros tres estudios: en torno al influjo de Josefo en la literatura española, *RPh,* 23:4 (1970), 412–48 (= *Ramón Menéndez Pidal Memorial,* Part 1). [412–24: Las infancias de Moisés; 424–32: Los pilares de la sabiduría; 432–8: El ave y el arquero; 438–45: El escarnio de Paulina; 445–6: Nota exegética [de Y.M.]; 446–8: Anotaciones sueltas].

Cr.: Gillian Weston, *YW,* 35 (1973), 218.

See also 769, 771, 779, 783–7.

783 Túbal, primer poblador de España. *Ábaco,* n° 3 (1970), 9–48. (Nota preliminar de Y.M.: 9–10).

See also 769, 771, 779, 782, 784–7, and especially 30.

784 Las sectas judías y los "procuradores" romanos (En torno a Josefo y su influjo sobre la literatura española), *HR,* 39 (1971), 183–213. ("Nota preliminar" de Y.M.: 183–5.)

See also 769, 771, 779, 782–3, 785–7.

785 La dinastía de los Macabeos en Josefo y en la literatura española, *BHS,* 48 (1971), 289–97. (Epílogo de Y.M.: 297.)

See also 769, 771, 779, 782–4, 786–7.

786 En torno a Josefo y su influencia en la literatura española: Precursores e inventores. In: *Studia Hispanica in Honorem R[afael] Lapesa,* 1,15–61. Madrid: Gredos, 1972. (Epílogo de Y.M.: 59–61.)

Cr.: Gillian Weston, *YW,* 36 (1974–75), 218.

See also 769, 771, 779, 782–5, 787.

787 *Jerusalén: El tema literario de su cerco y destrucción por los romanos.* Universidad de Buenos Aires: Facultad de Filosofía y Letras (Instituto de Filología y Literaturas Hispánicas), 1972[–73]. Pp. 211 (Prefacio de Y.M.: 7–13.)

Cr.: Renata Donghi [de] Halperín, *La Prensa,* 30.IX.1973.

See also 769, 771, 779, 782–6.

788 El 'romance', la *Comedia Pródiga,* las *Coplas a la muerte de un su amigo* y la *Carta al Rey* (1545) de Luis de Miranda [1943], *RPh,* 26:1 (1972), 57–61.

See also 774, 794.

789 Notas sobre Lope de Vega y los judíos (1. La diferencia fundamental entre Lope y Tirso; 2. ¿Contradicciones entre los retratos de Lope?). *La Nación* (Buenos Aires), 3ª Sección (Ensayos, poesía, narraciones), Oct. 29 and Nov. 5, 1972.

See also 791.

790 *Juan Ruiz. Selección del "Libro de buen amor" y estudios críticos*. Buenos Aires: EUDEBA, 1973. (Prefacio de Y.M.: pp. vii–x.).

[On May 11, 1976, Alicia [Colombí] de Ferraresi repeated at Mills College (Oakland) a lecture previously given at Harvard's Comparative Literature Conference, Spring 1976: "The Prison Revisited; on Juan Ruiz's *Libro de Buen Amor,* an Homage to M.R.L. de M.".]

Cr.: Gillian Weston, *YW,* 25 (1973–74), 228.

See also Alberto Vàrvaro, *FeL,* 17, 1–12.

791 Lope de Vega y los judíos, *BH,* 75: 1–2 (1973[–74]), 73–113. (Nota preliminar de Y.M.: 73–8; epílogo: 112–3.)

Cr.: Varii, *YW,* 36 (1974–75), 277.

See also 789.

792 Elementos técnicos del teatro romano desechados en *La Celestina, RPh,* 27:1 (1973), 1–12. (Nota preliminar de Y.M.: 1.)

Cr.: Varii, *YW,* 37 (1975–76), 257.

See also 775, 777–8, 780, 800.

793 *Dido en la literatura española: su retrato y defensa.* London: Tamesis Books Ltd., Serie A: 37 (1974). Pp. xxx, 166. (Prefacio de Y.M.: ix–xxix; Agregados y notas exegéticas: 141–56; Índice analítico: 157–66.) [Expansion of 1942–43 article in *RFH.*]

Cr.: Lía S. Lerner, *RPh,* 30:1 (1976), 303–9; Elias L. Rivers, *CL,* 28:4 (1976), 372–4; Nicholas G. Round, *BHS,* 54 (1977), 233–5; Gillian Weston, *YW,* 36 (1974–75), 248.

See also 795.

794 Fantasía y realidad en la conquista de América. In: *Homenaje al Instituto de Filología y literaturas hispánicas "Dr. Amado Alonso" en su cincuentenario 1923–1973,* ed. Frida Weber de Kurlat, 210–20. Buenos Aires, 1975. (Text of a lecture delivered ca. 1960.)

See also 774, 788.

795 *La tradición clásica en España.* Letras e ideas (dir. Francisco Rico), Serie mayor, 4. Barcelona (Esplugues de Llobregat): Editorial Ariel, 1975. Pp. 436. (Introducción de Y.M.: 9–32; Índices: 399–436; scattering of "Agregados inéditos de la autora": c. 15 pages.)

Cr.: Renata Donghi [de] Halperín, *La Nación,* Jan. 16, 1977 ("Tradición y creación").
See also 778, 792–3, 799.

796 La dama como obra maestra de Dios; esbozo de un estudio de tipología histórica y estructural [1954], *RPh,* 28:3 (1975), 267–324. (Nota preliminar de Y.M.: 267–70.) Rpr., *Estudios sobre la literatura española del siglo XV* (1977), 179–290.

See also 801.

797 *El cuento popular y otros ensayos.* Buenos Aires: Editorial Losada, S.A., 1976. Pp. 172. ("Tres apéndices" 123–46; "Índice alfabético de nombres, seudónimos, conceptos; títulos de libros y voces explicadas; temas narrativos y tipos humanos; zonas folklóricas y focos de cultura" [147–67] by Y.M.)

[Expansion of *El cuento popular hispano-americano y la literatura,* B.A., 1941.]

Cr.: Juan Carlos Ghiano, *La Nación,* Feb. 20, 1977; Harriet Goldberg, *RPh,* 35:3 (1982), 544–51; J.P., *La Prensa* [Buenos Aires], Sept. 4, 1977.

798 *Herodes: su persona, reinado y dinastía.* Literatura y sociedad (dir. Andrés Amorós). Madrid: Castalia, 1977. Pp. 256. (Prefacio de Y.M.: 7–14; Bibliografía esencial: 209–19; Índice alfabético: 245–56).

Cr.: Lía S. Lerner, *RPh,* 35:2 (1981), 374–388, esp. 383–6; Ángel Mazzei, *La Nación,* Nov. 26, 1978 (Secc. 3a:5).

See also 769, 771, 778a, 779, 782–7.

799 *Estudios sobre la literatura española del siglo XV.* Madrid: José Porrúa Turanzas, S.A. [1977]. Pp. 417. (Prefacio de Y.M.: 1–20; Índice alfabético, 393–417.)

[With an *ineditum:* "La ciudad, tema poético de tono juglaresco en el *Cancionero de Baena*", 333–8.]

Cr.: Ángel Mazzei, *La Nación,* Nov. 26, 1978, Secc. 3a:5; Robert B. Tate, *BHS,* 56 (1979), 150–1; Charles B. Faulhaber, *RPh,* 34 (1980), 123–7.

Cf. K. Kohut, *Actas* [Roma, 1982] *del 7. Congreso de la Asoc. Intern. de Hispanistas (Venecia, 1980),* pp. 639–47.

See also 795–6.

800 La técnica dramática de *La Celestina;* texto de una conferencia inédita, pronunciada el 21 de octubre de 1961 en la Universidad de La Plata. In: *Homenaje a Ana María Barrenechea,* ed. Lía S. & Isaías Lerner, pp. 281–92. Madrid: Castalia, 1984. (Epílogo de Y.M.: pp. 290–2.)

See also 775, 777–8, 780, 792.

801 *Juan de Mena, poeta del Prerrenacimiento español,* 2 (rev.). México, D.F.: El Colegio de México, 1984, p. 609. (24 pp. of additions include: "Prefacio a la segunda edición" [by Y.M.], pp. 9–11; "Agregados de la autora"; "Comentarios" [by Y.M.], pp. 569–80.)

XVI. Translations

802 Paul Valéry, "Manchmal sagte ich zu Mallarmé. . .", *Die Neue Rundschau,* 47:4 (1936), 382–97. ("Quelquefois je disais à Mallarmé. . . ")

See also 820.

803 (With María Rosa Lida de Malkiel) "Cantar de la hueste de Ígor", *Sur,* N° 176 (1949), 43–64 (includes Introduction and Notes). Rpr., Buenos Aires & Montevideo: Arca Galerna, "Aves del Arca", 1967. Pp. 54.

804 (With Percival B. Fay) Karl Jaberg, The Birthmark in Folk Belief, Language, Literature, and Fashion, *RPh,* 10:4 (1957), 307–42 (= *E.C. Armstrong Memorial Issue*) German original ("Das Muttermal in Sprache, Volksglaube, Sitte und Literatur") published subsequently in K.J., *Sprachwissenschaftliche Forschungen und Erlebnisse,* Neue Folge, Romanica Helvetica, 75, 282–322, Bern: Francke, 1965, with some improvements of details suggested by the translators.)

See also 405.

805 (With Marilyn May Vihman) Émile Benveniste, Mutations of Linguistic Categories, ed. W.P. Lehmann & Y.M., *Directions for Historical Linguistics: A Symposium,* 83–94, Texas UP, 1968.

See also 434.

XVII. Shorter Encyclopedia Articles

806 Spanish Language, *EB* (1964), 21, 152*b*-154*a*.

807 Amado Alonso, Wilhelm Meyer-Lübke, *EB* (1964), 1, 66*b*; 15, 401*b*.

808 Historical Linguistics. *International Encyclopedia of the Social Sciences,* ed. David L. Sills, 9, 371*b*-380*b*. [New York:] The Macmillan Co. & The Free Press, © 1968. Rpr., *ELT,* 1–18 ("Genetic Linguistics").

Cr.: Posner (b), 445.

See also 9, 13, 24, 27–9, 31, 33–4, 36, 38–9, 41, 43–4, 46, 51–4, 57, 59, 62, 64, 67, 71, 78–81, 83–5, 89, 94, 101–2, 105, 107, 109–10, 112–3, 117a, etc

809 Jakob Jud, Ramón Menéndez Pidal, *EB* (1970), 13, 101*b*; 15, 155*a*.

810 (α) Rōmānīōt, Lᵉšānōt ('Romance Languages'), (β) Sephardīth, Lāšōn ('Spanish Language'); and (γ) 'Portuguese Language'. *Encyclopedia Hebraica* (Jerusalem); for (β) see Vol. 15 (1974), cols. 399–402.

811 [Romance Languages]. Six-page typescript (Spring 1962); presumably translated and published in *Kannada Encyclopedia,* sponsored by the government of Mysore (Bangalore 20, India).

XVIII. Memoirs

812 Autobiographic Sketch: Early Years in America. *First Person Singular,* Papers from the Conference on Oral Archive. . . (Charlotte, N.C., 1979), ed. Boyd H. Davis & Raymond K. O'Cain, 77–95. Amsterdam: Benjamins, 1980.

Cr.: R.A. Hall, Jr., *Lg,* 57 (1981), 701.

812a A Candid Retrospect.

See the present volume, 145–56.

XIX. (Auto)bibliographies

813 Bibliography of Romance Linguistics (1940–47), *RPh,* 1:2 (1947), 167–90.

814 Bibliography of Portuguese Linguistics [ca. 1935–45], *RPh,* 1:4 (1948), 363–9; with a Supplement, 2:2–3 (1948–49), 267–8.

815 Breve autobibliografía analítica (selection of 275 items), *Anuario de estudios medievales,* 6 (1969), 615–39, preceded by an "Advertencia" and by a "Semblanza" (609–13) from the pen of Francisco Rico. With a plate.

See also 764, 770 in regard to María Rosa Lida de Malkiel.

XX. Comments by Critics on Editorship of Early Volumes (I–IX) of Romance Philology

816 **Ch.-V. Aubrun,** *BH,* 51 (1949), 114–5; 52 (1950), 413; 54 (1952), 449; **P.M. Boyd-Bowman,** *NRFH,* 2 (1948), 407; 4 (1950), 81–2, 286; 5 (1951), 89; **J. Bourciez,** *RLaR,* 70 (1948), 75–6; **V. Buben,** *Čas,* 31 (1948), 75–6; **A. Dauzat,** *FM,* 16 (1948), 160; 17 (1949), 317–8; 18 (1950), 76; 19 (1951), 77; 20:2 (1952), 159; **L. M.-J. Delaissé,** *SCr,* 2:1 (1948), 164; **M. Delbouille,** *MA,* 57:1–2 (1951), 198–9; **W.T. Elwert,** *NSpr,* year 1956, 90–5; **A. Ewert,** *FS,* 3 (1949), 93–5, 195–6, 295, 384–5; 4 (1950), 94–5, 285–6; 5 (1951), 97–8, 193–4, 383; 6 (1952), 187–8, 286; 7 (1953), 194, 386; 9 (1955), 96–8, 289; 10 (1956), 194–5; **J.G. Fucilla,** *It,* 25 (1948), 269; **M. García Blanco,** *RFE,* 34 (1950), 338–45; 35 (1951), 186–93, 379–82; 36 (1952), 165–71; 37 (1953), 349–55; 38 (1954), 382–91; **I. González Llubera,** *YW,* 13 (1951–52), 117–9, 121, 123–7; 15 (1953–55), 136–7, 140; **G. Gougenheim,** *BSLP,* 42:2 (1947–48), 92; *FM,* 19:4 (1951), 316; 20:3 (1952), 237; **O.H. Green,** *HR,* 16 (1948), 90; **J. Jud,** *VR,* 9 (1946–47), 388; **R. Lida,** *NRFH,* 2 (1948), 222; **B. Migliorini,** *YW,* 15 (1953–55), 204; **B. Pottier,** *Ro,* 71:4 (1950), 534–41; 72:1 (1951), 132–5; 72:3 (1951), 412–5; 74:2 (1953), 263–4; **G. Rohlfs,** *ASNS,* 187 (1950), 137; **R.B. Tate,** *YW,* 14 (1952–53), 127; 15 (1953–55), 149–50; **L.T. Topsfield,** *YW,* 14 (1952–53), 119–20; **S. Ullmann,** *YW,* 13 (1951–52), 18; 14 (1952–53), 7; **R.-L. Wagner,** *BSLP,* 49:2 (1953), No. 46 bis; **B. Woledge,** *YW,* 14 (1952–53), 30–1, 33; 15 (1953–55), 32–4. Cf. *Íns* (June 15, 1948); *Leuvensche Bijdragen-Bijblad,* 28 (1948), 25; *Neoph,* 32 (1948), 94.

XXI. Juvenilia

817 Pamjati Ril'ke [In Memoriam Rainer Maria Rilke]. *Nov'* (Tallin, Estonia), October 1930, p. 7*a-e* (in Russian).

818 Rossija v pis'max Rainer Maria Ril'ke [Russia in the letters of Rainer Maria Rilke]. *Rossija i Slavjanstvo* [– La Russie et le monde slave] (Paris), May 1931, pp. 3*a-d,* 4*ef* (in Russian).

819 Russischer Literaturbrief. *Die Literatur;* Monatsschrift für Literaturfreunde, April 1933, pp. 404–7.

820 Paul Valéry; l'homme et son œuvre. Thesis for the 1933 Matura Degree (Reifezeugnis, Abitur) of Werner Siemens Realgymnasium, Berlin-Schöneberg [closed in the 'thirties]; 40 typescript pages.

See also 802.

821 *Einführung ins Spanische für jüdische Auswanderer.* 42 two-column pages. Varia Verlag: Berlin, 1937. [Photographically reproduced from a feature, "Spanische Unterrichtsbriefe", in the weekly *Israelitisches Familienblatt.*] Exact information unavailable; ca. 1936–37.

822 *Einführung ins Portugiesische für jüdische Auswanderer.* 42 two-column pages. Varia Verlag: Berlin, 1937. [Photographically reproduced from a feature, "Portugiesische Unterrichtsbriefe", in the weekly *Israelitisches Familienblatt.*] Exact information unavailable; ca. 1936–37.

Appendix A: *A Candid Retrospect*

I concluded my nine years of secondary study at a Berlin-Schöneberg *Realgymnasium* early in 1933, by submitting an optional baccalaureate thesis ("Jahresarbeit"), written in French, on a modern poet and essayist still living and active at that time, Paul Valéry, and by vindicating my claim to a Latin major through interpretation of an ode by Horace as the center-piece of my oral examination on March 3, 1933—exactly two days before the German Revolution. My published juvenilia included a few bits of literary criticism, channeled through appropriate (*émigré* Russian and German) periodicals and bearing, in particular, on another major modernist poet, Rainer Maria Rilke.

I had to overcome serious difficulties before I was admitted to the Friedrich Wilhelms Universität (Berlin)—the forerunner of today's Humboldt University; upon entering it and observing the scene, I was horrified to discover how contemporary art, including *belles lettres,* could be distorted by a fanatic régime organized with diabolic efficiency and, possibly worse, how far until then highly respectable literary figures, known for their discretion and good taste, suddenly could go in currying favor with that essentially anti-intellectual and anti-artistic political order.

The resulting spell of aversion to contemporary fine literature prompted me to turn my attention, at first, to medieval literature, principally as set in the Western key and studied through the prism of medieval languages–still a highly prestigious field all over Europe in those years. I concentrated on medieval (beside Classical) Latin, Old Provençal, Old French, and Old Italian, without neglecting Slavic philology and Semitics (Hebrew, Arabic); the roster of my teachers included such star performers as Eduard Norden, Karl Strecker, and Eugen Mittwoch.

My next step was even more radical: By 1935 I decided to turn my attention, at least temporarily, away from literature and toward historical linguistics—a discipline not taught experimentally in those days—which, so I naïvely assumed, was an exact, slightly rigid science and therefore above all political turmoil (and above any politically-motivated distortion of humanistic scholarship). Within the vast Romance domain, persons more experienced than myself urged me to shift the core of my attention from French and Italian, whether old or modern, to Spanish and Portuguese, for two separate, mutually complementary reasons: There remained more to discover, factually and analytically, in those fields, in terms of enrichment of pure scholarship, and it seemed easier, at that juncture and in the foreseeable future as well, to forge ahead in the real world with a solid command of those two key languages to one's credit. As a university student marooned in Berlin throughout those grim years, I indeed earned my living in part, and even managed to support my aged parents, by teaching would-be emigrants to Argentina and Brazil elementary Spanish and Portuguese, even though my doctoral dissertation still bore on a problem of French.

Realizing that my future could not possibly lie in Central Europe, I began to scan the horizon for some possible escape route—at first not energetically enough. A short trip to France, in 1936, and a series of encounters with my more mature cousins who at that time lived—or vegetated—in Paris made it clear to me that a transfer to that lovely country and beautiful city would amount to a blind alley. Italy's brusque realignment in 1935 entailed the closure of that briefly promising gate. The following year Spain plunged into a bloody, mercilessly extended Civil War. I began to think of emigration to the New World; the delay in reaching that goal allowed me to file my dissertation and to send off manuscripts of post-doctoral articles to Denmark and Finland, where they actually were published in due time.

Shortly thereafter, as a newcomer to this country, I witnessed in New York (where I was eking out a meager existence through tutoring and occasional translation assignments) the pathetic collapse of France and the temporary near-extinction of long-standing American concerns with and about French culture, coincident with a dramatic rise of curiosity about Latin America, in tribute to hemispheric solidarity. In 1942, after a brief prelude at the University of Wyoming in Laramie, I was privileged to join a distinguished Department of Spanish and Portuguese on the Berkeley Campus (although its French Department had likewise been alerted to my availability), and thus the dice were cast: The voice of wisdom made it unmistakably clear to me, especially in the critical 1940–42 period if not before, that, in order for me to achieve an academic breakthrough, my record of research had better display an unmistakable emphasis on issues Luso-Hispanic.

This limitation was at no time strict, since part of my effort started to be deflected, before long, in the direction of Romance philology, many-voiced by definition, and the confinement to a single culture altogether ceased to prevail after 1966, when I was persuaded to transfer to the local Department of Linguistics. However, at that advanced stage my private curiosity about far too numerous problems Hispanic had been aroused for me to turn away entirely from that field, still insufficiently ploughed over. To my own amusement, there has since occurred a partial return to pristine preoccupation with Old French (witness the recent etymological inquiries into *concierge* and *sergent,* the lexico-phonological probing of *fieble/feible,* the suffixal analysis of medieval verbal abstracts in *-ëiz*); also, several other languages, modern English included (with special reference to its elusive adjectives in *-y*), have each received a long-overdue share of my concentrated attention, in addition to general linguistics, to the extent that it is diachronically skewed.

The problem examined in my doctoral dissertation ("The Substantivated Adjective in French", 1938) was, essentially, syntactic or located near the border-line between syntax and lexicology, but also abounded in loopholes of possible concern to the student of affixal derivation; suffice it to state that *les ridicules* is tantamount to 'ridiculous ways, little absurdities'; that *le comique de (l'histoire)* corresponds to 'the funny part of (the story)'; whereas for 'oddity, oddness' *singularité* and *bizarrerie*, and for 'attractiveness' *attraction* are available. The shift of certain lexical units from one form class to another is, then, in keen competition with such devices as the use of certain suffixes to produce adjectival and verbal abstracts. This is how intensive work on a given syntactic problem, to my own surprise, led gradually to self-immersion in issues in word-formation; and since, at least in the Romance domain, the exhaustive inquiry into practically any series of words, tied together by a suffix (as a sort of common denominator), includes a residue of lexical units not entirely transparent as to origin, an urgent need for occasional etymological probing before long made itself felt. The rise, in Late and Medieval Latin, of the types *attractīvu, initiātīva* is a question that ties in with the substantivized use of certain adjectives; almost independently, it is also connected with the vicissitudes of the Latin suffix *-īvu*. Thus, in older French, certain adjectives in *-if* (the normal local outcome of *-īvu*), among them *juif* and *soutif,* invite additional investigation under an etymologist's magnifying glass.

Before long, I came across questions similarly straddling two or more disciplines in my early post-doctoral explorations. Among Latin present-participial abstracts, ancestral *-antia* and *-entia* justified close attention, not least on account of the early disappearance from Spanish of the vernacular outcome of the latter, namely *-iença,* to the benefit of its learnèd counterpart, *-encia.* But even after clarifying that abnormality, noteworthy in itself, one remains with the uncomfortable problem on his hands as to how to treat such opaque monstrosities as *pendencia, primencias/primicias,* and *fe-, fi-, hemencia.* These three items were examined apart, in a companion article (1944) **(31)** flanking my first major monograph written in English and written in this country (1945) **(2)**. My only regret today is that I failed at that remote juncture to pay attention to *andulencias* and *garridencia* (later investigated by Spitzer and Dworkin, respectively), and to recognize the need for similarly examining the contrast between Sp. *menudencias* and Ptg. *miudezas.*

I mention these autobiographic details, despite their triviality, because the question is often raised as to just how "any serious person" can at all warm up to the challenge of etymology in this day and age. To this a straightforward answer can be supplied: Any failure, on the part of a whole generation of workers, to pay heightened attention to the stubborn residue of unsolved etymological "riddles" will tend to distort the diachronic projection under survey.

To sum up: In exceptional constellations of circumstances, one becomes an etymologist by accident, if not against one's will. In such a situation one must be properly preconditioned to reap the full benefit of a lucky coincidence. Even though I confess to having been a willing victim of those circumstances, the lesson that I had learned at the outset, to the effect that broad-gauged structure "on the move" and individual word history were tightly interwoven, has continued to haunt me ever since. One day, in slowly turning over the pages of a heavy volume of the *Thesaurus Linguae Latinae* (in search of what?), I chanced upon the rare gastronomic term *iecuāria* 'giblets' (from *iecur* 'liver'), transmitted by a single glossographer of Late Antiquity. It impressed me instantaneously, for the simple reason that my intensive readings—precisely at that time—in older Portuguese texts had inculcated into me a sharp awareness of *iguaria* 'tidbit', stressed on the second *i*. But I realized at once that, without a patient discussion of certain peculiarities, starting with the change in the position of the main stress, any attempt on my part to trace *iguaria* to *iecuāria* would amount to a wild guess, politely camouflaged as a "conjecture". On balance my article, published in the 1944 volume of *Language* **(129)**, reserves a more generous quota of space for the elucidation of these side issues than it does for the advocacy of the kernel of the solution proposed. This time, counter to what had happened in the earlier case of OFr. *soutif*, actual word-identification, despite the slight semantic discrepancy, preceded the analysis of grammatical paraphernalia.

Over the next few years, enthusiastic concern with problems in Hispanic suffixal derivation—including the formation of indefinite pronouns based, in the last analysis, on parental *ali-* plus *-quī*, *-quem*—claimed virtually all my leisure time, with subordinated etymological explorations, one by one, branching off from them, unless the looming target of derivational (or compositional) curiosity was, conversely, itself a spin-off from a previous spontaneous etymological illumination—with hits, one hopes, outnumbering misses. A new skill acquired in the process was the growing ability to cut a path through the thicket of dialect vocabularies—especially those illustrative of present-day conditions in Northern Spain. The documentation, imperceptibly, was growing heavier and heavier, and its control more and more difficult, while the problems themselves, alas, threatened to become ever narrower. Late in 1948, at the peak of a four-month season I was spending in the East, Roman Jakobson called me to order, insisting that an evening-filling talk I had volunteered to give under the aegis of the Linguistic Circle of New York (a group he was skillfully piloting during the years of his own affiliation with Columbia) bear on a topic of broad implications, one apt to be of potential interest not exclusively to the tiny group of Romance experts. I agreed, and thus set out to prepare the original version of my "Hypothetical Base in Romance Etymology", a radical elaboration on which soon thereafter appeared in Vol. 6 (1950) of the Circle's mouthpiece, namely the journal *Word* **(164)**. (A fresh revision and even bolder expansion, carried out in 1983, is awaiting a benevolent publisher.)

In the fifties and, on an ever increasing scale, throughout the sixties and seventies, down to 1982, my responsibilities as editor-in-chief (and founding editor, to boot) of the *Romance Philology* quarterly—the first of its kind in the English-speaking world—prompted me to deflect a not insignificant portion of my time and energy in the direction of managerial and editorial duties, for which, at the outset, I was unprepared. What threatened to sap my strength at the start was a heavy quota of commitment to unavoidable routine transactions, such as the processing of manuscripts received—whether solicited or spontaneously submitted; or the assignment to trustworthy critics of review copies, with which publishers the world over began to shower us. Once this facet of my involvement had begun to function like a well-oiled machine, I could afford to turn my attention to more creative and imaginative dimensions of editorial labor—those that bore fruit deserving to be recorded, albeit peripherally, in a subsequent inventory of writings: the preparation of review articles, standard book reviews, and bibliographic notices of my own, which were to alternate with those—obviously, far more numerous—which I continued to elicit from others; the writing of necrological essays and of pithy obituary notes; the phrasing of introductory remarks designed to usher in special expanded issues; and the like. While there was nothing especially original, let alone particularly controversial, about an editor's shouldering such a combination of conventional burdens, their cumulative weight, in the end, became crushing.

Less self-explanatory and less likely to have earned me unanimous approval was the long string of "editorial comments" which, after a weakly delineated prelude, started for good in 1961. Originally intended to function as mere space-fillers where the last page of an issue had been left incomplete, and entirely harmless, not to say banal, at that opening stage ("West Coast Learnèd Journals", "Library Subscription List", and similar crumbs), they soon began to acquire more sharply profiled characteristics and, in harmony with this inner growth, to extend, upon occasion, to two or even three pages. Some of them simply involved extra-short notes and queries, factual or didactic in content ("Stressed *nós, vós* vs. weak *nos, vos* in Old Spanish"; "Special Punctuation Marks for Quoted Translations?"). Others attempted to highlight long-forgotten episodes in the history of our discipline, or to bring to life colorful personalities of pioneers undeservedly neglected by posterity ("August Fuchs [1818–47], the Founder of Comparative Romance Dialectology"). Yet others aimed at mediating between the chosen field and other domains of intellectual endeavor ("The Portrayal of Philologists and Linguists in Fine Literature"). A few dealt, in semi-feuilletonesque—but seldom if ever eyebrow-raising fashion—with the human aspect of austere scholarship, with all sorts of passing fashions, quirks, and bizarreries unavoidably accompanying serious spade-work. Opinions on the ultimate value of such incidental comments were, I suspect, divided; but I happen to know for sure that they were widely read outside the very narrow circle of hard-core specialists; that they greatly increased the circulation of the quarterly, which might otherwise have remained pathetically low; and that they contributed to shattering the image of the philologist as a hopelessly dull person, devoid of any spark of humor or self-criticism. While the titles, at rare intervals, may have sounded flamboyant, frivolous, or downright flippant, the author's prime intention, even in those exceptional instances, was to bring to mind objectively valuable, if slightly marginal bits of knowledge, some of which also happened to be amusing in nostalgic retrospect.

What the ultimate merit (assuming there was any) of those scattered anecdotal reports actually was must, almost needless to add, be some day determined by qualified judges and annalists. In one category of editorial messages, I make bold to state, my respect for editorial etiquette has influenced my own private research. As I moved on, from originally short, or at most, middle-sized necrologies, such as those that I deemed it my duty to write on Leo Spitzer and Karl Jaberg, to discernibly more circumstantial essays—represented by the pen portraits of Menéndez Pidal, Migliorini, Gamillscheg, Elise Richter, Tomás Navarro, and Benveniste—all of whom I had known, at the very least, through correspondence—, my curiosity about the growth of diachronic linguistics and philology advanced by leaps and bounds. Using, at first as an excuse, the momentum produced by the genre of formal necrologies, I gradually started to develop an acquired taste for re-creating the climate of research (and lecturing) that must have prevailed at certain peak periods. This bent has ultimately led to a number of thumb sketches of personalities (and their respective environments) with whom, for transparent chronological reasons, it has not been my privilege to entertain any direct relations: Diez, Pott, Miklosich, Schuchardt, Tobler, Gröber, Michaëlis, Meyer-Lübke, Cuervo, Hanssen, Lang, Sapir (anticlimactically, I did meet Georg Cohn once, shortly before his tragic death).

As an example of this newly-awakened interest let me cite the case of my protracted concern with Menéndez Pidal's many-pronged *œuvre*. While the death (1968) of the *doyen* of all Hispanists—whom I had known through extended correspondence and through two personal encounters, in 1959 and 1962—almost at once produced the expected necrological article (half portrait, half *tableau*, in a memorial issue of *Romance Philology*, **412**), further reflection and new reverberations, obviously unforeseen seventeen years ago, led to two extended papers channeled through entirely different journals as late as the opening and mid eighties: one on Menéndez Pidal viewed exclusively *qua* etymologist **(288)**, the other on the three concluding decades in his remarkably long productive life **(294)**.

To my profound sadness I cannot entirely separate from the involvements just described those obligations that I spontaneously incurred as the executor of the intellectual legacy of my unforgotten wife. The biographical sketch and the tentative bibliography of María Rosa Lida that appeared in Vol. 17:1 (August 1963) of *Romance Philology* **(763)** were just the start of a long chain of activities, including introductions to collections of her articles and to book-length fragments carved from the torso of her unfinished monograph on Josephus. Twenty-four years later, these activities have not yet come to a stop, since unknown drafts or blueprints of studies she planned to engage in can still be unearthed in her archive, with a measure of luck.

In the meantime, the outward organization of research in my field, on a world-wide scale, was rapidly changing, and these modifications before long began to influence everywhere the discipline's content, slant, and styling. Approximately until the mid-century point, most of the significant original contributions to the increase of our knowledge about language were channeled either through self-contained books (including monographs), or through article-sized papers published in learnèd journals (typically, quarterlies, academy bulletins, yearbooks, and the like). Peripheral for a while to this mainstream of events was the sporadic appearance of memorial and testimonial volumes, or of transactions of *ad hoc* conferences and symposia. After 1950 (or thereabouts) the center of gravity began to shift in the direction of a category of scholarly communication found previously only on a vestigial scale: individual sections (almost invariably prepared by invitation) of major books; as a forerunner one may cite the contributions to time-honored *Grundrisse*. These pieces, as a rule, could be expected to cover distinctly wider patches of ground than precision-tooled etymological studies, known for their sharp focus, would have tended to do. By responding positively to flattering invitations of this sort, which around 1960 began to reach me in a steady crescendo, I felt obliged to adjust myself to a set of conditions new to myself. The papers thus produced would range, pleasingly enough, over 25 to 125 printed pages; might take into account the evidence of several languages, not necessarily closely akin to one another; and would, to the point of predictability, attack broad problems of wide appeal—with the twin ideals of exhaustive documentation and of a neatly chiseled *historique du problème* becoming practically unattainable and thus allowed to recede discreetly into the background.

Landmarks of this development, which to the present has not entirely lost its momentum, have included such characteristic items as: "Distinctive Traits of Romance Linguistics" (1964) **(28)**; "Genetic Analysis of Word Formation" (1966) **(33)**; "Hispanic Philology" and "The Inflectional Paradigm as an Occasional Determinant of Sound Change" (1968) **(35–6)**; "[English] Lexicography" (1971) **(41)**; "General Diachronic Linguistics" alongside "Comparative Romance Linguistics" (1972) **(43–4)**; "Changes in the European Languages under a New Set of Sociolinguistic Conditions" (1976) **(54)**; "Derivational Categories" (1978) **(59)**; "The Lexicographer as a Mediator between Linguistics and Society" (1980) **(72)**; "Semantically-Marked Root Morphemes in Diachronic Phonology" (1982) **(79)**; "Alternatives to the Classic Dichotomy: Family-Tree/Wave Theory?" and "Models of Etymological Dictionaries: Abandoned, Thriving, or Worthy of an Experiment" (1983) **(80, 83)**; "A Linguist's View of the Standardization of a Dialect" (1984) **(85)**; "Spontaneous Speech versus Academic Constraints in Medieval and Renaissance Europe" (1985) **(96)**; "Regular Sound Development, Phonosymbolic Orchestration, Disambiguation of Homonyms" and "Old Spanish Language" (both to appear in 1988) **(107–8)**.

As some of the titles just adduced, one hopes, demonstrate, and as could easily be shown on a far more liberal scale, such topical changes as can be culled from the bare mention of titles involve not only an increasing preference for larger slices of theory and bigger chunks of illustrative material, but also a deliberate shift of focus away from one-sided concentration on etymology and suffixal derivation, or else on the zigzagging history of past linguistic gropings. A wholesome expansion, in several by no means incompatible directions, of initially stringent curiosity has taken place over the last thirty-odd years, so as to include domains, perspectives, and approaches either previously neglected or far too long taken for granted. A few illustrations must suffice: key points and salient segments along the curved lines of linguistic trajectories; multiple vs. simple causation; strong vs. weak phonetic change; phonological irregularity; economy of sound changes; a speech community's preference, under select conditions, for bi-, as against mono-, syllabicity; patterns of morphological leveling; controlled and wild leaps from one conjugation class to another; constellations of morphological conditions as a stimulus of sound shifts; instances of lexical loss and, conversely, of lexical proliferation; agency of taboo; etc. Puzzling details of individual sound development and of erratic grammatical architecture, to be sure, continued to titillate my imagination; and there was always room for a modicum of attention to residual chance discoveries, which fitted no exploratory pattern. But little by little a certain premium began and continued to be placed on the precise identification and analysis of newly-discovered classes of change, as well as of courses followed by changes; also of specimens of material particularly subject to transmutations. Hence my increasing concern with such phenomena and processes as lexical polarization and serialization, interfixes and suffixoids, excessive self-assertion (in dramatic contrast to hypercorrection), and the like.

The one conclusion that I drew from intense and progressively critical observation of the contemporary scene was that excitement about new theories, however legitimate, and response to exotic data, however beguiling, must not, under any set of conditions, be allowed to blunt one's loyalty to the historico-comparative type of research, especially when brought to bear on Romance, where that approach is known to produce such highly satisfactory results and where, counter to rumor and folk belief, so much that is crucially relevant remains to be ascertained. The nearly-pervasive policy of the simultaneous use of title and subtitle (which might have been supererogatory half a century ago), has of late simply served to convey to generalists (i.e., theorists) and specialists alike the dual message that the facts distilled in the paper at issue and the technique invoked to achieve that goal could be of equal relevancy to both groups of readers, whose paths, in general, rarely coincide these days. Selecting as the title for a relatively short article something like "In Search of 'Penultimate' Causes of Language Change" and as the corresponding subtitle "Studies in the Avoidance of /ž/ in Proto-Spanish" is tantamount to announcing to theorists of all hues and glottogeographic areas of specialization that the piece deals with causation of change and, in one concrete instance, attempts to hierarchize such causes, while giving notice to the more alert type of Palaeo-Hispanists that here a specific point of diachronic phonology is likely to be threshed out. There is no harm if occasionally title and subtitle, so defined, are interverted.

It would be both inaccurate and boastful to maintain that in every single instance the topic, size, and slant (or tone) of a shorter piece have all been brain-children of the author alone. That the initiative for writing a piece may stem from a journal editor rather than from a critic-investigator need not be laboriously demonstrated in the case of book reviews (including review articles) and of contributions, of varying length, to encyclopedias. The situation is a shade more delicate with other genres of scholarly inquiry; yet, when summoned to contribute a piece to a volume launched in honor of a noted Catalanist (a label that denotes a student of that language, but also connotes a staunch supporter of its autonomy), one ordinarily selects, as I indeed did, a subject encompassing Catalan to a significant extent, if not mandatorily confined to it. In my contribution to the posthumous Stephen Ullmann miscellany, I aimed at offering a major pendant to the long article on hypercharacterization which he himself, *qua* editor-in-chief of Glasgow's *Archivum Linguisticum,* had previously encouraged me to write for that journal. A host of other examples are available to prove that an ensemble of studies, often starting with one's doctoral dissertation, far from continuously reflecting the preferences, however well-advised, of a single individual, often depend on the reiteration of consensus of tastes and opinions.

No problem is apt to cause so much embarrassment in an interview as the question, directed at a senior scholar, as to exactly what, in his earlier writings, he has resigned himself to regarding as superannuated, erroneous, or, at least, being in urgent need of elaboration. As regards matters of presentation, terminological styling, and the like, it goes without saying that any piece older than, say, a quarter-century has ceased to make enjoyable reading on account of the rapid obsolescence of fashions in all social sciences and, to a smaller degree, in the humanities, too! Not for nothing are linguists (including those of the diachronic persuasion) reputed to move ahead in the fast lane. A more serious matter is one's readiness to admit that certain causal explanations offered, certain temporal sequences reconstructed, or certain etymological identifications propounded have turned out to be untenable, either by virtue of self-criticism or in deference to outside criticism, sometimes brought forward in alliance with alternative or, worse still, preferable solutions advocated by the critics of one's own earlier gropings. Yet, the existence of weak spots, recognizable in retrospect, cannot be denied.

To offer a few candid admissions of defeat: My attempt (1946) **(141)** to derive Sp. *lerdo* 'slow, heavy, obtuse', just because there is on record a (rare, obsolete) verb *enlerdar* 'to render obtuse', from zoönym *glīs, glīris* (or its by-form **glēs, *glēris* 'dormouse'), via the supposititious verb **glīr-, *glēr-itāre,* lit. 'to transform s.o. into a sleepy dormouse', may or may not have been witty, but was certainly lacking in persuasiveness, although the mistake, ironically, was something of an eye-opener as regards the survival, into Romance, of the two rival forms *glīre* and **glēre*. In studying, around 1975, the Italian suffix *-(t)aggine* **(243)**, often jocose, I might have more heavily stressed its semilearned transmission, emphasizing that *-ana* was the normal rural reflex of ancestral *-āgine*. While busying myself, as a rank beginner in 1944, with the provenience of Sp. *sosiego* **(130)**, I should have shifted the emphasis onto the corresponding verb, *sos(s)egar* 'to tranquillize' if *subsecāre* was indeed the sought-for source, and might have striven to account for the numerous medieval variants: *aso(n)segar, assessegar,* etc.

One matter about which I have thought a good deal, but which it seems impossible for any author to tackle in a climate of good taste, even at a distance of several decades, is the spectrum of critical reactions to my writings, over a period of almost a half-century. Just why two reviewers–the one a Belgian, the other a Southern Frenchman—have roundly rejected, to the point of near-predictability, almost every single solution of a pending problem advocated by me is not readily understandable, but may be unimportant; I have never had the slightest contact with either person. As a neophyte, I had to endure the wrath of at least two senior scholars of considerable prestige, while in the stormy sixties a few—obviously, very young—critics, entirely unknown to me, apparently mistook me for an "establishmentarian" target of their general impatience with tradition in organized scholarship. All relevant details of these episodes and interludes can be easily culled from the pertinent entries in the body of the Autobibliography. I wrote a single rejoinder, and at present regret having done so. At the opposite end of the ledger, I must not leave unmentioned the striking generosity of the Zurich Romanist Jakob Jud, to whom, in the mid and late forties, I never dispatched a batch of reprints without promptly receiving from him detailed and constructive comments on every single one of them—a display of helpfulness and true leadership the like of which I never encountered before or after. (The wisdom of ever publishing these *prises de position* is a point that I later ventilated in my correspondence with Jud's closest friend Karl Jaberg; he was less than sanguine on that occasion . . .)

Over against explicit criticism, public or private (including its epistolary variant) one may place the varying responses of readers, real or potential, to the challenge of a book, an article, or an editorial notice. There are several ways of measuring it, by making use of statistical data other than actual sales figures, for book ventures. As regards the demand for reprints, my study of irreversible binomials (ultimately absorbed into the miscellany *Essays on Linguistic Themes*) seems to have been published at the right moment and/or to have placed the stress on the right languages (English and German, in large part through a liberal dosage of help from Archer Taylor); at any rate, a goodly supply of reprints that I had, optimistically, ordered was exhausted in a few weeks through insistent requests, in large part from unknowns. One rival technique for measuring readers' reaction is to count epistolary comments spontaneously submitted. To my utmost surprise, the one piece from my pen that seems to have caused a certain commotion was my rather short necrological essay ("From Rome to New York City" **(431)**) written in a conciliatory tone, or so I thought, on a figure as controversial as Mario A. Pei. I received about fifteen letters, of which one chided me for excessive leniency, while the others accused me of unwarranted severity.

There has been in the past, and I am confident that there will continue to be, a fair proportion of instances of a straight or circuitous return to a given topic. In only very few cases would I own up to a sort of obsession or infatuation. Typically, there has been a complex interplay of causes at the root of any baffling change under inquiry; of these–often hidden–factors, only one at a time has been recognized, so that a later presentation of the problem does better justice to the intricacy of coöccurring processes than does an earlier sketch, unavoidably one-sided. Let me cite one example: My earlier analysis of certain Spanish indefinite pronouns, conducted in the forties, aimed at explaining the genesis of forms such as *álguien, nádie, ótrie* (for older *alguién, nádi, ótri*), through all sorts of blends within the system, as when the pressure of *álgo* 'somewhat' (from ancestral *aliquid*), was made responsible for the shift from *alguién* 'someone', its stress guaranteed by rhyme, to mod. *álguien* **(18)**. This explanation still holds, I am convinced, but it happens to be incomplete, since the real crux of the problem, viewed in this perspective, recedes into the background: The most noteworthy feature of the more recent forms is the appearance of a rising diphthong in an unstressed, or lightly-stressed, syllable. Only a quarter-century later, in turning my attention to verbal paradigms, did I stumble across cases like mod. *atiesar* 'to stiffen, harden' (for older *atesar,* beside the adj. *tieso* 'tense, taut, stiff') or *amueblar* 'to furnish' (alongside *muebles*), which showed me the parallel penetration of the same diphthongs into another category—this time the pretonic—of lightly-stressed syllable. From this parallelism I would at present extrapolate, as the nuclear problem underlying both situations, the gradual slackening of the bonds that, initially, tied the occurrence of such diphthongs to the locus of extra-heavy word stress.

Upon other occasions, the return to a subject–not infrequently after the lapse of many years–either carries with it the need, or is, to begin with, prompted by the need for a rather thorough review of vital presuppositions, far beyond the appeal to supplementary factors. A single example will suffice. There existed in Latin a pattern of abstract formations in *-ium,* frequently deverbal (*cōnsil-ium* 'deliberation', *domin-ium* 'absolute ownership', *imper-ium* 'command, order, authority', beside *cōnsulĕre, domināre, imperāre*), and neatly observable in compounds (*nau-fragium* 'shipwreck', *stīpend-ium* 'tax, tribute, tariff', *trifurc-ium* 'three-forked shape'). Romanists, following in the footsteps of Meyer-Lübke (*Rom. Gramm.,* II, § 404), allow for the growth of this schema in Roman folk speech and are willing to identify the Romance traces of such formations, but steadfastly deny the continued productivity of the model at later stages of the development (unless *-ium* entered into the composite suffixes *-ārium, -ĕrium,* and *-ōrium*), arguing, as if an unshakable axiom were involved, that such derivational tools as carried no heavy stress were doomed to petrifaction if not downright extinction in Late Latin. Accepting the "axiom" at its face value as a beginner, I consequently steered clear of any thought of *-ĭum* in coming across Sp. *ahoguío* 'shortness of breath', *poderío* 'power' (and, in its wake, *señorío* 'domain'), It. *brividío* 'cold shiver', and the like, declaring them–in 1941–to be extensions of such clear-cut cases as Sp. *umbrío* 'shady', *estío* '(late) summer', etc., which unmistakably point to Lat. *-īvu(m).*

Having meanwhile, with the passage of time, developed a wholesome disrespect for alleged axioms, I have started paying close attention to contexts previously overlooked, such as Sp. *albedrío* (orig. *alvedrío,* 'free will', from *arbĭtrĭum,* and as *rocío* 'dew', from *rōscĭdu* 'dewey', alongside adj. *rocío, rúcio* 'wet, moist' (in dialect speech). It has become clear to me that primary *-́io* and even secondary *-́io* can, under certain conditions, undergo an accent shift and emerge as *-ío.* It now seems much simpler and more realistic to link the above-mentioned Spanish and Italian *-ío* words with reputedly extinct *-ium,* an idea I am henceforth prepared to espouse and defend, without categorically excluding the possibility that the parallel pattern *-ío* < *-īvu* (i.e., my original choice), favored especially after dentals (*-dío* < *-tīvu,* as in *regadío* 'irrigated [land]'), could have had its share of influence in bringing about the necessary stress shift. Yet other pressures are conceivable; consider the structure of Ptg. *assobio* 'whistling' against the background of the corresponding verb *assobiar* < *sibilāre,* with labialization of the first *i* by adjacent *b* and loss of the *l* between vowels—a point that I completely missed forty-five years ago.

July 19, 1986

Appendix B: Selective Topical Index

I. Range of Languages

II. Key Words and Key Concepts

Appendix C: Samples of Lexico-Etymological Research

The items listed in this Index—the longest but hardly the most elaborate of all those included—are estimated to comprise actually less than 5% of all problems of this sort and size attacked over a period of almost a half-century. Hence the wisdom of speaking, at most, of "samples". The material falls into three major sections, which are all further subdivided, albeit not the same way.

Section I is a record of the most characteristic bases, either identified or, if starred, reconstructed. The overwhelming majority of them are Latin—immediately recognizable here through use of capitals; other bases appear in italics and are specifically assigned to the given source language. This section is subdivided into (A) an inventory of lexical units and (B) a distinctly shorter list of grammatical morphemes: prefixes, interfixes, and suffixes, in this order. For simply structured Latin etyma the "oblique" case has been provided, especially in regard to nouns, with -A standing for -AM, -E for -EM, -U for -UM, etc.; alternatively, one finds nominative plus genitive endings. For other lexical units the standard rather than the assumed colloquial forms have been selected, and vowel quantity has been marked, one hopes, consistently for length, yet selectively for brevity.

Section II is, basically, an alphabetic sequence of Romance "products", without any sharp distinction between medieval and modern, or literary and dialectal, forms. The major subdivision here is according to the vernacular language involved, an arrangement which carries with it the advantage of allowing one to respect the orthographic caprices of each major language in regard to the succession of certain letters (or combinations of letters).

Section III, offering the reader by far the sketchiest list of those here compiled, involves an attempt to organize the material with a modicum of attention to semantics. What has been caught in the compiler's dragnet is a certain number of vitally important glosses; these have been reduced to Standard English as a sort of common denominator, even where the original article had been worded in, say, French or Spanish. Even though there are in existence rather sophisticated schemata for further subdivisions, it has been deemed simpler and more practical, given the modesty of the size of this list, to set off groups of glosses solely by the form classes involved: verbs, substantives, adjectives, etc., in admittedly conventional manner. For the purpose of future etymological probings to which this highly selective compilation of denotational raw data has been squarely subordinated, the alternative of operating with any more experimental classifications, however thought-provoking per se, might have turned out to be downright anti-climactic.

I. Ancestral Bases

a. Lexical Units

b. Pre-, Inter-, Suf-fixes

II. Vernacular Lexical Items

Portuguese (Old and Modern; Galician)

Spanish (Old, Modern, and Dialectal)

Catalan / Provençal (Occitan) / Gascon (Literary, Dialectal)

French (Old and Modern, Literary and Dialectal)

Rhaeto- and Istro-Romance (Romaunsch and Friulano)

Italian (Old, Modern, and Dialectal)

Sardic (Old and Modern; Various Dialects)

Rumanian (Including Macedo-Rumanian)

English (Including Older, British, American English; Slang)

bandit 299; *betwixt and between* 200; *bitch* 306; *bloody* 79; *blustery* 79; *Bob* 236; *boo-boo* 293; *boogie-woogie* 200; *bootsy* 79; *brave* 184; *bubble, bubbly* 79, 293; *bumpety-bump* 79; *burly* 79;

calve, cub, pup, whelp (v.) 306; *cash and carry* 200; *cat and mouse* 200; *catchy* ~ *captious* 79; *chilblain* 79; *chilly* 79; *choos(e)y* 79; *chummy* 79; *clammy* 79; *cloggy* 79; *clumsy* 79; *cock-a-doodle-doo* 293; *colt* 306; *comfy* 79; *contraband* 299; *cookie* 293; *cosy* / *cozy* 79; *crack-ed, -y* 79; *craft-y, -sy* 79; *craichy* 79; *crazy* 79; *creepy* 79; *cross-legged* 79; *crotchety* 79; *crumby* 79; *cuckoo* 293; *cuddl-y, -esome* 79; *curb* 318d;

dad(dy) 79, 293; *(by) day and (by) night* 200; *disjunctives* 123; *dizzy* 79; *dodder* 293; *dop(e)y* 79; *drear(y)* 79;

each and every 200; *early* 79; *economic(al)* 123;

fancy 79; *feeble* / *foible* 399; *fidget-y, -ing* 79; *fishy* 79; *flimflam* 79; *flimsy* 79; *fluky* 79; *foal* / *filly* 306; *fog(gy)* 79; *foot(s)ie* 79; *frisk(y)* 79; *fuddy-duddy* 79; *fuzzy* 79;

gargle 293; *gas and oil* ~ *oil and gas* 200; *giddy* 79; *girl and dog* 200; *grisly* 79; *grizzle, -ly* 79; *gutsy* 79;

hammer and tongs 200; *handy-dandy* 79; *happy and gay* 200; *hard-and-fast (rule)* 200; *hasty* 79; *haughty* 79; *head off* 291; *heckle and jeckle* 200; *historic(al)* 123; *hit or miss* 200; *hoity-toity* 79; *hokey-pokey* 79; *holy* 79; *(by) hook or crook* 200; *husband and wife* 200;

iffy 79; *Ike* 293; *inceptives* 123; *ivory* 79;

Jew 20; *jolly* 79;

kiddy 79; *Kike* 293; *knife and fork* 200;

Ladies and Gentlemen 200; *law and order* 200; *(by) leaps and bounds* 200; *leggy* 79; *lengthy* 79; *leopardess* 306; *lioness* 306; *logic(al)* 123; *lohs* 306; *lousy* 79; *lulu* 293;

male and female 200; *man and woman* 200; *mangy* 79; *measly* 79; *meow, miao* 293; *merry* 79; *messy* 79; *miry* 79; *moist(y)* 79; *motley* 79; *mucky* 79; *muddy* 79; *muffy* 79; *muggy* 79; *mum(my)* 293; *murky* 79; *murrey* 79;

naggy 79; *namby-pamby* 79, 200; *nanny* 293; *narcotrafficker* 299; *nasty* 79; *naughty* 79; *nesty* 79; *newsy* 79; *nifty* 79; *nippy* 79; *noisy* 79;

odds and ends 200; *old-tim(e)y* 79; *on and off* ~ *off and on* 200; *ounce* 306;

paltry 79; *paly* 79; *panicky* 79; *pantheress* 306; *parnickety* 79; *parrot* 293; *party* 79; *paunchy* 79; *peep* 293; *perceptives* 123; *pernackery* 79; *persnickety* 79; *perspire* 404; *petticoat* 79; *pettifogger* 79; *petty* 79; *phony* 79; *pop(s), poppy* 293; *(to) pop* 293; *propaganda* 299; *puny* 79; *puppet* 293; *pup(py)* 293;

quakey-shakey 200;

race 236; *razzle-dazzle* 200; *reel* 332; *rickety* 79; *rise and shine!* 200; *Rob(by)* / *Bob(by)* 293; *roll* 332; *roly-poly* 200; *rough and tough* 200;

sassy 79; *shabby* 79; *shad(ow)y* 79; *shaggy* 79; *shilly-shally* 200; *shoddy* 79; *shoes and stocks* ~ *stocks and shoes* 200; *shoes and stockings* 200; *showy* 79; *shuttle* 332; *silly* 79; *sis(sy)* 79; *skimpy* 79; *sleezy* 79; *slippery* 79; *sly* 79; *smarmy* 79; *smirk-y, -ing* 79; *smuggle* 299; *snappy* 79; *snazzy* 79; *sooner or later* 200; *sorry* 79; *spiffy* 79; *spooky* 79; *spry* 79; *spunky* 79; *stark* 291; *stern* 291; *stiff* 291; *stop* 291; *straight* 291; *strain* 291; *strait* 291; *stretch* 291; *strung* 291; *stub* 291; *stubble* 291; *stubborn* 291; *stump* 291; *sturdy* 79; *sultry* 79; *surly* 79; *swanky* 79; *swart* / *swarthy* 79; *sweet and sour* 200;

tardy 79; *taut* 291; *then and there* ~ *there and then* 200; *thight* / *thite* / *theat* 291; *tight* 291; *tigress* 306; *tipsy* 79; *tip-top* 200; *tit for tat* 200; *tit* / *teat* 293; *toil* 332; *toil and moil* 200; *Tom, Dick, and Harry* 200; *topsy-turvy* 200; *touchy* 79; *tough* 291; *town and gown* 200; *track* / *trail* / *train* 332; *traffic* 299; *trafficker* 299; *transpire* 404; *trawl* 332; *tried and true* 200; *truht* 306; *trundle* 332; *tug* 291;

ugly 79;

very 177;

weak-kneed 79; *weal(th)y* 79;

German (Including Older and Low German)

Russian

Polish (All in 200)

(o) chlebie i wodzie, chuchać i dmuchać, głodno i chłodno, (na) łeb (na) szyję, orzeł i reszka, prośbą i groźbą, (od) stóp (do) głów, śmiech i łzy, tam i zprowotem, tędy (i) owędy, to i owo

Greek (Mostly Classical)

abrótonon 229; *amphoreús* 229; *amygdálē* 229; *átta* 293; *chroniká* 229; *diábolos* 229; *Hierṓnymos* 229; *ídios kaì dēmósios* 200; *kákkē* 293; *kálamos* 229; *karkínos* 229; *kámmaros* 229; *kóphinos* 229; *krithídion* 236; *kýmbalon* 229; *lýnkeios* 306; *lýnx* 306; *monachós* 229; *orphanós* 229; *óstrakon* 291; *páppas* 293; *páppos* 293; *pápyros* 229; *parabolḗ* 229; *parádeisos* 229; *petrosélinon* 229; *plateîa* 236; *pyrrós* 306; *pýxis, -idis* 229; *pýxos* 229; *symphōnía* 306; *sýndikos* 229; *théma* 291; *titthḗ* 312; *-issa* 312

Hebrew (Mostly Biblical)

ʾāb 293; *ʾarye* 306; *ba-yōm uβa-laylā* 200; *dōd(ā)* 293; *Kᵉīr* 306; *(lᵉ)ʿōlām wāʿaed* 200; *šen lᵉšen* 200; *taqānâ* 291; *ʿayin lᵉʿayin* 200

III. Glimpses of Semantic Counterview

a. Adjectives

axis 'abundant' – 'sparse' / 'lonesome' 126
axis 'calm' – 'angry' 234
axis 'cheerful' – 'sad' 264
axis 'diligent' – 'lazy' 141
axis 'equal' – 'diverse' 148, 258
axis 'expensive' – 'cheap' 285
axis 'faithful' / 'loyal' – 'treacherous' 16
axis 'firm' – 'slippery' 358
axis 'free' – 'tied' 258
axis 'full' – 'empty' / 'hungry' 249
axis 'handsome' / 'ugly' 16, 140
axis 'happy' / 'lucky' – 'wretched' 143, 230
axis 'hard' – 'soft' 156, 271
axis 'healthy' – 'sick' 17, 399
axis 'hot' – 'cold' 16, 174
axis 'intelligent' – 'stupid' 76, 245, 260
axis 'rich' – 'poor' 314
axis 'strong' – 'weak' / 'tired' 190, 399
axis 'sweet' – 'bitter' 241
axis 'thick' – 'thin' 152
axis 'true' – 'false' 177
axis 'young' – 'old' 344

color 183, 189, 371
dimension 66, 90
direction 62
peculiarity, resemblance 42, 56, 124
pertaining to anatomy 170
pertaining to an animal 162, 202
pertaining to social conditions 165
pertaining to time or season 160

b. Substantives

anatomy: inner organs 129, 183, 196
anatomy: visible parts of the body 4, 37, 175, 180, 185
animals – domestic 90, 147; female 301, 306; young 86, 90; herds 169; zoönyms 47, 90, 141, 166, 310, 329
art (forms, objects) 82, 175, 289
authority (religious, lay) 362
behavior 48, 61
birds 47, 361
child language 272, 293
concepts of action 45, 63, 118, 123, 305
concepts of quality 1, 2, 87, 136, 243, 260
containers 287, 336

c. Verbs

d. Pronouns

e. Numerals

f. Prepositions

Appendix D: Index of Authors of Books Reviewed

Included in this Index are also the names of authors of certain articles, as well as those of organizers of collective book ventures and of honorees of testimonials and memorials.

Appendix E: Index of Obituaries, Necrologies, and Celebrations